Stripped

Stripped

Inside the Lives of Exotic Dancers

Bernadette Barton

NEW YORK UNIVERSITY PRESS
New York and London

NEW YORK UNIVERSITY PRESS
New York and London
www.nyupress.org

Library of Congress Cataloging-in-Publication Data
Barton, Bernadette.
Stripped : inside the lives of exotic dancers / Bernadette Barton.
p. cm.
Includes bibliographical references and index.
ISBN–13: 978–0–8147–9932–1 (cloth : alk. paper)
ISBN–10: 0–8147–9932–9 (cloth : alk. paper)
ISBN–13: 978–0–8147–9933–8 (pbk. : alk. paper)
ISBN–10: 0–8147–9933–7 (pbk. : alk. paper)
1. Stripteasers. I. Title.
PN1949.S7B37   2006
792.7—dc22   2005032450

New York University Press books are printed on acid-free paper,
and their binding materials are chosen for strength and durability.

Manufactured in the United States of America

c 10 9 8 7 6 5 4 3 2 1
p 10 9 8 7 6 5 4 3 2 1

For Anna

Contents

Preface

What kind of woman dances naked for money?

The first time I went into a strip bar I was nineteen, on spring break from college, visiting my friend, Charles, in Minneapolis. We were downtown looking for lunch and passed a storefront advertising dancing and a buffet. Hopelessly naive, and a former ballet dancer to boot, I said to Charles, "Oh, dancing, wouldn't that be fun." He looked puzzled, and said, "It's not that kind of dancing, Bernadette." Then I understood. "Well, I want to go anyway. I've never been to one before." But Charles wasn't interested. Later that afternoon, when he had left for work, I bravely marched in alone. My first impression was that the place was very dark. Heavy metal music blared from the speakers, a thin scattering of men hunched at the bar, while one customer sat at the stage, a woman gyrating her crotch in his face. One patron asked if I was the next dancer. I fled, feeling vulnerable and afraid. He thought I was the next dancer, and I realized I could have been. I was young and sufficiently attractive. I had even studied dance most of my life—ballet, Pointe, modern, and jazz— so I felt oddly qualified for the job.

The next time I entered a strip bar was in Las Vegas. I was twenty-eight, a graduate student attending an academic conference and exploring future research projects, and I was considering studying exotic dancers. By coincidence, there was a dancer/academic on my panel who agreed to go with me to an all-nude dance bar off the strip. This club was decorated exclusively in shades of dark burgundy. Walking in was like entering a giant vulva. Although I was in researcher mode and avidly entranced with the space, I still felt uncomfortable. I first noticed that the dancers lacked rhythm and grace; they literally could not find the beat. This lack of skill was incredibly distracting. Nor did their acts reflect any trained aesthetic, consisting largely of random gyrations in front of men, interspersed with apathetic meandering around a pole in the middle of the dance floor. These listless performances were accompanied by faces masked by boredom and contempt. My companion from the conference, however, saw something I had missed. She repeated throughout the evening how nice the place was, how tasteful, how empowering dancing was for women. It seemed important for her to convince me that the club was classy, the dancers powerful women carving out their own fate. As the evening progressed, our communication only deteriorated. She became defensive, and I felt threatened. Clearly our different perceptions of the same environment sprang from our dissimilar life experiences, for she was an exotic dancer and I was not. I wondered then how dancing naked for money changes one's view of strip bars, influences one's perception of how women and men interact, and impacts how one understands the saliency of cultural taboos, especially what is considered "respectable" femininity?

Since then, after meeting, interviewing, and growing close to women who work in strip clubs, I have gradually become more comfortable entering and socializing there. Dancers are individuals whose motivations I well understand. Most are intelligent risk takers, surviving in a world where women have limited economic options. In this world, dancing is a choice with clear, practical benefits. "My time is important to me," more than one dancer told me. "Why should I work eighty hours to make the same money I can in eight?" For many women, dancing is also personally gratifying. "I like dancing," they said, "the music, the attention. I like being told I am beautiful." A job that supplied me with large sums of cash, an attentive audience, and free booze doesn't really sound so bad.

At the same time, however, my research has confirmed rather than disproved my original sense that sex work exacts a high cost from those who engage in it. Outside the club, dancers combat social stigma daily. They avoid discussing their work because, when they do, others react with a mixture of shock, disgust, and salacious curiosity. Dancers have trouble finding housing. They do not easily form or keep friendships or intimate relationships with those who are not dancers or otherwise in the business. Inside the club, dancers cope with many other difficulties: men who assume they are prostitutes or who are abusive in other ways; the ever-present smoke-filled air, bright stage lights, and deafening music; and an environment that encourages excessive drinking and provides access to illegal drugs. Also lost in most personal narratives and academic research on exotic dancing is an exploration of stripping as an economic exchange between dancer and customer. In other words, stripping is work. And, like all work, sex work requires emotional labor.[1] The emotional labor required of sex workers, moreover, is more demanding than that of individuals in most other professions. The costs of this emotional labor on a dancer's self-esteem, together with the environmental hazards and social stigma, make up what I dub "the toll" of sex work, which I discuss at length in the chapters that follow.

Much of the scholarship and popular discussion of stripping addresses the issues of control, power, and agency that dancers have, or do not have, over their lives.[2] These ongoing debates ask: Is she in charge or is she exploited? Is she a creative entrepreneur of her own body or a dupe of cultural expectations? To my mind, however, the issue of who has "control" or "power" in the strip bar—the man buying a sexual fantasy or the woman delicately extracting a man's entire salary—seems beside the point. After all, depending on one's political orientation or how one defines these slippery terms, different and incompatible pictures emerge. Victim or villain? Slut or sinner? Like most people, exotic dancers are complicated. Simply characterizing them with a one-dimensional label— good or bad, sinner or saint, whore or mother—perpetuates the stereotype and neglects the more subtle nuances of good and bad, exhilarating and devastating, not to mention the mundane, boring, rewarding, funny, ironic, annoying, and downright weird aspects of being a stripper. *Stripped* breaks down this polarized binary of exploitation or empowerment, slut or victim, that frames most academic and feminist work on the sex industry, as well as popular myths about the lives of strippers because the unnatural dichotomy defining stripping as either good *or* bad is simply inadequate to the task of understanding the lives of dancers.

We can only unpack the complexities of stripping by talking with many dancers and letting their narratives drive our understanding. I particularly wanted to know what the women who dance naked think about their jobs. My goal in this book, then, is to slake popular curiosity with an even-handed, multifaceted examination of the current lives of exotic dancers in the United States. I am also motivated by the desire to add to the general library of information about stripping—a little-studied aspect of women's work lives. Unfortunately, as Lily Burana noted in her witty book *Strip City,* "In stripping there is no sense of continuity. Women take their stories with them when they go."[3] Because stripping is such a socially stigmatized employment, the average performer has few opportunities to share her stories—not in the classroom, not with researchers, not with friends, and especially not with parents and partners. Although strip clubs are a burgeoning industry in the United States, now employing more women than at any other time in America's history, we still know little about the women who work in them. And, as you will read in the following pages, the experiences and insights of exotic dancers have much to teach us about women's lives, the cultural construction of sexuality, and what it means to live in a male-dominated society.

Exotic dancing is just beginning to develop a devoted group of sensitive researchers, including Katherine Frank, Wendy Chapkis, Ron Weitzer, Jill Nagle, Lynn Chancer, and Carol Queen, among others.[4] Even so, there are few collections of stripper narratives, no rigorous "history" of stripping, and no work that systematically explores how, over time, the career of stripping changes the women who dance; in short, little public knowledge about dancers and dancing that is not titillating or condemning exists. Attentive to this gap, *Stripped* explores the ideas and experiences of dancers at *every* stage of their careers in the sex industry—from novice to experienced dancer to ex-dancer. To accomplish this, I examine both women's daily experiences in strip bars—unpacking the emotional vicissitudes of an evening's work—and the ways that dancers' feelings about their labor evolve over time. For when we see popular culture's representations of exotic dancers, in mob movies and crime dramas, or even visit a strip bar on a Saturday night, we glimpse only a snapshot of a woman completely defined by her nudity and her relationship to a brass pole. We have no idea how she ended up on that pole, why she dances, and what she thinks about her work. In *Stripped,* I pull apart the mind-numbing stereotypes of strippers as stupid, sleazy, whore mongering, and drug addicted, you name it. In their place, I reveal unique individuals expressing complex reasons for their labor and how they feel about tackling that pole, depending not only on their personal history and place of employment but how long they have worked as a stripper.

At the center of this book are interviews with exotic dancers themselves—voices missing from much research on the sex industry. In these pages, dancers describe their own journeys into, and sometimes out of, the sex industry. And although each woman is differently located on her journey, the trajectory of entry into, within, and out of stripping shares strikingly similar features for all the exotic dancers interviewed for this book. A dancer's journey from novice to expert to ex-dancer significantly changes the ways that she perceives her sexuality, gender, connections to others, and overall sense of place in a world driven by the engine of capitalism. Stripping forces a woman into what Gloria Anzaldúa dubbed the "borderlands"—a liminal location between titillating and scandalous, powerful and powerless. For the exotic dancer is both revered and reviled, subject to the worst of men's behaviors and yet adored by the same men in extremes women rarely experience outside the sex industry. Simply put, the act of taking off one's clothes for money has a dramatic and life-altering impact on a woman's life. In *Stripped,* I take you inside the topless bar and into the lives of the women who feign sexual desire for money. In illuminating their experiences, we will uncover not just the *kind* of women who dance naked for money but how that act changes their lives. I hope that, like me, you will find this exciting, even harrowing journey one well worth taking.

Acknowledgments

It is a great pleasure to thank all the individuals who helped make this book possible. By sharing their time, attention, resources, and suggestions, many individuals and institutions shaped this work. Most significant are the dancers whose interviews form the core of this book, and I am profoundly grateful to them. Whether we were talking in coffee shops, at kitchen tables, on futons, or, in one memorable instance, in a rental car in a mall parking lot, our conversations were always inspiring and rewarding. I especially thank Angie and Morgan, whose insights on dancing are a background pulse in this work.

This book would not have been possible without my academic mentors and peers. At the University of Kentucky, Shaunna Scott, Dwight Billings, Ellen Rosenman, Joan Callahan, Adrienne McMahan, and Howard Grotch each provided intellectual, material, or emotional support, or all of the above, through the early stages of this book. Without Susan Bordo's attention, advice, editing, and general academic influence, this book simply would not have happened. Susan was my original inspiration and shepherd. Special thanks to Kathy Blee both for her feedback on this work and for being my first professor ever to believe in me. The University of Kentucky's Graduate School and College of Arts and Sciences each provided crucial funding sources for this book.

My colleagues and students at Morehead State University in Morehead, Kentucky, created a supportive environment for the expression of ideas. I thank Connie Hardesty, Becky Katz, Alana Scott, Ed Reeves, Shondrah Nash, Misty Dyer, Ted Marshall, Ric Caric, Mike Seelig, Cindy Faulkner, Sam Faulkner, Judy Stafford, Suzanne Rolland, Greg Goldey, Tom Kmetz, and Jennifer Madden. Special thanks to Eric Swank who generously gave me substantive criticism on much of this book. I also express my gratitude to the Office of Research and Creative Productions at

Morehead State University for funding the Honolulu portion of my data gathering; that support greatly benefited this book.

I am tremendously lucky to have stumbled onto the talented and experienced Ilene Kalish to edit this book. Ilene plucked my proposal from a pile and, with a marvelous mixture of critique and compassion, brewed a book. Thanks also to the thoughtful reviewers and staff at NYU Press.

My family and friends keep me anchored in this world, and this book is better because of them. I thank my brother, Colin Barton, who visited strip bars and waited in gay bars while I gathered data in Honolulu. I appreciate my sister, Joelle Nims, whose commitment to the craft of writing inspires me. My father, Colin Barton, even before I could form a sentence, believed that I would be a writer. I credit my mother, Catherine Ziesmer, for my love of books. At every new home, my mother's first act was to give her children library cards. I thank both my parents for encouraging me to do and be anything I imagined. My friends and family, Charles Combs, Patricia Jennings, Shondrah Nash, Dina Schaper, Marie Miller, Jordyn Steig, Jeff Jones, Teri Wood, Lisa Tolliver, and Matt Gallaway, were faithful sounding boards and provided support at varying stages of this book. I also thank all those I dragged to strip bars. Finally, I acknowledge my partner, Anna Blanton, who has been an unwavering rock through the journey from idea to research to book. Anna has cooked dinners, pushed me toward the computer, "popped" my back, visited strip bars, and spent endless hours talking with me about exotic dancing. I cannot overestimate her impact on this book.

Introduction

Come Inside and See the Show

Brandy is considering becoming a dancer. Before she musters the courage to audition, she wants to see what the dancers actually do. Bringing a male friend to an upscale club near her home, Brandy enters the lobby of the Velvet Lounge. Mötley Crüe's classic rock song "Girls, Girls, Girls!" is playing while an attractive, elaborately made-up woman flanked by a burly bouncer takes their money at the door. Brandy gets in free because she's a woman. The lobby has a comfortable couch, some tasteful, artistic photographs of nude women, and an ever-present pot of coffee.

Brandy walks down a hallway to a hazy room lit by black lights. There is a huge-screen TV playing the sport of the season. The club is two-tiered. The first floor includes a main stage and side stages for the dancers on which at least two women perform, one clothed in an evening gown, the other topless or nude. Dancers, waitresses, bouncers, and customers maneuver through a maze of tables and comfortable, padded chairs. While Brandy is grateful that they obtained seats in a relatively inconspicuous area of the club, she is, nonetheless, acutely conscious of being a clothed woman among so many near-naked ones.

She listens to the DJ's banter encouraging the men to applaud and tip the dancers, "Hey guys, give it up for Selena!" and "Who's drunk enough out there to give me a 'Hell, yeah!' " This DJ commentary is also spiced with raunchy remarks about the performers, "Shit fellas, somebody take over the booth, I got to get me some of that," and homophobic quips like "Clap if you're not a fag!" The DJ frequently announces special dances: a two-for-one table dance, and, later, the dancers parade through the club, each in a T-shirt she sells off her back with a couch dance at a reduced cost. At one point, a dancer circling the room offers to sell Brandy's companion a video of sports highlights with a table dance. These are all gimmicks organized by the club to increase the cash flow.

1

When she glances up, Brandy spots couches ringing the entire space on the second floor; on each couch is a patron with a dancer undulating over him. From the customer's vantage point, it is a voyeur's dream. People downstairs can see the backs of the dancers performing while the clients purchasing the dances are shadowed and anonymous. Brandy buys an overpriced beer and watches the dancers circling the room soliciting table dances as well as the women performing onstage. One dancer walks to the center of the stage, removes her evening gown, displays her breasts, pivots slowly, and thrusts out her buttocks. Brandy has the opportunity to peruse the dancer's body from every angle while the performer struts and sways, eyes glassy or shut. There is a pole in the center of the stage running from the base of the floor to the ceiling. After a period of languorous posing, the dancer twirls on the pole, twisting into a back flip and hanging upside down by her ankles. Brandy is intimidated and impressed by the acrobatics. Later, she learns that most dancers balance themselves with the pole. As the dancer is virtually naked on a raised stage in front of any number of fully clothed men, the pole provides both a psychological and physical balance. When she feels vulnerable, when the stage is wet, when she's dizzy or intoxicated, the pole is something the dancer can literally hang onto.

By the time Brandy and her friend have had two or three drinks, he wants to buy a table dance. He signals the attention of the woman he finds most attractive, and she joins them. She swivels his chair, smiles and winks at Brandy, disrobes, and gives her undivided attention to the paying customer. While he is forbidden to touch her, the dancer presses her body inches away from him, revealing her breasts, turning around, and bending over to show her buttocks. Most men sit, their bodies quivering with restrained lust or slightly limp with desire, intently watching the performer, admiring the curves of her body. When the song is over, the dancer, just as casually as when she began, shrugs on her dress, sits, and chats for awhile about carefully neutral, flattering, noncontroversial topics: What business are you in? Where are you from? Do you like the club? My, aren't you the nicest looking man here! Brandy notices that if a patron wants to continue to spend time with a dancer, he will have to spend more money. He may request a couch dance.

Couch dances are an even more graphic expression of simulated sex than table dances. Most clubs reserve a special area for couch dances, away from the main floor to ensure more privacy for the client and, often, more supervision for the dancer. Bouncers usually patrol the area to make

*sure neither the customer nor the dancer violate club rules about touch-
ing and body contact. At the Velvet Lounge, a dancer takes a client by the
hand and leads him upstairs to a deep fake-leather couch. He gets comfortable and watches while she strips off her dress, standing just above
him. The angle and depth of the sofa provide the patron with an eye-level
view of her crotch. Although she must have both feet on the sofa or floor
at all times, if the bouncer is turned away, she might manage to maneuver her body to grind against his genitals. Most clients know this type of
body contact is against the rules of the club and might therefore increase
her tip.*

*The Velvet Lounge closes at 1:00 A.M. Having watched the dancers per-
form, Brandy has a better idea of what stripping generally involves. Still
a bit scared but aware that she is totally broke, Brandy fills out a waitress
application, thinking that she can make good money serving drinks and
not have to take off her clothes. She is hired on the spot.[1]*

Getting Inside

I started my research on exotic dancers in 1998 and continue my study of
women's experiences in the sex industry to this day. My first task was simply getting inside. Entering a strip club and sitting down with the clients
on the floor rather than joining the dancers onstage, I am breaking a cultural taboo: a woman watching other women perform erotically. The unwelcome feeling I often had doing so was reinforced by the reality that
most clubs across the United States have rules preventing unescorted females from entering. When questioned, clubs offer a number of reasons
for this policy. The most diplomatic response to my question about why
I could not enter a club alone came from a manager at the Pink Cave, an
upscale chain club in "Silverton."[2] With disingenuous sexist suave, he
chivalrously explained that there were a number of drunk and horny men
in the bar, and he could not guarantee my safety. Showing little regard for
the dancers, however, he never mentioned how he guaranteed *their* safety.

One bouncer refused to let me into Vixens, a local family-owned bar
in Silverton, the site for much of the research for this book.[3] When I again
asked, "Why not?" he told me they did not want prostitutes in the club.
Although he did not strike me as the swiftest of fellows, as I glared at him,
it eventually did occur to him that I might not appreciate being called a
prostitute, and he added, grumpily, "Not that you're a hooker or any-

thing." I learned another reason why unescorted females are unwelcome as patrons from Brenda, the owner of Vixens:[4]

[We have to] protect our customers from a wife coming in or jumping one of the dancers. We've been there and done that. You can always look up and see that look in their eyes. They come storming through and Bobby's over there with Suzy and nine times out of ten they don't hit Bobby, they hit Suzy. And it's Bobby's fault.

She added that increased security at the door helps to prevent such scenes. Beyond the official and unofficial reasons managers and owners cite for curtailing women's access to strip bars, this policy also performs the function of regulating female sexuality—"bad girls" are inside and "good girls" are outside. By simply walking into a strip bar, a woman risks turning from "good" to "bad" as she crosses the threshold. Just as the magazine *Playboy* advertises itself boldly on the cover as "the magazine for men," so do strip bars engender atmospheres that cater almost exclusively to conventional male fantasies of control. The presence in the audience of wives, girlfriends, co-workers, or neighbors observing the spectacle not only of naked female flesh but of naked male desire potentially disrupts this fantasy.

Being a lesbian with no male spouse whom I could badger into accompanying me, just getting into clubs was a challenge at first. Before beginning my research, I toyed with the idea of doing participant observation and dancing myself. I was drawn to the idea of dancing for many of the same reasons of my more privileged informants: I certainly needed the money, I liked to dance, I had a "good" body, and I thought it would be interesting to break a taboo and test the boundaries of "respectable" femininity. Moreover, what better way to solve all my research problems? I could obtain access to the clubs and gain the trust of informants. For a couple of months I weighed the pros and cons of becoming a dancer both by visiting strip bars and interrogating my feminist consciousness.

I soon discovered that simply watching the show swiftly drained most of my emotional reserves. In the beginning, I felt depressed and exhausted after only forty-five minutes in a club. After a few months of visiting the bars and getting to know some of the dancers, I learned to tolerate the noise, the smoke, and the undiluted testosterone for about one to two hours before I had an irresistible impulse to leave at once. Clearly dancing was not an option for me. And while I am extremely supportive of dancers' rights to dance topless, I do not enjoy spending a lot of time in the strip clubs. I quickly grasped that the role of sympathetic outsider would more easily facilitate researching this book.

With the help of male friends and female dancers who used their influence on my behalf, I logged in extensive observation time. I researched strip clubs in "Silverton," San Francisco, and Honolulu. Silverton's location in the Southeast was convenient for me, as that's where I live. I chose San Francisco for its sexual diversity and Honolulu for its racial and national diversity. Because I performed extensive observation at three different sites, my research is arguably more representative of a range of dancers. Of the nine clubs I frequented in Silverton, I focused on two in particular—one upscale establishment, the Velvet Lounge, and one working-class club, Vixens.[5] The time I spent in San Francisco and Honolulu was more concentrated, and hence I visited a variety of bars daily. Of the more than thirty strip bars I visited, Vixens and the Velvet Lounge are each emblematic of a certain type of gentleman's club and local strip bar.

I found, surprisingly, that the process of making contacts and establishing rapport took far more time and was more difficult than I had imagined. This is partly because dancers are a stigmatized group, wary of the voyeuristic curiosity of outsiders. Likewise, some might have thought that their life stories were unworthy of scholarly research. Indeed, Tracy, a Vixens dancer I interviewed, told me that no one had ever been interested in hearing what she had to say before. Perhaps the most exasperating problem I experienced was simply getting the dancers to attend our pre-approved interview session. In Honolulu, for instance, I arranged to meet interview subjects outside the Honolulu zoo, at an open, safe, public park. Six women stood me up on six separate occasions. Some simply changed their minds, and others claimed their boyfriends didn't want them to participate. Others, I think, originally agreed to be interviewed because they are socialized not to say no to any request in the strip bar. In playing the stripper script, the more agreeable and accessible a dancer appears to the prospective client, the more money she will make. Finally, exotic dancing is not a nine-to-five job; the work discourages routines and introduces a dimension of chaos into the lives of many dancers. Hence, carving out two hours for an interview was not necessarily a high priority for them.[6]

In spite of my efforts to be respectful, affirming, and considerate, I sometimes ventured into topic areas that the women did not wish to discuss. For example, when I questioned Mandy, a Vixens dancer, about her perception of the sexual orientations of the women working at her club, she replied that that was none of her business and changed the subject. Most dancers, however, were rarely insulted by my questions. Indeed, the majority of my informants thanked me profusely at the conclusion of our interviews, saying that they had not had the opportunity to reflect on their experiences before and that doing so had been immensely rewarding. Questions I was not comfortable asking were those that probed an informant's childhood, especially experiences of sexual and physical abuse. This was partly because my aim in this study was not to explore the relationship between childhood sexual abuse and sex work and also because I wanted to avoid questions that might cause dancers to mistrust me.[7] I feared that the women I interviewed might interpret questions about sexual abuse, and alcohol and drug use, for example, as reinforcing negative stereotypes about sex workers, and I wanted the dancers to feel that I was sympathetic to their concerns. Nevertheless, because several dancers voluntarily discussed these controversial subjects, they are included in the book.

Despite the many difficulties I experienced in researching exotic dancers, I had at least one advantage in the research process. My sexual identity invited the trust not only of lesbian and bisexual dancers but of heterosexual informants as well. However they defined their sexual identity, all the dancers are marginalized in mainstream culture and hence are sexual outlaws as well. This generally encouraged them to be more open-minded about alternative sexual identities and consequently more sympathetic to me as a lesbian researcher.

Sizing the Women Up

The first dancer I spoke to was April, who was introduced to me by a contact at the university where I taught. She, in turn, graciously introduced me to a few of the women she worked with at the Velvet Lounge.[8] I also asked friends and acquaintances if they knew any dancers who would be willing to participate in my research. Finally, I walked into clubs, introduced myself, and asked those women present if they wished to be interviewed.[9] In addition to these more formal interviews, I spoke informally with more than a hundred dancers, patrons, bouncers, and waitresses about their experiences in topless bars and peep shows, and these conversations informed my collective analysis of the effects of the sex industry on performers. Although I mainly focus on women's experiences in and out of strip bars and peep shows, I also observed that the kinds of sex work my subjects performed overlapped. Most of the women I interviewed had been or continue to be involved in other aspects of the sex industry, including prostitution, phone-sex work, and acting in pornographic films.[10]

The years of paid dancing of the women I interviewed ranged from six months to seventeen years.[11] Broadly classified, I interviewed and informally spoke with roughly three types of dancers: students aged nineteen to twenty-five dancing their way through college, taking a break from college, or supporting themselves after college while they decided what to do with their lives; "career"[12] dancers aged twenty-five to forty who generally began dancing when they were young, perhaps with children to support, who continued because of low educational attainment and few equally lucrative job options;[13] and artists, bohemians, or "free spirits" of any age who liked the flexibility and economic advantages of sex work.

I also classified my subjects into "early" or "late" career dancers, as I found that the length of time they worked as strippers proved to be an important distinction on many levels. Whether a dancer was "early" or "late" in her career bore some relationship to her age but not always. For example, one twenty-five-year-old woman I interviewed had been dancing for six years, while a forty-year-old woman had only been dancing one year. Early-career dancers included women who had been stripping up to three years, and late-career dancers included women who had been stripping for more than three years. I chose three years as the dividing line because it most closely coincided with dancers' descriptions of when the negative aspects of dancing began to outweigh the positives.[14]

The Sex Industry

How many strip clubs exist, and how easy is it to get a job at one? Recent totals of strip clubs in the Unites States vary from twenty-three hundred to twenty-seven hundred nationwide.[15] In his meticulously researched book *Reefer Madness: Sex, Drugs, and Cheap Labor in the American Black Market,* journalist Eric Schlosser estimates that patrons spend $2 billion each year in strip clubs.[16] Nor are strip bars evenly distributed among the states. Texas sports the most strip clubs (219), with Florida a close second (214) and New York a distant third (152), while the New

England states of Vermont (2), New Hampshire (3), and Maine (4) have the fewest strip bars.[17] San Diego alone has eighteen nude bars employing 1,500 women, averaging 187 women per club. Because sexually graphic images are so pervasive today—in fashion, advertisements, and music videos, as well as in explicit pornography outlets—one can easily lose sight of how quickly the sex industry has grown. A 1970 federal study of pornography estimated the total value of hard-core pornography at $10 million.[18] This is only a fraction of the billions now spent per year in the twenty-first century. The fact is that more women are employed in the sex industry now than at any other time in U.S. history.

Table 1.1 indicates the number of strip bars in each state, and Table 1.2 shows the number by country. The information in these tables came from an Internet website called the Ultimate Strip Club List, which is regularly updated. Because of the frequency with which strip bars open, close, and change owners and names, this information is always changing. For specific names of clubs and their locations, one need only click on the state link at the website.

TABLE 1.1

Strip Clubs in the United States

Alabama	31
Alaska	9
Arizona	59
Arkansas	11
California	204
Colorado	35
Connecticut	46
Delaware	5
District of Columbia	12
Florida	214
Georgia	71
Hawaii	24
Idaho	10
Illinois	91
Indiana	78
Iowa	34
Kansas	34
Kentucky	53
Louisiana	60
Maine	4
Maryland	61
Massachusetts	31
Michigan	82
Minnesota	35
Mississippi	11
Missouri	45

Montana 9
Nebraska 17
Nevada 43
New Hampshire 3
New Jersey 127
New Mexico 11
New York 152
North Carolina 99
North Dakota 7
Ohio 137
Oklahoma 40
Oregon 92
Pennsylvania 131
Rhode Island 12
South Carolina 56
South Dakota 14
Tennessee 40
Texas 217
Utah 16
Vermont 2
Virginia 41
Washington 17
West Virginia 53
Wisconsin 84
Wyoming 8

SOURCE: http://www.tuscl.com/.

TABLE I.2
International Strip Clubs

United States 2,770
Canada 275
Africa 6
Asia 31
Australia 47
The Caribbean 33
Central America 27
Europe 248
Guam 8
Mexico 115
New Zealand 9
South America 32
South Pacific 1

SOURCE: http://www.tuscl.com/.

If the numbers in the tables are accurate, or even close, the irony is self-evident that in spite of the United States' professed public commitment to family values, Americans lead the global community in the number of strip bars available for "gentlemen's entertainment." Moreover, Americans spend $8 billion to $10 billion per year on the sex industry, including consumption of strip bars, peep shows, pornography rentals, phone sex, sex acts, sex toys, and sex magazines. As Schlosser noted, "Americans now spend more money at strip clubs than at Broadway theaters, regional and nonprofit theaters, and symphony orchestra performances—combined."[19] Logically, this highly lucrative, resilient, exponentially expanding sex market employs an increasing number of women and men. On a more local level, this means that most strip clubs are always hiring dancers, and many run continuous ads for dancers and support staff such as waitresses, hostesses, bartenders, and bouncers. Thus, a woman who conforms to conventional, media-driven standards of age and beauty can dance almost anywhere at any time in the United States. Given the increasing presence of the sex industry in our daily lives, and the increasing number of women and men employed in the business of sex, it is more important than ever to understand both the nature of sex business and sex labor.

Inside the Strip Bar

Clubs in the United States range from upscale, pricey places like the national chain Pure Gold and the locally owned Velvet Lounge to down-home family country bars such as Vixens.[20] Door fees run no higher than five dollars in clubs in Silverton and up to thirty dollars at the most exclusive club in San Francisco. Clubs make most of their money from the clients' purchase of alcohol. Drink prices are comparable to those in moderate to expensive hotels: a beer or mixed drink will cost three to eight dollars, depending on the location of the club and the class background the clientele. At certain clubs, management requires dancers to solicit drinks from the patrons by making them fill a drink quota. At Vixens, each dancer must sell ten drinks per shift or pay for them herself. At clubs without liquor licenses, dancers share with the club a percentage of the profits from each table dance and couch dance.

Individual clubs attract a range of clients by class and race, although wealthier men are drawn to the more expensive clubs and blue-collar men are more likely to visit the less class-conscious environments of the inexpensive bars. Each club I visited, including those in Kentucky, Tennessee, Idaho, California, Las Vegas, Minnesota, and Hawaii, is different depending on the customer base it hopes to attract, but all the clubs share some similarities. They are all dimly lit with black lights, play loud music, and have one to several stages for the dancers, including a main stage centrally located. This is where out-of-town or "feature" dancers perform during the club's special attractions. All clubs have comfortable, sturdy chairs that can tolerate a great deal of activity. In areas that allow cigarettes, they are all smoky, and the drinks are overpriced. Most clubs have large-screen televisions tuned to a sports channel. In one strip bar on Oahu, I watched, with rising amusement, as the clients tried to split their attention between a competitive basketball game and the women onstage. I felt I was observing primary id in action—basketball, naked women, basketball, naked women—eyes darting from breasts to balls. Carl, a client, described this particular plight:

> If there was a really important sports game on, it would dominate the males' attention over the dancers, and, on commercial breaks, the guys would look at the girls. I even saw one guy run over from the bar at the commercial break and give one of the dancers money. He said, "You're doing great, baby, you're doing great," and went back and sat down and watched the game. In that way, it seemed like the guys were just there to watch the sports, and the women were more a peripheral bonus.

The more expensive the club, generally the more regulated the environment. Rules lay out how much physical contact is allowed between dancer and client and what acts are prohibited and permitted. Patrons may inquire from any club employee the rules of that club. If a client breaks a rule and touches a dancer, for example, a bouncer will warn him. If he continues to break a rule or more generally disrespects or distresses a dancer, he will be thrown out—after paying. In certain cities, dancers must maintain six inches of space between themselves and the customers; in others, they must be six feet from the client.[21] The laws dictating the space allowed between dancer and customer are idiosyncratically determined by state, city, or district.

In some clubs, dancers cannot carry cigarettes or drinks between tables or eat with the clients. When a dancer breaks a rule, she is fined a small amount. If it is a serious infraction like drug possession, she may lose her job. Often, however, clubs turn a blind eye to certain kinds of drug use at work, especially smoking marijuana. Typically, dancers have access to many types of illegal drugs working in the clubs but make at least a moderate effort to hide their drug use from managers. The more upscale clubs require that dancers attend nightly meetings to discuss new promotions and the day's events. Predictably, the dancers who feel comfortable in structured environments prefer the more expensive clubs, whereas those who enjoy their autonomy work in the less expensive bars.

Evaluating the Talent

The dancers vary by club as well. Every club employs at least a few "classic beauties," women with slender bodies, large breasts, and blonde hair. The more fashionable the club, the more conventionally attractive the dancers are, particularly in the chain clubs such as Déjà Vu and Pure Gold. Just as consumers expect their Quarter Pounders to taste the same from Miami to Boston to Taipei, clients frequenting chain clubs expect a franchised standard in the club layout, service, and even the very bodies of the dancers.[22] To meet these expectations, and increase their incomes, many dancers have breast augmentation. After only a short time stripping, dancers quickly realize that the women with the biggest breasts get the biggest tips. Since the cost of breast implants have been decreasing— a friend of mine just purchased a pair of saline implants for three thousand dollars—a large percentage of dancers make the investment. In the strip clubs I observed, it appeared as though 30 to 50 percent of the women had implants. The percentage was smaller among my informants, closer to 10 percent. Clients told me that it is not unusual for the men to make a game out of deciding which dancers have breast implants.

Like a dancer's height, weight, hair color, and breast size, race is another facet of a woman's appearance that clients evaluate and choose. The strip club is largely a buyer's market. In the world of sex for sale, the consumer has the "right" to buy whatever "product" he prefers. Although the blonde, blue-eyed, big-breasted dancer is always popular, many clients enjoy viewing a variety of women. For instance, during a special dollar dance at the Velvet Lounge in which women circled the club and danced for thirty seconds per customer per dollar, a client remarked happily to me, "Time for the buffet!" as he assembled a number of single bills.

Skin color, like one's economic power and educational level, affect people's interactions both within and without the sex industry. In the strip bar, however, where a woman's physical attributes are constantly on display—being evaluated, rejected, or admired—many dancers explained that a woman's race was less a site of stigma than just another distinguishing characteristic that enabled her to make either more or less money on a given night. Conscious that her white skin might inhibit her insight, Morgan stated,

> This is coming from someone who is of Caucasian descent so I don't know how much validity this has. From what I saw, all the other things we have talked about today, the personality types, the social stigma, I think race is less of a factor there than a lot of other places. Is a woman of color's experience different? I'm sure just like someone who is blonde is different, because everyone has their preferences. For the most part you are talking about a visual art, a visual milieu. All the discussion of biological characteristics by clients to me was kind of lumped together. They said racial things, but they said a lot of things that were about physical characteristics.

Maxine, an African American dancer in Atlanta, explained that she felt her race had less of an impact on her experience of dancing than her ability to negotiate the environment and manage the money she made:

> It's all about—not being black—it's all about being educated to do what you're supposed to do with whatever amount of money you made. It wouldn't made a difference if I was black or white. I made all that kind of money and get caught up in that drug thing just like some actress do and they become broke at the end.

Ideas about race shape both the customer's desire and the dancer's performance. Rick, a burly bouncer and a mixed Pacific Islander, Hawaiian, and local, described the racial attitudes of some customers:

> Have you ever heard "fucking Howie"? It means foreign person in a negative way. When they [foreigners] go to the strip bar, the first girl they head for is the white girl with the blonde hair. The black women that are at the club, and they are like, "fuck you, give me a dollar." There are some Asian women that try to pull that off, but they don't make much money. A lot of guys come in looking for the Asian women at the club. Then you have local guys claiming that they don't like white girls. You are expected to like the Asian women. I find myself stereotyping my own race.

Racial images permeate our culture. Representations of the "Asian flower," "Hoochie Mama," and "Blonde Playmate" color the expectations of customers.[23] Dancers understand this. In the strip club, in which every interaction is a market transaction, dancers may deliberately perform customers' fantasies to extract more money from them. These fantasies include both racialized fantasies, such as the subservient lotus blossom, and fantasies that have nothing to do with race, for example, the dominatrix or schoolgirl. Politically correct language and attitudes about race are largely irrelevant to the dancers. Customers want what they want: boobs, long legs, blondes, Asian girls, black girls, the girl next door, and so on. Dancers read racial preferences much like they do a client's interest in breast size or legs: as information they can manipulate to make money. Mary, a white woman from Colorado dancing in Honolulu, described how customer expectations and preferences for a certain type change daily: "You can tell if it's a blonde day or if it's a local girl or Asian day. There are some days in here where the customers want the local girls, and I don't make any money."

In this environment, then, what distinguishes a good client from a bad one in the eyes of dancers is not his racial consciousness but the respect he shows the dancer. To illustrate, a client may behave as described by Trina, a dancer of white, African American, and Native American ethnicity:

> One time I danced for this guy who was like, "I am a complete racist but you are so beautiful." He wanted to talk to me, and he spent money on me. Another time I danced for a customer and he was like, "I don't even like black woman." I was like, "Well, I'm not just black," but whatever. He was like, "That was great," and he tipped me hard. Some guys are like, "I don't like black girls," and that's cool. I'm sure it ends up at the end of the day is people have their own flavors; some guys like blondes, some guys like redheads, and if you play into all that, then you are going to find all that.

As Trina's customer shows, clients have preconceived notions about race and are liable to make racist comments. Yet if these comments are made in a supposedly complimentary fashion, no matter how obnoxious or insulting they actually are, a dancer will generally respond with deference. After all, the strip club is a place where men get to pick who they want to look at; a casual compliment is to tell a woman she has a "nice ass." As

Trina explained, each man has his own favorite flavor of dancer. The financially successful dancer swiftly learns to read customer desires and perform his gendered and racial fantasies.[24] Does he want a college student? A biker? Big breasts? A rap dancer? Does he expect the struggling artist? The hot Latina babe? The suffering single mother? The blonde bombshell? Does he want the potpourri?

The dancers' heights vary, as do their hair length, style, and color. As an observer, it is difficult to determine exactly how tall dancers are in the club. The dancers and audience are often on different levels—I am sitting, she is standing; I am tipping her while she dances on a raised stage—*and* the performers wear four- to six-inch platform shoes. These shoes are standard dress and are the only part of the dancers' costumes, besides the g-string in the topless-only bars, that the dancers do not strip off. Dancer after dancer complained about the shoes during our interviews: the heels give them back aches and knee problems and make it difficult to balance, especially on slippery floors. The shoes weigh one to three pounds each and usually have spike heels. More than one dancer has described fights between a dancer and a client or between dancers where the woman took off her shoe and threatened to hit someone. The shoes can therefore double as weapons. In the middle of one of my interviews, we paused when April let me try on her shoes. Standing carefully, I found that the thick platform section weighted my foot while the extremely high heel threw me off-center. It was instantly clear why exotic dancers spend so much time writhing on the floor and wrapping their bodies around poles. As I wobbled across April's living room carpet, I winced at the prospect of maneuvering between crowded tables, mounting stairs to a stage, and negotiating my way to the toilet, not to mention actually dancing in these shoes. After this exercise, I was even more impressed with the dancers' balance, athleticism, and flexibility.

The Work

Women perform both private and public dances for patrons. Dancers on each shift sign up with the DJ to rotate onto the main stage and sometimes onto the side stage or stages. Performances on the raised stages generally last for two songs. During the first, the dancer remains clothed, but in the second she strips to a g-string or completely disrobes. Dancers will receive tips, usually dollar bills, from patrons or other dancers while on the main stage. These tips are often small and rarely add up to much money. They are more symbolic in nature, a gesture of appreciation or a signal that a client wants to purchase a private dance. The bulk of their money is made dancing one on one with a client. This includes table and couch dances in Silverton, while in other cities dancers may perform lap dances or other kinds of nude shows.

Unlike most strip clubs in the continental United States, the dancer in Hawaii makes a substantial chunk of her money onstage in dollar tips. At Desire, a popular local strip bar in Waikiki, the majority of dancers simply sat, legs awkwardly akimbo in front of them on the main stage during their shifts, waiting for a client to approach them. When a customer did join her, a dancer's posture and expression changed from boredom to seduction. She rose to her knees, protected by a foam mat, and performed a personal show for the client, opening her garter at thirty-second intervals for dollar tips. Or as one customer, Carl, colorfully described Desire,

> Well, you go in there and it's just a bunch of women sitting around waiting for someone to give them money so they'll dance. It looks like a dingy bar, with disco lights sometimes under the dancers, and set up like those little fountains, like little women fountains in the middle. And you sit around the fountain, and you throw money into it.

The number of times a woman dances on a main or side stage depends on the number of women working that shift: the more women working, the fewer times a dancer performs onstage. During an average shift, performances might be once every hour and a half; on a busy shift, a dancer may only perform on the main stage once every three hours. Because a dancer makes the most money through table and couch dances, as noted, a dancer will usually make a round of the room every half hour or so to see if patrons want to purchase a table dance or couch dance. All the dancers obviously face some rejection during an evening, but that does not prevent them from trying again with a client who has said no. Melinda always returns to solicit patrons who have declined her invitation:

> They say no, right now they just might not have had enough beer. So I'll give them another half hour, another beer and a half or whatever, and come by and hit them up again. And eventually you wear them down if you're always friendly and you pop up and are like, "Hey, are you ready

now?" And then eventually they'll be like, "Yeah, sure. Why not?" You just keep going around and around, and you'll find people who will want to buy you a drink, and you'll just sit down with them and chew the shit for twenty minutes, sell a couple drinks, and get up. You might find someone who wants to keep buying a lot of dances, and they'll buy you a drink, and you'll stay there as long as they're going to be there doing the same thing, buying dances and buying drinks.

Table dances occur right at or on the customer's table. In the more fashionable clubs in Silverton, table dances run ten dollars and couch dances twenty. In the less expensive clubs, table dances are five dollars and couch dances fifteen. Couch dances are even more explicit than table dances. Some dancers prefer couch dances because they offer greater financial rewards, but others find the crotch-to-face contact demeaning. Clubs tend to enforce more rules for couch dances: for example, a dancer must have both feet on the ground or on the floor at all times. Some clubs have video cameras trained on the couches or bouncers watching the couch rooms during dances. The number and variety of city and club regulations may strike the uninformed as surprising. The purpose of these regulations is threefold: ostensibly to protect the dancers from aggressive clients but mostly to protect the business interests of the owners and to protect the club from violating any city statutes.

When performing a table dance, the dancer maintains an air buffer between herself and the client, but during a lap dance she sits directly on the man's lap and rubs against his genitalia. She may wear a g-string or be nude during the "dance." Prices for lap dances, and nude dances, vary by club. Beatrice, a San Francisco dancer, describes the different dances in the first club she worked:

We had a room which was called the lap dance room. We had couches lining the wall. So, the customer would sit down, and you would either sit on them with your back facing them or straddling them. We would just sit on their lap, move around, and try to just be sexy. Do small talk . . . in the VIP booths there was just one chair and a curtain, so we would do naked dances in there. I always felt very safe working there. We had a lot of bouncers. There were times when a customer would get too rowdy with me, and I'd just tell one of the guys who worked there, and they'd have them removed. If someone touched me in a way that made me feel uncomfortable, they'd be removed. There was very little bodily contact. The men had to keep their hands on my hips; they could-n't touch my breasts or any other private parts of me. I didn't permit them to lick or suck me or kiss me. It was very clean-cut there. And it was nice. It was good money. We would charge twenty dollars for a reg-ular lap dance, forty dollars topless, and forty dollars plus for private booths, [the price] going up as clothes came off. We would go around to customers and ask them if they would like some company, a lap dance or private dance. We took the money first.

With this kind of friction, one might imagine that customers would some-times ejaculate during the dance. But most of the time this is not the case. Strip bars are about arousal, not satisfaction. A man who wants to mas-turbate goes to a peep show, not a strip club. New to the research, I asked a dancer at the Pink Cave if the men ever climaxed. She shuddered, dis-gusted, and said, "No, the men never come. It's not that kind of place." However, Melinda, a Vixens dancer told me that, although a man rarely reached orgasm, it occasionally happened. If he did, she would demand a hundred dollars from him on the spot. The men always paid, knowing that ejaculating was forbidden and that they could face repercussions for doing so—except in San Francisco. The regulations in San Francisco are considerably less rigid. At the Mitchell Brothers Theater, where Beatrice worked, some dancers engaged in more explicit sexual acts with cus-tomers for a price, including hand stimulation, oral sex, and intercourse, in addition to the various erotic dances.

Cities have different regulations and licensing procedures about selling alcohol in the presence of nudity. Totally nude clubs often do not have liquor licenses, and those that provide alcohol might be topless only. An exception to this rule occurs on the island of Oahu. Dancers in Honolulu can get completely naked, and liquor is served. But a local quirk in Hawaii is that lap and table dancing have been prohibited for years. Most clubs leave nudity to the dancer's discretion: she can strip naked, leave her g-string on, or even keep her breasts covered. The third "choice" is rarely taken, however, as a dancer who refused to go topless would make little money and the dancers that reveal more skin get bigger tips. The power of the purse drives women to reveal their genitals and increase skin con-tact with clients. I have observed that the women who remove their g-strings when most of the other performers remain covered tend to be those that are physically heavier in build. Dancers who do not match the "centerfold" figure compensate for their body size by taking more off and performing more graphic moves on the stage and on the floor. This kind of hierarchy by weight, breast size, and appearance was evident in every club I visited.

A typical shift for a dancer lasts between six and eight hours. In most establishments dancers are not allowed to leave the club while they are working. When they are hungry, they order food in or eat a sandwich they brought to work. In the more relaxed clubs, a customer can even order a pizza to share with the dancers. But if there is money to be made, the last thing dancers want to do is leave the floor. The nature of a dancer's job is to be on public display: hanging out, drinking, and entertaining. Hence the slow times in a club, when few customers are present, are the best opportunities for dancers to take breaks. Mandy explained:

> We're not allowed to leave. We order food. Basically you eat when you want, but you don't get, per se, lunch break. We're making money; we don't want to take that break. We may be tired, but we don't care. We're going to keep going. Because if there's money to be made, we're going to make it. We'll take that break when we're able. If the money's there, you're not going to stop, "Well excuse me, I'm going to go take a break." But then again, you got customers who say you need a break, and they pay you for a song to sit down. So you'll get a break that way. They'll buy you a drink and give you ten dollars just to sit there for a song.

Fees and the sharing of tips with the staff vary by club. In Silverton, at the more expensive clubs, dancers are considered independent contractors and pay a stage fee of approximately twenty-five dollars. They are also expected to "tip out"—meaning that they share a percentage of what they've earned with the bartender, waitresses, bouncers, house mother, and DJ. This may come to about fifty dollars a shift. In other clubs, like Vixens, dancers are required to sell a drink quota. In many cities, dancers are classified as independent contractors and do not receive any salary from the club. In Silverton my informants seemed fairly comfortable with this arrangement, but dancers in San Francisco complained bitterly about expensive stage fees. There, a woman might pay up to $150 for the privilege of working in a topless bar and then have to tip out on top of that. San Francisco is the site of the first exotic dancer union in the United States, galvanized largely by exploitative working conditions.[25]

Who's Running the Show

At the end of the last shift at upscale clubs, dancers attend a meeting with management to review what transpired during the day, and what they liked and did not like. Management also informs dancers about upcoming events, featured dancers, and policies. Although dancers who worked in clubs that required nightly meetings expressed no strong feelings about them, those employed by clubs without meetings were happy to escape them. Having worked in clubs with and without meetings, Melinda believed they were a waste of her time:

> Some clubs have meetings, but those are just bullshit. They don't do nothing. When they have meetings, they don't listen to the dancers; they just bitch about things, about how it's going to be, and then they ask for our opinion. And then they tell us how it's going to be once again, and then they let us go. Vixens doesn't mess around with that; they know better.

Strip bars are, for the most part, highly regulated environments staffed by trained employees. Like most businesses in America, the owners' goal is to turn a profit. The bar is regulated and the dancers protected to the extent that this guarantees a profit. For example, most dancers reported that they made more money when they drank because it lowered their inhibitions, and, for some, using drugs helped them cope with the more difficult parts of the job. It is therefore in the interest of management to permit dancers access to substances that improve their job performances, and they often do. But if a dancer's behavior threatens an owner's profits —for example, if she misses work, is too intoxicated to perform, or creates conflicts with other employees—she is predictably sanctioned. Thus, despite the sordid reputations of strip clubs in some circles, they are a significant source of revenue to owners and are usually modeled after standard business principles.

As I explore in detail in the following chapters, working as an exotic dancer in the early twenty-first century is a reality for an increasing number of women. The exponential proliferation and accompanying standardization of strip bars, with the recent incarnation of chain strip clubs, make working as a dancer a conceivable choice to a range of women who might not have considered this profession thirty years ago. Although still a highly stigmatized career, exotic dancing is creeping into the continuum of possible job options alongside modeling, acting, and beauty pageants as a means for young women to make money from their physical attributes. For that reason, it is more important than ever to explore what stripping entails and how it affects the women who dance for a living.

Outline of the Book

I was initially drawn to this topic because it combined a number of personal areas of interest, including feminism, sexuality, dancing, and the experiences of marginalized groups. Answers to many of the big questions I wanted to resolve could be found in the stories of strippers. Our interviews touched on weighty issues such as sexual hypocrisy, moral Puritanism, conflict, oppression, the balance of power and powerlessness, sexual agency, and the overall transformation of self, as well as the day-to-day details of managing menstrual cycles, hair removal, and alcohol consumption. Central, then, to each chapter of *Stripped* are the voices, stories, and experiences of the women who work as strippers both inside and outside strip bars. These conversations form the basis of a detailed examination of strippers' lives and provide a cultural context to sort through contemporary tensions about women's sexuality.

The book begins with the question of why, and how, women decide to strip. Many start dancing when they are young and penniless with few familial, educational, or occupational resources. Women often described their decision to dance as a last resort for economic survival, both their own and their children's. Some of the attendant circumstances, such as breaking a taboo and exploring their rebellious side, also appealed to certain women but was a secondary motive to the money that could be earned. A few dancers also spoke at length about how childhood sexual abuse colored both their decision to enter the sex industry and their understanding of the abuse they endure as sex workers.

Chapter 2 examines both the positive and negative events women experience daily working in strip bars. Dancers describe what it is like to dance, how much money they make, the pleasure they derive from performing, how the clients treat them, and alcohol and drug use in the clubs; in short, they share their stories of what they like and do not like about being strippers. Dancing in strip bars, in my view, cannot be neatly broken down into an either/or experience of empowerment or oppression for women, as partisans of the feminist "sex wars" claim. Instead, it is a mixture of the two, an unexplored theoretical terrain that I see as a Möbius strip of rapidly changing feelings and events that wear on women the longer they dance.[26] In this chapter I introduce the toll on women that the sex industry takes over time.

Chapter 3 moves us from inside the strip bar to outside, to the range of problems women endure hiding their work from others, and the discrimination and stereotypes they experience when others learn what they do. Managing stripper stigma requires convoluted psychological techniques to maintain one's self-respect and avoid internalizing the negative stereotypes about strippers. Exploring all the many facets of stripper stigma, and its overall impact on a dancer's life, is a crucial foundation to understanding the toll of stripping.

Chapter 4 closely examines the toll of stripping, the central theme of this book. This toll is specific to stripping and working in the sex industry more generally. As will become apparent, a complex network of experiences tax the energy and self-respect of women the longer they work in the sex industry. The dancers' comments demonstrate that stripping distorts their perceptions of money and sexuality, encourages them to blur their personal boundaries about previously unacceptable sexual acts, teaches them to develop contempt for men, reduces their sex drives, and causes problems in their intimate partnerships. Several late-career dancers told me that stripping itself became literally toxic to them, that just the idea of going into work made them feel sick.

In chapter 5 I explore the first of several creative strategies dancers develop to respond to the toll of stripping. The strip bar is an environment that exposes women to the worst of men's behaviors while providing them access to beautiful women. Because this space also encourages them to break sexual taboos and feign sexual intimacy with one another for men's pleasure, many dancers I interviewed explored their romantic, emotional, and physical attractions to other women. A high percentage of the women I spoke with identified as bisexual or lesbian.

One of the most fascinating and socially significant responses to stripping, according to the women I interviewed, is bonding closely with one another and developing a deeper understanding of inequality. In chapter 6 I examine how the sex industry can engender female solidarity and the capacity to think critically about the industry itself. In the highly unpredictable club environment, a dancer's greatest source of stability comes from the company, respect, affirmation, and friendship of other dancers. In fact, the women who form stable communities with other dancers, like the Vixens dancers, danced the longest. The dancers who learn to critically analyze the sex industry and other forms of social inequality best survive the toll of stripping.

In chapter 7 I describe the historic unionization at the Lusty Lady in San Francisco and speculate on future directions that feminist analyses of the sex industry might take. Experiencing workplace solidarity and developing a critical consciousness logically precede political organization and social change. Performing comparative research in San Francisco afforded me an opportunity to interview some of the key women involved in forming this union. At the Lusty Lady, greater oppression led to a deeper understanding of systemic inequality and to a collective effort to change unfair and discriminatory workplace policies.

Stripped, overall, is a unique compilation and analysis of women's experiences as strippers. I briefly visited the world of the women I interviewed, gathered their stories, and here interpret their experiences. Our richest and most intimate conversations took place, significantly, not in clubs but at kitchen tables, in coffee shops, on living room sofas, and in public parks. In the following chapters you will learn what the dancers themselves want you to know about their lives, not what you might want to hear nor what the popular stereotypes try to make you believe.

1

Becoming a Stripper

Maureen was seventeen when she decided to support herself and her child doing the most lucrative job she knew she was qualified for: exotic dancing. Pregnant at sixteen and the victim of wretched parenting, Maureen found herself cast adrift when her mother kicked her out of her home upon learning of the pregnancy. After Maureen had the child, she felt her options for supporting herself were limited:

> I just had a kid, and I didn't want to get in welfare. Actually it was a friend that used to hang out in the bars that got me the job and stuff. He's a fireman. He said, "Why don't you be a dancer?" I said, "Well, I'm not old enough." And they worked around that.

Maureen is not unusual among the women I interviewed. Several found themselves homeless or with a child to raise or both when they began dancing. Most turned to dancing with little formal education; some chose stripping to help them finance college tuition and living expenses. Nancy, a dancer working in a Honolulu club explained, "I ran out of gas in Florida. I had to do something, and I looked it up in the newspaper, and eleven years later I'm still doing it." The single most common reason why any woman starts dancing (and continues) is for the money.[1] Dancers in most locations in the United States can count on making an average of at least two hundred dollars a shift, and, on some days, and in certain clubs, they may make much more. This means that for women with little formal education and few professional skills, dancing is among the most well-paying occupations available.[2] Stripping offers a higher salary than most pink-collar jobs. For example, in 2004 secretaries averaged $13.38 an hour, totaling a gross annual salary of $27,830 for a forty-hour work week.[3] The dancer earning two hundred dollars a shift (and this is the low end of the salary range for stripping) and working three shifts a week will bring home $31,200 for a twenty-hour work week, and much of this is untaxed. Furthermore—feminists take note—sex work is the only occupation in which women make more money than men. The question, then, could easily be, why don't *more* women start stripping?

Many women begin dancing after struggling to support themselves through more conventional means and after exhausting other employment options. Finding work that supports oneself without a bachelor's degree—and, unfortunately, sometimes with one—is increasingly difficult in the twenty-first-century United States. With deindustrialization—the outsourcing of relatively high-paying manufacturing jobs from the United States to foreign countries—the number of jobs that pay a living wage is decreasing. Meanwhile, as sociologist Jennifer Johnson eloquently documented in her insightful book *Getting By on the Minimum: The Lives of Working-Class Women,* over the past thirty years the number of service-sector jobs has increased. Today, three-quarters of American workers are employed in the service sector in highly stratified jobs that are compensated accordingly. The low-paying end includes cooking, cleaning, serving, and general care work available to anyone, although traditionally performed by working-class women, and the average service-sector job pays only $7.94 an hour.[4]

Work is work. Some jobs are better than others. In her pivotal book, *Nickeled and Dimed: On (Not) Getting By in America,* journalist Barbara Ehrenreich described the difficulties individuals in low-paid service-sector jobs faced to meet their daily expenses. These included problems finding affordable housing, transportation expenses to and from work, drug testing, and an overall lack of time to look for better-paying alternatives. A woman who needs to make fast cash can avoid most of these problems through exotic dancing.[5] Dana, for example, had just gone through a divorce and, like Maureen, also had a child to raise:

> Actually I went through a divorce, and I had so many people telling me what to do, what to do, what to do, and I just kind of wanted to be able to be financially secure on my own. So I tried it once and just stuck with it from there on out. . . . I was always curious, always. From the time you were young and you see the ads for dancers—make two hundred to three hundred dollars, so much a week.

Delia, like Dana, decided stripping was her most practical option for making ends meet:

I think that my major motivation for doing it was twofold: first, I could make a fairly good living for myself and my daughter, and I think that that was the only thing I had. I could sell myself through dancing, but I didn't think I had the ability to do anything else. I didn't have any education until my daughter graduated from high school. When she went away to college, I went with her. So, I really think that that wasn't such a bad choice at the time, because it was an easy way to make money, and I had fun, for a while. It wasn't much fun after a while, but for a while, it was a lot of fun. . . . I think that one of the reasons I did it for a while was because it was an ego boost at that time.

Although many dancers spoke about enjoying the attention they received when they first began dancing, no one I interviewed decided to enter the sex industry for the "ego boost"—to feel better about her body or for the attention. Flattery, adoration, attention, and control were the unexpected perks of the job, not the main motivators for entering the business. Several women, however, did share that they were attracted to dancing specifically because they found the idea of breaking a taboo both exciting and liberating.

"I Was Curious. It Was Exciting!"

Performing in a strip club is also attractive to women with a certain kind of adventurous, experience-oriented, I'll-do-it-if-you-dare-me attitude. It's taboo, but it isn't illegal. It's dangerous, but the financial rewards may be high. It's risky, but it can also be exciting to live on the edge of a morally correct society. Moreover, strip club managers, owners, and dancers encourage this attitude of reckless abandon when they recruit women into stripping. Often, they will ply a potential applicant with alcohol, tell her she is as beautiful as any woman up there, and ask her, "Don't you want to know what it's like to dance?" This is especially attractive to women who feel repressed, bored, or frustrated with their lives. Morgan, who left home at seventeen, was looking for a way to make ends meet and was not averse to the idea of combining her sexuality with her work life.

I had several people tell me that it was a good way to make money, enough money to live on. Just yeah, I thought about dancing before, and

I worked for a guy named Chris. The name of the company was Playful Entertainment. I'd done the lingerie shows at the hotel they used to have on Monday Night Football. I guess my profile fits a certain moral flexibility, but I wasn't absolutely revolted by the idea.

Topless bars are environments in which some women feel they can act out their own fantasies (not just their clients') and resist familial and cultural expectations that they behave virtuously. Kelly, a women's studies major in college, started dancing in a peep show in Chicago before she moved to San Francisco. At first, she interpreted dancing as a feminist expression of her sexuality:

It just allowed me a lot of freedom. I could pick my own schedule. I thought my job was cool and interesting. It was a side of life I hadn't seen before, and I was really attracted to it. I thought it was great. I had this very idealistic, feminist opinion about it at the beginning. I thought it was really empowering; I'm using my sexuality and getting paid what I'm worth.

Most women start dancing when they are very young—when they are more likely to lack economic alternatives, when they are perceived as most attractive by club managers, and when they are best able to thrive in a physically taxing occupation. Mandy was unusual in that she did not begin dancing until she turned forty. Although she started dancing largely for the money, she was also curious about dancing and wanted to experience it for herself:

I wanted to 'cause I didn't know about it. I wanted to experience it because per se you hear this, you hear that, and I'm a person that wants to find out for yourself. My ex-husband used to go, and I wanted to know why. Then I got there, it's different, it's different.

Joscelyn, like Mandy and Dana, investigated a strip club before she auditioned to see if the way she imagined stripping matched reality. At first, she found that dancing met some of her emotional and financial needs. Being in a wholly different world freed her creatively in the beginning—she designed her own innovative costumes and choreographed complicated dance performances. This was exciting for Joscelyn:

I had a friend that was working at the Market Street Cinema, and she was a single mom. She auditioned and got a job. And she told me it was great and she was making three hundred dollars a day. So, of course, I was curious. I had been a dancer before. I had done dancing and gymnastics growing up. So I knew how to do it. But of course, for that job, if you can walk, you can have a job! So, I didn't really need those skills.

I also did fashion design, so I would make some of my costumes. And I had that creative outlet, so it was exciting for me. When I first started, it was a whole new world. I had never been in a strip club before. I just had a stereotypical image that I had gathered from TV and media. I had no idea what to expect. I was exposed to lap dancing. It was very interesting. This was totally new to me. At first, when I saw the lap dancing, I was like, okay, there's this woman on stage tying herself in a knot, and these women look like they are having sex with these men in the audience with the gyrations back and forth, was something I hadn't seen before, and it didn't even occur to me that that happened in these places. I just had no idea what to expect. Needless to say, that is where it all started, and that was my little part-time job during school.

Approximately one-third of the women I interviewed were dancing to support themselves while they worked on an undergraduate degree. As tuition for higher education continues to rise and government funding for education declines, and as popular figures like Brittany Spears and Janet Jackson dance provocatively on prime-time television (in Jackson's case actually going topless herself at the 2003 Super Bowl), some young women consider stripping a practical way to meet college expenses. Indeed, a 2004 issue of the *Nation* explored the trend of stripper-inspired consumer habits: young girls exercising to stripper workout videos, buying thongs in droves, and asking their parents for poles to practice in their bedrooms.[6] "Slutwear," as I have dubbed the latest fashion in girls' and women's clothing, has never been more "in." As I write this, female fashion trends feature crop tops, stiletto heels, low-cut pants, impossibly short miniskirts, and latex body suits. For many of the women I interviewed, it was only a short step across—an admittedly large taboo—from mainstream expectations about their sexual desirability to stripping for money. As Joscelyn admitted wryly, "I already had all the clothes."

"I Was There. I Got Drunk"

Several of the women I interviewed intended to work, or began to work, in some other capacity at a strip bar. Few were certain from the beginning that they wanted to dance. Three of my informants waitressed before they started dancing. It's easier for a woman to decide to dance after she has worked in a club in another capacity, for example, as a waitress or bartender, because she has had the opportunity to watch what the dancers do, as Dana and Joscelyn explained, and become acculturated to the environment. Julie had waitressed at Polished Pearls for a few months before coming to the conclusion that dancers made more money than she did, doing less work. She explained why she changed jobs from waitress to dancer:

> Waitressing, you work very hard. You're always on your feet; you're on five-inch heels. But dancers get to sit most of the night. Big difference. Waitresses cannot sit. They don't get any breaks. It's only a five-hour shift. You're on your feet constantly, and if it's real busy it's very, very frustrating. You deal with drinks, you deal with bartenders, you deal with time period, like if you're impatient like me, it kills you to wait on drinks. You deal with everything in the club, where dancers don't have to. Dancers are pampered: they sit down, they work when they want to work 'cause their money is all on tips, so they're making their own money at their own pace. You get to party if you want to, you sit down, you can socialize. It's a lot different. Waitressing, you can't do any of that. Waitresses, no one cares, no one notices you, no one's polite with you. Most men are in there typically for the dancers. They want to spend their money on the dancers. So whereas you're getting seventy-five cents maybe to a five-dollar tip, they're getting a fifty- to a hundred-dollar tip. And if you're in need of money . . .

The prestige of stripping relative to the other employment possibilities for women in strip clubs—waitress, hostess, bartender—is reinforced by management, which generally allows dancers more leeway in their job responsibilities. Most clubs constantly require a fresh supply of women because of the extremely high turnover rate among dancers. Dancing is difficult, demanding, and draining. It is not unusual for a woman to try dancing for a night or two, feel overwhelmed and uncomfortable in strip bars, figure working at the factory or in the copy room isn't so bad, and quit. Also, dancers regularly switch clubs when the money dries up at their current establishments, hoping to increase their income elsewhere.

Managers routinely try to turn women workers into strippers. One method management uses to replenish an unreliable labor pool is to coerce waitresses into dancing. Frequently alcohol is involved in this recruitment strategy.[7] In Darby's case, the management at her club employed alternating techniques of bullying and coaxing her to drink alcohol to propel her onstage. Darby was sixteen years old when she started waitressing at Lace and Lashes, a small, working-class club in Silverton. It was not long before she found herself performing onstage instead of serving drinks.

> I started waitressing at Lace and Lashes. My girlfriend got me the job. Up in Silverton. And she got me the job waitressing. I waitressed for like two or three months, and I got used to the money. And then they told me, they got me real drunk one night, and they told me that they really didn't need as many waitresses and they were going to have to cut back, so I needed to dance or find me a new job. And so they got me a little bit drunker, and I got up there. That's all it was.

In this case, the intimidation tactics are unmistakable. Management employed Darby when they knew she was a minor, encouraged her to drink vast amounts of an inhibition-reducing intoxicant, and threatened her livelihood in order to "encourage" her to dance topless for men two to three times her age. This was the most blatant example of being coerced into dancing that I encountered, but most dancers reported similar intimidation by management. For example, April, who originally worked as a waitress, was persuaded onto the main stage on a slow night after the management had gotten her very drunk:

> I was coaxed into doing it. I was so drunk I can't remember exact sentences or exact dialogue. I never thought I could do it. When I started, I thought my boobs are too small. I thought I was too ugly to do it, and then to have that sort of acceptance was in itself kind of flattering I think.

To indicate how common this transition is, April told me that the week I interviewed her three women in her club had changed from waitress to dancer.

Since clubs will apply a variety of techniques to recruit dancers, including economic threats and bribes, flattery, peer pressure, and alcohol, management predictably prefers to hire waitresses with dancer potential. Once in the club, however, and having learned that there were only vacancies for dancers, several of my informants auditioned to dance on the spot. This is how Melinda became a dancer:

> I walked into a bar. I was going to be a waitress. A little hole in the wall, a backside country bar, and I walked in and they told me they weren't hiring for waitresses, but they were like, "We're hiring for dancers." And I was like, "I don't know if I want to be a dancer." They're like, "Try it anyway." So they put me onstage like ten minutes later. They had this girl take me in the dressing room and put me in her clothes, and they put me onstage. I stayed, and worked the rest of the night, and made a lot of money. I was pretty happy. I was like, "I guess I'll keep doing this."

As a further incentive, novice dancers are heavily tipped their first time onstage. Melinda continued:

> Well, I was nervous. They put me onstage, but as soon as guys come up and start handing you money, you start feeling a little bit better about being up there. It took me—like I said, that night I went to work and got put onstage—I was nervous for about two minutes, and then after that, I had a lot of fun because I was the new girl. And when you're the new girl, people will give you all kinds of money that first day so you get all geared up feeling good about yourself. And then, after that, dancing seems a little bit easier.

Becoming a dancer entails overcoming personal and cultural taboos about being perceived as everything from sexually available to a "hooker." Women shared that their motivations for battling this taboo were generally very compelling: the need to support a child, financial insolvency, a chance to go to school, a personal dare. And, as I will discuss later, although it is an extremely controversial topic among sex workers and sex-radical feminist researchers—with some claiming that a large percentage of those in the industry are victims of abuse and others resenting the way this so-called stereotype undermines sex workers' ability to control their life choices—a few of the women I interviewed spoke at length about how their personal histories of sexual and physical abuse influenced their choice to dance and their lives as strippers.[8]

"My Mind Was Trying to Work It Out by Replaying It"

Sex workers embody a nexus of oppression: they are almost always women, often they are economically disadvantaged, many are women of color, and a substantial percentage are lesbian or bisexual. In addition, sex workers perform work that is considered dirty, dangerous, and immoral by critics as disparate as the religious right and feminists. Although committed to understanding the complexity of women's lives, feminists have too often participated in stereotyping sex workers by presenting polarized and static portrayals of sex work as either a site of unmitigated oppression or an arena of enormous power and creative self-expression. These opposing positions have existed largely in antagonism to each other, hence the phrase "sex wars" has come to be used to describe the competing theories and empirical findings brought forth by each camp.

The central debate of the feminist sex wars conceptualizes sex workers either as victims of patriarchy and perpetuators of sexism or as transgressive feminine warriors battling sexism through their resistance to "respectable womanhood." Borrowing from sociologist Wendy Chapkis's characterization of the feminist perspectives on the sex industry,[9] feminist theorists can be roughly separated into two groups: (1) radical feminists who find any kind of sex work, and often even sexuality itself, inherently and irrevocably exploitative within patriarchy,[10] and (2) sex-radical feminists who theorize sex work as subversive of patriarchy's definition of conventional femininity and who strongly support sex workers' rights to perform erotic labor.[11]

But even among feminist partisans, there is common ground, as sociologist Lynn Chancer reminds us in *Reconcilable Differences: Confronting Beauty, Pornography, and the Future of Feminism*. As Chancer illustrates, at stake in the sex wars are potentially reconcilable goals: for women to enjoy sexual freedom (the emphasis of sex radicals) *and* to experience freedom from sexism (the emphasis of radical feminists). It's no wonder that we have trouble theorizing these goals in an inclusive fashion—with the sexual and the sexist as closely intertwined as they are in our culture, it's difficult to assess what is truly freeing and what is subtly undermining to women's long-term health and happiness. Nothing illus-

trates this difficulty more vividly than unpacking the relationship between sexual abuse and sex work.

Childhood sexual and physical abuse among sex workers is such a politically, ethically, and personally loaded subject, I did not independently
address it in my interviews. Only if a dancer broached the subject herself
would I explore incidents of abuse, and, even then, I was very cautious.
Like Katherine Frank, anthropologist and author of the book *G-Strings
and Sympathy,* I was conscious that the questions researchers ask of
dancers, including those about sexual abuse, tend to be colored by the researcher's individual unexamined cultural assumptions and stereotypes.
Frank elaborates:

> I began to realize that these basic assumptions about the nature of sex
> work and sex workers, along with the power differentials that often
> exist between researchers and their subjects in terms of gender, educa-
> tion level, economic resources and cultural capital, were influencing not
> only the questions that were asked, but also *who* was studied, in what
> manner, and how the findings were represented. This is not to deny that
> some dancers have been sexually abused, used drugs or alcohol, or have
> difficulty forming intimate relationships—just as many secretaries,
> lawyers, professors, nurses and housewives do. Rather, it is to point out
> that the kinds of information sought out by researchers and the ques-
> tions that one asks are in and of themselves political and based on cul-
> tural assumptions.[12]

Partly, Frank is responding here to the popular conception, advocated especially by radical feminists, that all sex workers were once abused and
that they are driven into the sex industry because of this abuse. One example of an organization that operated with this perspective was the
Council for Prostitution Alternative (CPA), based in Portland, whose goal
was to help prostitutes leave "the life." The organization's orientation
was to see the prostitute not as a victim or a criminal but as a survivor,
one who should confront her past and move on.[13] The following excerpt
from the CPA handbook described the organization's philosophy of why
women enter prostitution:

> Somewhere in your life, someone pointed the way to the street. Either it
> was fast money, you were doing a favor for your boyfriend, or someone
> turned you out—but a lot had to happen before you turned your first

trick. . . . a psychologist who works with post trauma stress syndrome victims suggests that women who are prostituting are "retelling the story" of abuse, neglect, and incest that happened to them. They will tell the story to the world until the pattern is broken or until they are themselves broken.[14]

This theory that all sex workers are abuse survivors understandably angers some dancers, sex activists, and sex-radical feminists.[15] Feminists like myself, who want to freely analyze all parts of a dancer's experience, have to be careful neither to unwittingly feed cultural stereotypes about sex workers and abuse nor, if we do not discuss issues of abuse, to contribute to a conspiracy of silence and omit a relevant component of dancers' experiences. A few of my informants, however, independently discussed personal experiences of sexual, mental, and physical abuse and theorized how those experiences affected their lives as sex workers. In articulating how her own history of abuse influenced her choice to enter the sex industry, Janeen, an African American San Francisco dancer, discussed the time she was raped, and then blamed for that rape, as a teenager.[16] Her powerful story is quoted at length:

When I was fourteen years old, I had this horrible incident on the roof with a boyfriend where I had to perform oral sex. And in black culture, when I was growing up, that was the worst thing you could do. If you had sex on someone's dick, you should just kill yourself, because it was the lowest, most demeaning thing you can do. You can get pregnant at thirteen, but you can't do that. This was a situation that I did in order to get off this roof. It wasn't a pleasurable act. I felt I was either going to get raped vaginally or I can do this. That was the option. What happened as a result of this incident is that everybody found out about it, and it became this scandal. It spread in a way that was unbelievable in the neighborhood I grew up in, in Queens. I went to school across town, and it spread there. Someone would say something to me and I would just cry. And had I had a good home environment, I would have been able to say, "I had no choice. Fuck you!" or I could have called the police; but I didn't have that. The problems have already started before that. My life was already the way it was because of what was going on in my house. So, this spread all over Queens, and I had this reputation wherever I went. I would go outside, people would make slurpy noises and would call my mom and ask her if she knew her daughter was a cocksucker. That relates, because I had that up until I left for college. So, from fourteen to eighteen years of age, I had that going on, as well as whatever was going on in my house.

I had no peace for four years. But it wasn't just teenagers. It was people's parents saying, "I don't want you playing with her." Because of my reputation. Just this one incident. I was fourteen years old and had never had sex or been on a date, but I'm considered the "Slut of Queens." I think that I was so affected by that, that I was affected all throughout college. I couldn't get it out of my mind. I felt like I was that person. It affected my dating in college.

So, I think what went through my head was that everybody says this about me anyway. I don't think it was as simple as just making money from it, but on some level I was like, "Let me make a choice to take this job. I'm going to make a choice to go make money. People always said this about me. Let me go and really be sexual in a way that I don't seem to be able to be sexual in my personal life." In my head, that's how it worked.

It was my mind trying to work it out and heal it. On one level, it obviously doesn't heal it. But I did have to work it out because the next thing I know I was a lap dancer and was right in the middle of all this stuff. And it exacerbated the problems I already had, but it also forced me to work it out. So, it's a complex issue. When people say, "Do you think it was degrading?" Honestly, yes, I do. But I don't want that to be the end of the sentence, because it is complex. Yeah, it was totally fucked, but at the same time—this is corny—but it was also very spiritual. I played out this whole thing, like trying to work it out. This may not sound like it relates, but someone was saying that they had an obsessive-compulsive disorder and they would check things fifty times. And they thought that it was because they were so out of control and beaten up as children that their mind was desperately trying to control something, but it just had to pick something at random, like the mind wasn't able to think it through. "Okay, I'll control moving this glass fifty times." My mind was trying to work it out by replaying it.

Janeen understood her decision to enter the sex industry as partly a way to reframe a degraded sexual self on her own terms: "People always said this about me. Let me go and really be sexual in a way that I don't seem to be able to be sexual in my personal life." Similarly, Tyler, formerly employed by the navy and dancing in Honolulu, explained to me, "When you're in the military they grope you anyway, and you don't get paid for it. Here at [Déjà Vu], you don't have to get groped and they pay you."

At the same time, Janeen described sex work as a complex means of trying to work out the abuse by replaying it: "Yeah, it was totally fucked, but at the same time—this is corny—but it was also very spiritual. I played out this whole thing, like trying to work it out." In the clinical psychology literature, this process is called "repetition compulsion." Repetition compulsion is a common response to post-traumatic stress disorder. Survivors of traumatic abuse reenact the trauma to gain mastery of the situation. In psychoanalytic theory, to quote Jacob Lindy and John Wilson,

> the irrational, persistent psychopathology is seen as an unconscious repetition of psychological tensions (conflicts, deficits, traumas) unresolved from earlier times or life-events. The repetition compulsion infuses current-day perceptions, relationships, and self-esteem. As a consequence, the repetitions dictate fixed configurations of affects, defenses, and object relations that do not adapt well to changing current circumstances. These repetitions then become organizers of the ongoing psychic life of affected individuals.[17]

Clinical psychologists theorize that abuse survivors sometimes seek out situations that reflect past abuse in order to gain control over situations in which they once felt powerless. At first, this may even help survivors cope with the trauma. Unfortunately, replaying and even gaining mastery of a situation that reflects a past trauma is not itself sufficient for an individual to fully heal. It is not unreasonable, then, to imagine that women who experienced childhood sexual abuse are consciously or unconsciously attracted to sex work as a way to replay and try to heal from abuse, as Janeen suggested. Linda, a Honolulu dancer and certified public accountant, also shared that she was strongly attracted to the high income of stripping partly because of childhood experiences of mental abuse and deprivation:

> I will tell you this industry attracts a lot of people who have been abused. I was mentally abused, never sexually abused. My mother mentally abused me. I've been told this industry is attractive to people like that like a magnet. Why does it attract me like a magnet? I think it's because when I was seven years old my mother told me I would have to eat lima beans every meal for a month because we didn't have any money to

buy food. She had no money. She spent all her money. She said, "You like those lima beans? Get used to them. You're going to eat them every meal for a month." Then she turned around to mentally abuse me. We haven't spoken since I was eighteen. Because of stuff like that, I want the money. I want to be secure with money.

Linda left accounting and started dancing to get out of debt. She explained that she made three times as much money dancing—up to three thousand dollars in a shift, with an average of eight hundred dollars—than she did as an accountant. Linda further rationalized exotic dancing by saying bluntly, "If people tell you that you are a dirty lowlife, you might as well get paid for being a dirty lowlife."

The shame and secrecy that shadow sexual abuse make it difficult to generate accurate statistics of abuse victims.[18] Because of the stigma and pain associated with abuse, victims are reluctant to report it. This makes identifying a random sample, measuring the experience of abuse, and trusting that the data are reliable extremely challenging. Not surprisingly, then, figures that indicate the prevalence of childhood sexual abuse among sex workers and in the general U.S. population can vary by as much as 20–50 percentage points. This variation occurs both within each group and between groups. For example, the National Resource Council estimates the percentage of the U.S. population that has been sexually abused to range from a low of 20–24 percent to a high of 54–62 percent.[19] In contrast, studies included in the anthology *Prostitution, Trafficking and Traumatic Stress,* written primarily by clinical psychologists, sociologists, and feminists, suggest that 40–90 percent of sex workers experienced childhood sexual abuse.[20]

Although these figures suggest that a large number of dancers may have been victims of sexual or physical abuse, it is also apparent that childhood abuse is rampant in our culture. A researcher could potentially generate statistics to support the argument that a history of childhood sexual abuse is more prevalent in other professions and is therefore a likely motivating factor for people who enter into those professions, whether they are therapists, coaches, doctors, social workers, or attorneys. This is possible because, as Frank articulates, researcher bias colors the questions we choose to explore. Thus, the sexual behaviors of sex workers, both past and present, are more visible, and salient, to researchers, feminists, religious leaders, and politicians. Similarly, academics are less likely to explore a possible correlation between experiencing childhood sexual abuse and becoming a social worker, lawyer, or doctor, for example, because these are not sexually stigmatized professions.

Cultural biases aside, although studies measuring sexual abuse in the general population and studies on the childhood experience of sexual abuse among sex workers vary enormously, there is, on average, at least 20 percent more childhood sexual abuse cited as experienced by sex workers than by women in the general U.S. population. It is important to note that sexual abuse is never far from sight when you are studying the sex industry, whether it's being singled out by radical feminists, clinical psychologists, and criminologists as the most important illustration of the deviant nature of sex work or being deliberately and actively ignored by sex activists. Further research on the relationship between sex work and childhood sexual abuse has the potential to be both illuminating and problematic for dancers. Such research will require a delicate negotiation: how does one explore the ways in which childhood abuse influences a woman's decision to enter the sex industry without reinforcing the stereotype that it is impossible to make a healthy decision to be a sex worker? Furthermore, although sex work may consciously or unconsciously attract an abuse survivor to work through, and sometimes replay, the abuse, it is not the only reason women begin dancing. But it is the reason most likely to tantalize a voyeuristic public and, consequently, drown out other findings.[21]

Lisa, who was pursuing a master's degree in social work at the time of our interview, and who also was April's partner, hypothesized that women who have been sexually abused dance not only to replay the abuse but also as a way to punish men. Taking money from men, then, is a kind of revenge for previous suffering. Lisa explained:

> I'm thinking of four dancers off the top of my head who have all been sexually abused. If my abuser were a male, it would be easier for me to punish men than it would be to punish women. When you have been abused—and that was the one thing that first intrigued me, when my first girlfriend was dancing, about being a dancer is the power over men. I've never been sexually abused. But to have power over men, at that time in my life, was just exciting to me, because that's what I thought she did. That she could go in and take all their money. And I kind of saw that as humorous at that time. I don't know why. I don't now. I have many men in my life who are good people, and I value them, and that would bother me. But I think the dancers do see it as a way to take back from the men who took from them, and dancing is a way for them to do that.

Although Beatrice did not share a personal history of abuse with me, she did partially support Lisa's theory when she discussed how vindicated she felt taking large sums of money from her male customers. She rationalized her attitude as getting even for the oppression she has experienced as a woman in a male-dominated culture. Beatrice elaborated:

> I totally would feel comfortable using men in a way that I wouldn't with women. In general, so many women feel that they are used sexually by men, and it starts at a young age. Teenage sex is for boys, not girls. Girls will often have sex with a guy because they think that the catalyst to the emotions they want from the man is through sex. And some girls just don't learn that lesson until they've slept with fifty men. So, in a way, it's payback. You're getting money for a service, and it's still not enough money. It's still not what it's worth. But, if you come home with a thousand dollars and think of all the men who paid you to sit with them on their lap and talk to them and be fake to and fulfill what they think of women as being. They come in there thinking women are stupid or slutty and they just do this job because they don't have a brain and that's all they can do. And a lot of women let them think that. "Fine, I'll get their money. That's okay if they think I'm some stupid bimbo. But, I'll be laughing all the way home with my thousand dollars in my pocket that I made in eight hours." And a lot of girls see it that way.

With this comment, Beatrice illustrates some of the ways that sex workers justify to themselves performing stigmatized labor, that is, that what strippers do is little different from what women are socialized to do for men anyway. And furthermore, the dancer thinks, "You may be treating me like a whore, but I am getting hundreds of dollars out of you." But, as Beatrice says, "It's still not enough money. It's still not what you're worth." This sentiment came up over and over in my interviews as part of the toll of stripping, the emotional and psychological costs of sex labor. The dancer may well be getting paid for acts she might have done for free before, and she may be receiving enormous sums of money, but acting sexy for revenge and money do not foster a happy, self-actualized self over time.[22] Ultimately, the negative parts of sex work—rejection, tying money to sexual attractiveness, hearing abusive comments, and constant propositioning—reinforce the original abuse. Most dancers recognize this.

Manufacturing Strippers

Exotic dancing attracts women for both cultural and personal reasons. Interested in how a woman initially overcomes her social conditioning about dancing naked for money, I began each interview by asking, "What made you decide to start dancing?" I started with this question because an individual's first impressions of a high-risk experience, such as bungee jumping, sky diving, engaging in hand-to-hand combat, or taking off your clothes and dancing naked in front of a group of men, is frequently an intense, colorful, and profound experience. I expected that the women I interviewed would have strong feelings associated with both their decision to dance and their recollection of the very first time they danced. Many women wonder what exotic dancing is all about; some toy with the idea of auditioning to dance in times of emotional or financial crisis. I wanted to see if the reasons the women I interviewed chose to dance were adequate to enable them to sustain the toll of dancing, including societal condemnation and familial disapproval. Dancing is not static; it is a journey that occurs over a changing landscape of experiences—and significant changes in perception.

Women's decisions to dance were influenced by a few common elements: economic need, the pleasure of doing something forbidden, access to the environment, and sometimes childhood abuse. Dancing naked on a raised stage for cash might have been a powerful way for some of my informants to resist feelings of inadequacy about their bodies. Many of the women I interviewed were intoxicated the first time they stripped on a stage. Alcohol is a great loosener of inhibitions, and inhibitions are not what one needs when first learning how to strip. Indeed, most dancers shared that they had no idea how to strip at first and "faked it" by copying the woman who danced before them. Several women, such as Morgan, Kelly, April, and Joscelyn, were intrigued by the aspects of the strip club that they felt satisfied their emotional needs to be rebellious, sexy, glamorous, and adventurous. All of them wanted the money. Sex work is a relatively high-paying occupation that does not require a high school diploma, bachelor's degree, résumé, cover letter, or references. The work is obviously attractive to women in financial straits. Eventually, though, whatever their reasons were for beginning to dance, women reported various reasons—some very positive—for remaining employed in the sex industry.

2

Dancing on the Möbius Strip

When I asked Kelly, a dancer of six years, what she thought about the debates over sex work—whether the work is empowering or oppressive—she made a face and said that she was "totally bored" with talking about sex work in those terms. Kelly not only thought categories of empowerment and oppression were limiting in framing her experience she was also "sick to death" of hearing the same tired rhetoric replayed endlessly. Few researchers or journalists have questioned whether sex workers themselves find these categories useful to describe their experiences. And few wonder whether these categories are accurate in the first place. To tease out what dancers think, feel, and experience as sex workers, when I spoke with them I avoided framing my questions into these polarizing categories and asked each woman to explore the range of experiences she had in the clubs.

I found that although there are elements or periods of dancing that the women I interviewed reported as positive and pleasurable, these feelings and moments are transitory. Though one might expect that sex workers, of all women, would have well-developed defense mechanisms to protect their feelings of self-worth, I did not find that to be the case among the women I interviewed. Subjects' responses to questions about the positive and negative aspects of dancing demonstrated that they had surprisingly fragile self-perceptions. The instability and unpredictability of the club environment, which I will be exploring in detail in this chapter, affects dancers profoundly. For example, a dancer may one moment feel that she is the "queen of the universe" when a man tips her a hundred dollars. The very next moment she may feel humiliated and violated when a stranger sticks his tongue down her throat.

To fully understand exotic dancing, it is important to understand the actual work the dancers do and the environment they do it in and, only then, whether or not aspects of the work can be considered empowering, exploitative, or something else altogether. Depending on the length of time a woman has danced, the amount of alcohol or drugs she's consumed, the patrons present, or the mood in a club, a dancer may feel more or less powerful in the act of taking off her clothes on a raised stage or on the floor for men. But to say, in the terms of the feminist sex wars, that dancing is altogether empowering or oppressive, even within the confines of a single evening, is limiting and inaccurate. Good, bad, and just plain weird incidents follow each other with dizzying swiftness. Dancers constantly negotiate these sorts of contradictory and extreme experiences with customers and consequently have extreme emotional responses to them. Dancers are only one comment away from hearing, "You are the most beautiful woman I have ever seen," as well as, "You ugly slut." What emerged from my subjects' narratives was a new way to understand exotic dancing: not empowering *versus* exploitative or even empowering *and* exploitative but, rather, how easily what is empowering can *become* exploitative in the strip bar. Thus, I use the metaphor of the Möbius strip: a roller-coaster ride of male scrutiny, adoration, and rejection to illuminate the multifaceted experience of exotic dancing. Again, the key to understanding stripping lies not so much in the individual psyches and experiences of the dancers but in the length of time they have spent working in the sex industry. There are, of course, exceptions, but overall and over time the toll of sex work is high.

What Women Like about Dancing: Money, Money, Money

The number-one thing that every dancer said she liked about dancing was the money. Most women expressed that, at least in the beginning, to be given rolls of cash for making conversation, drinking freely, and giving the occasional table dance was very exciting. Dancers shared specific experiences that illustrated the pleasures of receiving a large amount of money for doing relatively little physical work. Some told stories of men who gave them a large sum of money without expecting any sexual favors in exchange. These experiences are important to dancers not only because it is gratifying to receive a gift of money but also because they reaffirm the woman's belief in the generosity of clients. Dana's story is typical of these lucrative encounters with clients:

I had a really good customer come in, a younger guy, and I totally didn't trust him either, but he always wanted to go out and everything, and I totally didn't trust him. I thought he was married. I still wonder to this day if he was married. But he came in, and on my birthday last year he brought in seven or eight hundred dollars: here you go, no strings attached, no anything. I thought that was really neat. Most of them are just like that, people that were just being nice. An older guy—he was a car dealer—he came in around Christmas time, and I sat with him for a little bit, and he asked me what I bought for my daughter. And I said I hadn't bought her anything yet. I wasn't able to. And he said, "you need to get that baby something, here," and he slaps two hundred dollars on the table. "Tell her this is from me." And I had just met the guy. So it's just people like that, people who do nice things out of the blue, out the ordinary, and it's nice. I know it's money things; but it's just the thought that went behind it giving you the money.

April experienced something similar:

I was single and everything, and I was kind of depressed, and he comes in and we go up to the VIP room. We're up there twenty minutes, and he has to leave because he's having a New Year's Eve party, and he gives me five hundred dollars. So that was pretty cool. Because that doesn't happen as much as people think. I mean that was twenty minutes of work—five hundred dollars. And I didn't do anything. I was dancing for him. I was a neurology major at the time, and we were talking about the structure of the brain while I was dancing for him, and it was really weird. It was actually the least sexual dance I'd ever done. We were sitting there talking about serotonin levels and dopamine levels and neurons and all this stuff, the limbic system, the temporal lobe, the parietal lobe, all this stuff. I'm sitting here dancing for him, and he just gives me five hundred dollars and leaves. They just give you great compliments, and at the time you totally believe them because they look like they're honest. And they're telling the truth.

Like Dana, April appreciated that the customer recognized her as a person and, in her case, as an intelligent woman, in addition to giving her a large gift of cash. The desire for money, the need for money, and the impact of money on dancers' lives and self-esteem are central to their choices to enter and remain in the industry. But, as April's reflections indicate, the meaning of money for dancers goes beyond its purchasing power. It may signify, as for Dana, that the customer appreciates, and can empathize with, her struggles. But dancers may also have conscious or unconscious expectations that the money men give them is a recognition of their beauty and charm, thus tying one's level of self-esteem directly to one's level of "take-home" cash.

Still, from what I could see, the amount of money a woman makes on any given night is unpredictable and tied to factors as diverse as the weather, the economy, the time of the month, the number of other performers working, and the dancer's own mood and presentation. Working at the Pink Cave, Beverly has made as much as five hundred dollars and as little as three dollars a shift, and she averages between two and three hundred dollars a shift. The bar might be fairly empty early in the evening and become more crowded as the night wears on. If so, a dancer may relax, chat and drink for most of her shift, only collecting money through table and couch dances near the end of the night. Beverly described nights when she made no money at all for four hours and then, at the end of her shift, collected $250 on last-minute table dances. Although money is the number-one reason women choose to dance, and continue to dance, money is not the only positive aspect of the job.

Flexibility, Free Time, and Control

Single mothers, students, and artists explained that the free time dancing allowed them was invaluable to their overall quality of life. Although the public tends to perceive stripping in terms shadowed by morality or lechery—terms of which the dancers are well aware—stripping is also just a job with positive and negative aspects as with any occupation. And for the early-career dancer the positives of stripping are quite salient, especially the advantages of flexible hours and high wages. Dana, a single mother and former paralegal whose time with her daughter was extremely important to her, was able to support herself and her child working only fifteen to twenty hours a week exotic dancing, in contrast to the fifty-plus hours she used to work in a law office. She explained:

I like the free time. It's easy, and I can make my own schedule. I don't have to worry about telling someone I can't come in to work today or worry about finishing a deadline, making a bid go through. You don't have to worry about all that stuff. It can be stressful in a regular job. But I think more or less I like the freedom of it. I'm able to do whatever I want. I can live on my own and not have to worry about having someone because I make more than enough money to live on. That's the overall gist of it. And I have a little girl; my free time with her is really important. I like to spend as much time with her as I can.

It is important to note that Dana's child was only three years old at the time of our interview, too young to understand what her mother did for a living. Dana explained that she planned to stop dancing before her daughter started school, and, indeed, she quit dancing about six months after we spoke. So, for a short while, dancing helped Dana support and spend time with her child. (I will address the stigma of stripping in further detail in the next chapter.)

Stripping, particularly in the less-regulated clubs, is a job whose duties remain nebulous. The work necessitates what appeared to me to be a tedious amount of hanging out, chatting, and waiting to dance. Informants expressed that they liked the fact that they were largely their own bosses. For example, Melinda appreciated being able to control when, where, and for how long she worked, as well as what she does in her work space:

> Yeah, the good thing about working in clubs is the money is all up to you. If you want to make twenty dollars that day, then you sit on your butt all day. If you want to make four hundred dollars, then you're really working hard. And management won't tell you how much you need to work. They won't push you for how much you need to work. You have a certain number of drinks you need to sell. If you don't sell them, you pay for them by the end of the night. But that's all on you, that's up to you. You don't have anybody breathing down your back, checking up on you. You have bouncers who keep you safe, but other than that you're left alone to work by yourself. So that's a good thing.

Hence, dancers drink, laugh, socialize, lounge, visit one another or the DJ or the bouncers, check their makeup, and fix their hair during work hours. Although management requires a dancer to perform in the stage rotation and perhaps spend a certain amount of time on the floor chatting with the customers, it is within the control of each dancer to generate her income. No one is checking up on her to make sure she circles the room every half hour hustling for dances.[1] Consequently, dancers must be self-motivated and avoid getting too distracted or intoxicated partying with one table while the evening slips away.

For many of the women I interviewed the flexible hours topped the list of the positive aspects of dancing. In most establishments, dancers can choose their shifts weekly, call in if they are sick, or simply not show up, with few repercussions. Moreover, dancing is a good job for those unable, or unwilling, to work a nine-to-five job. For Sarah, exotic dancing was an appealing job option because unpredictable health problems prohibited her from committing to a full-time job. She explained what she liked about dancing:

> Definitely being able to do my work and make it every single day. Like, when I was in college, I missed half my classes because of my health. And I've missed like two days of work in the six months I've been here, because my schedule is so lenient. That makes me feel good. It makes me feel like I'm getting over my chronic fatigue and I'm getting control of my life. Having the Lusty Lady giving me that, that freedom, I don't know what I'd do without that job right now. I really don't know what my life would be like without the Lusty Lady. And the schedule flexibility is definitely the number-one, top best thing.

Dancers all liked having more free time and flexible hours than they might in a "straight" job. This is a consequence of the relatively high pay per hour. Each dancer recognized the advantages of a flexible work schedule, even when the dancing itself was physically and mentally draining or just tedious.

The Pleasure of Performance

Some of the women I interviewed shared that, given the right combination of circumstance—lights, costumes, alcohol, music, clients, money—stripping was an incredible high. The early-career dancer accesses this high more easily than the more-experienced stripper because she is new to the world, its rhythms, and not thus far beset by the drawbacks. No one has denied her housing yet, ostracized her at a party, or refused to date her because she is a topless dancer. Her parents think she is waitressing at a club, and the burden of hiding exotic dancing from them has yet to emerge. The fledgling dancer has not felt the Sisyphean toll of dancing, and most are intoxicated by the attention, adoration, and rush of money from men. Beatrice, a recent UC Berkeley graduate who had been dancing for approximately two years at the time of our interview, described some of the pleasure she derived from dancing:

> I'm kind of a ham. I like to perform. I did a lot of music and dance performance before. I feel like that part is kind of an art. When I'm on stage, I feel everyone looking at me, and it just makes me shine in a way. I feel pretty. I try to do imaginative things in my dances. I try to get really classy music and beautiful costumes. I feel like some sort of model or priestess in the olden days, doing the very erotic thing. But I like it.

The women who had some training in dance enjoyed performing on the main stage the most. Morgan studied ballet for ten years. Her favorite time in the club was right at the beginning of her shift, at four in the afternoon, when the bar was almost empty. At this quiet hour, she used her first set to stretch out and move to music she particularly enjoyed, without worrying about any crowd-pleasing Mötley Crüe requests. While no real dancing is required of performers, Morgan felt her dance training has increased her appeal to clients. She explained:

> I think that's my thing. I don't have breasts. I'm not blonde. I'm certainly not willing to do a lot of the things a lot of the girls are. I think that's kind of my gimmick. That I can actually dance, as opposed to just walk around and wiggle. 'Cause me walking around and wiggling is just really not all that much to see; I mean I'm pretty well built like a fourteen-year-old boy. There ain't that much to see as far as wiggling goes. I don't have the wiggle power. Yeah, I can dance and I like to. I really enjoy it. And I think that that always shows when somebody really enjoys and is kind of spiritually with what they're doing, whatever it is. I like to dance. It's nice to be able to do something that you enjoy in an athletic and artistic way and get paid pretty good money for it.

A recent study of topless dancers categorized one subset of women as "dancers."[2] These individuals shared in common that they had all taken traditional dance lessons for many years, and most had considered becoming professional dancers. Among my informants, Morgan and Trina were in this category. Exotic dancing is a means for professionally trained dancers to use their skills to make a living dancing. Trina, a Honolulu dancer, explained that exotic dancing gave her the opportunity to actually make money with her art:

> I have my degree in economics and dance; I could be doing anything I want. I've worked in a Fortune 500 company. I've done lots of different work and I know lots of different people where I could network myself to work behind a desk, but that's not my true self. My true self is in my dancing body that is willing to go anywhere, even to this place of extremity of dancing. It's like the only dance place where you can actually make money as a dancer, as opposed to getting paid six dollars for ten days of hardcore work. It's amazing the juxtaposition of what is valuable.

Moreover, some of the women I interviewed explained that dancing initially made them like their bodies more. The power rush a woman can receive from dancing is especially potent if she previously thought her body was ugly, fat, short, flat-chested, and so on—the litany of ways women (and men) can critique their physical forms is seemingly endless. If a man pays to see her undesirable, "rejected" body nude, a dancer might feel that she is not as ugly or fat or flat-chested as she thought.[3] Exotic dancing is particularly rewarding for women who felt they were unattractive in junior high and high school. Many of the women I interviewed, like Tara, a former dancer and native Hawaiian, suffered from "ugly duckling" syndrome:

> In high school I was one of those girls that guys never paid any attention to. I was the chubby girl or the fat girl, the one that was good enough to be your friend but never anything more. After high school I lost the weight and got into shape, and all of a sudden I had all these guys that wanted to be with me and take me out on dates.[4]

As an early-career dancer, April's self-esteem increased working in strip bars. Having been raised by a critical mother who told her she was unattractive and, like Tara, having felt ugly and unwanted in high school, dancing freed April to perceive her body as beautiful. She confided:

> It's a power trip though. I'm getting it all back. After twenty years of that, of hearing that, it's still there. It takes hearing how beautiful you

are and how sexy you are and just, it takes just taking people's breath away, whether they're drunk or not. If you're hearing it twenty times a day, it's slowly healing you, and you start to believe it. That's how all of the girls are the same. You see, everybody thinks that girls that dance, they have this very high self-esteem and they believe that they're beautiful and all that. And that couldn't be further from the truth. It's your other personality there. The longer you dance, the more confident you become. There's almost a pattern of behavior. If you were told fifty times a day that you are the most beautiful woman that person had ever laid eyes on, wouldn't that make you feel better?

April was not alone in expressing how powerful it feels to be given money and told that she is beautiful. Mandy said succinctly, "I like it. I like dancing. I like music. I like control. I like power. I like to look good, and I like to feel good. And they make me feel good sometimes that I look better, more radiant." Maureen shared, "Sometimes you feel like a goddess with all the men looking at you. It makes you feel good. I like being spoiled with attention, attention you wouldn't get anywhere else. Any woman would." Delia, like April, discovered that dancing introduced the possibility that she could perceive herself as attractive: "I had always had a negative opinion about myself—always—and even though it didn't help my negative opinion about myself in most ways, I didn't feel ugly anymore. There were people coming and paying money to watch me, so I must not have been as ugly as I thought."

Trina, who called herself an "erotic improvisational artist" rather than striper or exotic dancer, interpreted her performances in strip bars as part of her journey to her authentic self:

I'm beginning my inward journey, lots of meditation, yoga, dancing, creative expression, lots of writing, lots of reading definitely. Just discovering all the different facets of myself that need to heal and to lift and to feel again. I reread my thesis, and at the end of my thesis my last sentence said, "I will continue to journey my life through dance." I was like, "What in the world gives me more meaning than anything else? Dance." It's real for me. It's my path. I was like, "OK. I want to dance. All right, how am I going to be a dancer and make money at it?" I didn't want to be a teacher in the school system because it's just going to be teaching technique. I don't want to do musicals. I'm not into that. I'm into this authentic expression. I want it to be this inward journey toward healing myself and becoming more of whoever I am and that sort of thing. What would that allow me to do with enough space to teach, feel, do, whatever?

Although Trina had only worked as a stripper for nine months at the time of our interview, she has danced since she was a child and received her bachelor's degree in dance. Eventually, Trina planned to continue her studies in dance in a Women's Spirituality and Dance program in San Francisco, then start graduate school at UC Berkeley. Trina was one of several women I interviewed who discussed feeling spiritual while she danced.

Spiritual Stripping

Not only did many of the women I interviewed describe dancing as a profoundly pleasurable experience at certain times, they also discussed exotic dancing in language that connected them to the divine. Some of my informants sought "redemption," like writer/dancer Meredith McGhan—they danced partly to feel that their bodies were "good enough" for at least a few hours a week.[5] Additionally, several of the women I interviewed, including April, Morgan, Trina, Kelly, Joscelyn, and Janeen, described exotic dancing as spiritually fulfilling, a way to reclaim power, a journey into their bodies and souls, and a release from a numb corporate culture. Trina articulated it this way:

> Spirituality and sexuality are one in the same when you are not using them to either dominate or control. When you are using them as this commingling dance, if you will, tango of sorts, you're finding a divinity that exists. It's finally a release from the pressures, all the limitations, all the judgments that we hold sacred and valuable to ourselves that keep us from really experiencing and letting everything go in the flow of an infinity. Do you know what I mean? You're experiencing a release, and it's finally like a breath of fresh air. I don't know if you've experienced for yourself anyone that you know was a closeted homosexual and finally came out. It's like complete release when you say, "It's okay to be me, however I am." I feel like in dancing you say, "It's okay to be me, however I am."

April, twenty-three and working on her bachelor's degree in psychology at the time of this interview, shared similar feelings:

> It's very spiritual. I love it. It's the only time I feel good about every inch of my body, every part. I get this totally different perspective that I never get to see. You know, I mean the black lights. I've liked them before I've ever worked in the bars. They cast like this dark glow on your skin, and the music is pounding and the alcohol. You're soothed. I used to, we used to be able to smoke dope very openly in the bars. We'd wrap up tampon wrappers full of dope and smoke it. And we'd come out, welcome to Paradise, and everybody'd walk out, and there'd be a big cloud of pot smoke following everybody. But it was everybody clapping and cheering, and you were just exhilarated. And I loved it though. But I love music; I love music more than anything. I love it. It goes down the very center of me.

Psychologist Abraham Maslow described moments such as the ones April and Trina shared with me as "peak experiences," when an individual transcends her normal state of consciousness and feels in harmonious contact with the "seen" and "unseen" worlds.[6] Unsurprisingly, the potential spiritual dimension of stripping has received little attention in a culture that associates spirituality with religion and strictly separates sexuality from religion. For most people, strip bars are about bodies, not souls, and the basest expression of lust at that. So how, and why, might an exotic dancer access her spirituality in such a place? To explore this question we must examine topless bars not only as places oriented for men and male desire but also as spaces in which women can subjectively experience themselves while performing their jobs. This finding is not only culturally counterintuitive, it also challenges the patriarchal domination and regulation of female sexuality. It suggests that one can mingle sexuality with spirituality and, further, that during a peak experience on stage a dancer may not be performing her sexuality at all but, instead, be engaging in a form of worship.

Dance and other forms of movements are common to many spiritual traditions. For example, in the mystical branch of Islam, Sufism, participants—called whirling dervishes—twirl their bodies round and round to induce a transcendent state of consciousness. Similarly, those who practice shamanism drink mind-altering substances and move rhythmically to a monotonous drum beat to enter a sacred space.[7] For shamans, sacred space is a liminal space, a place between worlds, in which the normal flow of time and perception is altered. Other elements present in shamanistic journeys include overcoming hardship, testing one's endurance, breaking taboos, and searching deep inside oneself to explore one's most vulnerable and hidden parts. Many of these elements are also present when a woman dances in a strip bar. Exotic dancing happens in a liminal space, between the "straight" world and a forbidden zone of vivid feminine sexuality. The dancer tests herself and evokes danger by breaking cultural taboos, facing her fears, twirling around a pole, and moving rhythmically to a repetitive drum beat. She is exposing herself—"her sacred parts," as Katrina, a Honolulu dancer, described—and may feel vulnerable. If she is drinking alcohol or using drugs, the "dreaming" self is even easier to access.[8] This finding complicates popular understanding of the strip bar. Exotic dancing can be a more multifaceted experience for women, and the strip bar a more nuanced work environment than most patrons realize. Strippers are not only objectified bodies dancing for male desire; at times their sensual movements can connect them to their own perception of the divine. A dancer may be tuned out, apathetic, and bored on stage. Or she might be dancing into her spiritual self, with the sea of faces a distant accompaniment to her worship.

The empowering aspects of stripping emerge immediately, despite some unpleasant experiences and consequences, for the early-career dancer. She enjoys a sudden cash flow, attention, adoration, free time, a flexible schedule, even access to deeply buried emotions and "peak experiences." After interviewing several dancers, however, I began to observe a pattern emerging from dancers' stories about their experiences in the sex industry. As early-career dancers, most women spoke about how exciting it was to dance, how much money they made, how powerful they felt, and how energizing it was to break the taboo about displaying their bodies for money. Those feelings of empowerment and excitement changed, unfortunately, in relation to the length of time they danced and to the greater number of negative events they experienced while working.

The Physical Cost to the Body:
"You Age in Dog Years When You Dance"

Physically, dancing wears out women's bodies. Dancers work late hours in dark, smoky environments in which they are encouraged to drink large amounts of alcohol. They dance in extremely high heels with little opportunity to get properly warmed up before each dance. Melinda explained:

> I plan to be a dancer probably no more than another year. That would put me at two and a half years total. That's not too bad. It's rough on your body. I dance so much that my joints ache a lot now. I get bruises real easy. I get stiff. I'll wake up in the morning and it's hard to move sometimes 'cause I don't stretch out enough too. 'Cause you'll find yourself doing a lot of dancing for ten, twenty, thirty minutes. If you get in that couch room and you stay there, that's a lot of hard work, a lot of sweating, and then you get out and you might sit for another forty minutes after that and never stretch out. Eventually your body gets more and more wound up and wound up, and it starts to hurt.

During each couch, table, or lap dance, depending on the type and depth of the surface the client is sitting on, as well as the size of the client, a dancer will have to adjust the amount and direction she bends and squats. The physical positions dancers maneuver themselves into during these dances are particularly taxing to their knees and lower back. Imagine getting into a half squat and varying it only slightly for three and a half minutes. Imagine doing this for four hours at different squat levels. It's a testament to dancers' flexibility and ingenuity that they don't fall on top of their customers more often. Mandy, the forty-year-old dancer working at Vixens, explained that she had an even harder time than some of the younger dancers with the physical demands of stripping:

> Squatting the legs, the bending, constantly in high heels, a lot of bad things. Your feet. I don't care, I've got shoes that are a size and a half too big, but your feet swell up so much they fill in that shoe when you wear a shoe that high. I take these things off, let my toes breathe. It's hard on you. The lights get intense; so much lighting all the time can get old. When you get onstage you're seeing spotlights in different colors and black lights. Now, see, they have to turn strobe lights off for me. I'll have

a seizure with strobe lights. Then the music gets old. It does affect your hearing. People don't realize it that you're sitting right underneath that speaker and you're yelling to speak up. Right now I know my voice is loud 'cause I'm still ringing in my ears from the loudness.

In San Francisco, dancers perform live sex shows in certain clubs, like the Mitchell Brothers O'Farrell Theater. These shows sometimes include penetration, with another woman or with toys. Inserting dildos caused internal irritation for Joscelyn. She described this unique job hazard during our interview:

> To be frank, one of the worst things is like when you're doing toy shows and you're doing girl-girl shows and just the constant penetration when you're not necessarily aroused can cause internal problems. So there were times I had bladder infections or yeast infections. So there's a discomfort. Obviously, if you're uncomfortable, you don't want to have sex, and you're not feeling that great about yourself because you're in pain. And you don't feel well, and one of your body parts isn't working like it's supposed to be working, so there's these occupational hazards that go along with it.

Similarly, Morgan explained that dancing fully nude increased the possibility of contracting an infection:

> Well, you have performers touching themselves onstage and elsewhere, touching objects and touching the customers. I am dancing, and if ten people have danced nude onstage before me, and their genital area touched, say, the pole, and then I touch the pole, and touch my face, or something that I am going to eat . . .

Morgan concluded that there are a limited number of things that could actually be transmitted that way, but it still made her uncomfortable.

April summed up the physical demands of dancing nicely:

> You age in dog years when you dance because it's so hard. I mean, you're walking around in nine-inch heels. Your body is in this totally different position. Your knees go out. You get out of bed, you sound like an old mattress. You throw up all the time. Your body weight goes up, it goes down, it goes haywire. You drink. So it's the physical part of it.

And it makes you age faster. And hearing some of the things that you hear, I mean, it makes your mind mature a lot faster.

In addition to the bodily wear and tear dancers endure, Melinda explained that working in a bar is exhausting:

It wears on me. It's just something that's—it's dark. The bars are dark so you hear a lot of music over and over and over again. If I ever listen to AC/DC ever again in my entire life, when I quit dancing I'll find the band and kill them all. Guns and Roses, Aerosmith, they're all good bands but geez . . . Even my own music, as much as I love it, I've got to try and change it up every now and again because I just keep something new in there. I got to, 'cause I get so burned out on the same stuff. The nights feel—every time you're in that club, you feel like it's the same day you were in there before 'cause there's no windows, nothing changes. It's always a dark, smoky place with the same music, the same people. I change clubs a lot, every three or four months. I often find myself quitting and going somewhere else, and that's because I can't take the scene.

To deal with the boredom, the noise, the strange men, and the aching joints, many strippers imbibe the easily available beverage of choice in a strip bar: booze. As a regular customer, Mike, quipped, "Who wants to be sober in a strip bar?"

Alcohol and Drug Use

An occupational hazard that virtually every dancer discussed was alcohol. In the clubs that serve alcohol, management expects the dancers to accept drinks from the customers because most club owners make the bulk of their profit from alcohol purchases. To combat the problem of drunken workers, and demanding clients, clubs often manufacture ways for dancers to order nonalcoholic drinks without alerting the customers. Dana explained the fake-drink system at Polished Pearls:

You can buy fake drinks, though, if they want you to drink. I'll try and almost always order something and make sure the waitress knows it doesn't have alcohol. They have little slang terms you can use to let the waitress know that you don't want alcohol. So if you want an Absolut and cranberry, you just give her this little phrase and she knows to make it a virgin drink.

Customers invariably want the dancers to drink alcohol and are savvy to the tricks dancers use to stay sober. A client reasons that if he can get a woman sufficiently intoxicated, it might loosen her inhibitions enough so that she'll have sex with him later. Consequently, he may insist on ordering shots for her, drinks that are hard to fake. Many of my informants discovered that they actually made more money when they drank or got high; one dancer explained that it relaxed her enough to hustle harder for table dances. Also, the more intoxicated a dancer is, the more uninhibited she might be during private dances. More exposure or more contact often means bigger tips.

Dancers may also use drinks from clients as a test of interest level. If a client is too cheap to buy her a drink when she sits down with him, she expects he will not spend money on table or couch dances later. Dana shared her strategy for gauging a client's level of financial commitment in the following exchange:

> *Dana*: My big thing is, if I sit down and the waitress comes over and automatically he says no, he gets about five minutes more of my time, and then I'm gone. Because, generally, if they're not going to buy you a drink, they're not going to buy a dance. So I'll get up and move or say hi to someone or whatever, and then I don't go back. Nine times out of ten I'm right about it. Sometimes you're wrong, but nine times out of ten you're right, and that person hasn't been taking up all your time for nothing. You have to kind of be careful about all that.
>
> *Bernadette*: So do you end up drinking a lot on a shift?
>
> *Dana*: You can. I don't always, but you can if you're not careful. If you find yourself just drinking and drinking and drinking, and then all of a sudden, before you know it, you're just drunk. So it happens, probably more frequently than it should among a lot of us. But that's how the club makes their money.

Several dancers discussed that it was not only the toll drinking took on their bodies in the form of hangovers and low energy that upset them but also that, when drunk, they sometimes said and did things they regretted. April described this phenomenon:

If you're just a raging alcoholic, you do not need to be doing this, because if you have blackouts, you end up prostituting yourself. I've just
seen a lot of girls get lost doing it, doing a lot of bad stuff. Everybody
makes mistakes. You make mistakes from the moment you start. You
just constantly learn. I mean, I did a lot of stuff that I regret. I may have
regretted that I did thirty shots the night before. I may regret that I ate at
White Castle after work.

Immoderate alcohol consumption was not the only problem employees of strip clubs shared. Allen, a DJ at Vixens and Melinda's partner, said
that working in strip bars provides dancers, and other employees of the
clubs, the opportunity to party excessively:

The real danger in working in the clubs is that it becomes one long
night, because you work until 1:00 A.M. and you've been drinking all
night. Afterwards you want to get a bite to eat maybe, so you go to
Perkins. That's an hour, an hour and a half, that's 2:30 getting home.
You want to relax, watch TV, that's 3:00 or 4:00. And if you're with
somebody, and you're going to be having sex or whatever, that's 5:00,
6:00. And then you go to bed at dawn and wake up at 4:00 in the afternoon, get ready, go to work, and start your night again. 'Cause as soon
as you walk through the doors, it's dark. It really is a life of excess. Some
of the clubs now that are doing the nonalcohol thing are a lot better to
work in because you don't have the opportunity to be perpetually
fucked up. You can actually maintain some kind of semblance of reason
while you're in that place.

One of the stereotypes about dancers is that they are all drug and alcohol abusers. Although I did not find that to be the case among my sample, six of the women I interviewed smoked marijuana before or during
our interview. Additionally, the subjects themselves spoke of a higher
than normal drug and alcohol use among dancers than in the general
population. Morgan, now a pre-med student, described the pattern of
drug and alcohol use on any typical night when she worked at Lips in
1999:

I think your pattern of drug use in a club on a given night . . . let's take
the ends of the bell curve: let's say you have a few people who are sober

for whatever reason, say they just don't drink, and then you have the people that are habitually so fucked up on their drug of choice that they can't stand and have been to the hospital three times out of the club for overdosing or whatever. There are a lot of people like you would see in a normal bar that don't necessarily even use any recreational drugs, but if it's here and somebody's buying, I might have four, five, six drinks throughout the night the same as they would if they were out. Then you've got the people who use, to whatever degree, recreational drugs, which I think fall into categories as well. You have cokeheads, pills, the benzo people, and the opioids—the people who like the Valium and Xanax.

This particular pattern may or may not be present at other strip bars. In any case, dancers do have greater access to legal and illegal intoxicating substances while they are working than most people in mainstream occupations. Moreover, because dancers work in environments in which they regularly experience rejection and emotional abuse, it is enormously tempting to turn to alcohol and drugs to alleviate this stress. Alcohol and drug use may not only relieve stress but allow the dancer to feel more powerful and in control.[9] The combination—easy access, more money, and emotionally and physically demanding labor—means that dancers may be on some chemical substance most of the time they are working. Lisa, April's partner, perceived drug abuse as rampant among dancers:

They want to numb themselves out, and if they do not have a good enough defense system in place, they use the drugs and alcohol to numb themselves out to enable them to perform. The first dancer I was with became addicted to drugs. And I watched her through the dancing. She began to use the dancing for a means to make money. In the end, dancing used her. She began to prostitute. The addiction to the drugs led her to prostitution. And where my current girlfriend works, I don't know of any girls in that club who don't drink, do coke, marijuana, or some type of drugs. They all do drugs. I think it puts them in a situation where it's easier to perform that job if you are fucked up and numbed out. That's one of the best defenses in the world. We feel a lot more comfortable in certain situations if we have that drug in our system. Just as alcohol can destroy a person, dancing can destroy. I watched my first dancer girlfriend be annihilated.

In this excerpt, Lisa supports every stereotype of exotic dancers and drug use: strippers use drugs and alcohol to numb themselves, dancing turned her ex-girlfriend to drugs, and the drugs made her a prostitute—in effect, drugs and dancing annihilated her. It's easy to single out strippers as uniquely troubled by substance abuse, especially when doing so obscures the bigger picture. Workers in many professions use alcohol and drugs to cope with job stress. The Substance Abuse and Mental Health Services Administration (SAMHSA) estimates that 8 percent of full-time American workers are current users of illegal drugs. The rate of drug use is highest among construction workers (16 percent), restaurant employees (11 percent), and laborers and machine operators (11 percent).[10] Alcohol use is even higher in each category. Consider how many people you know who need four cups of coffee to get going in the morning, who drink a six-pack or smoke a joint after work, who are on antidepressants or sleeping pills or Ritalin, who guard their smoking breaks religiously, who get high *before* work. I know someone who smokes a bowl of pot every morning before he does sales calls to help himself "get focused and alert." I interact every day with people on allergy pills, pain killers, heartburn medicine, benzodiazepines, and antidepressants. How many people do you know who have stressful jobs? If each one had the opportunity to drink alcohol or smoke marijuana during work, and see an improvement in job performance and income level, would she or he use?

Exotic dancers do use alcohol and drugs in their workplaces. So do Americans in many other professions. Although strippers may be more affected by the stigma of their work than individuals laboring in more socially acceptable occupations, performing any stressful, repetitive, physically demanding, underappreciated labor creates tension that some individuals alleviate through self-medication.[11] The problem with studying dancers' substance use, like researching strippers' histories of sexual abuse, is that such research can be used to further stigmatize dancers. The better question is: how do we change the labor force so that we can each perform socially useful and fulfilling work?

Rude Customers

Strip clubs exist on the borders of "morally correct" society. Although the simulated sexuality that takes place in topless bars is not illegal, the women that work as dancers are breaking social rules for respectable female behavior by playing the role of "tawdry slut" in public. Therefore, in the mind of the average customer, normal rules of social etiquette do not apply. Some feel entitled to make the dancer the target of all his most abusive, perverse, and obnoxious behaviors and ideas. Indeed, some patrons consciously or unconsciously assume that this is what they are paying for: their right to treat a naked or nearly naked woman with abuse and contempt. Consequently, in the minds of some customers, middle-class norms of social etiquette do not apply. Not all customers are rude. Dancers estimated that problem clients composed no more than 20 percent of all customers. However, even though the majority of men frequenting strip bars are affable, rude clients are common enough that every dancer shared stories of contemptuous male behavior. Rachel, a San Francisco dancer, felt that dealing with rude customers was the hardest part about working at the Lusty Lady:

> The job is bad because you have to deal with the customers, who can be problematic and rude. Most of the time, the customers are okay, but that one bad apple can really ruin your day. I guess they feel like the normal laws of etiquette that govern any other social or business interaction are suspended there. It is okay to call someone a bad name or use foul language. They'll say, "Turn around, bitch, I want to see your ass. I'm paying." Just to talk to someone in a way you'd never in a million years think of talking to someone in any other business or social interaction. That's just not allowed; they get thrown out. But still, to have to deal with that at all is a real drawback. That's not something you have to contend with systematically in other jobs.

Customers attempt to manipulate and intimidate dancers in a variety of ways: peer pressure, insults, rejection, or money. The most common act a client will attempt to pressure a dancer into is prostitution. A stereotype about dancers is that they are all promiscuous. As much as dancers dislike the stigma associated with this stereotype, they must also reinforce the idea that they are available, male centered, and sexually aroused to make money. Hence, a dancer will flirt with her customers and feign interest in them in order to encourage them to return to the club and spend more money on her. The drawback is that a client may not realize that the performance is a fantasy and may think that the dancer really desires him. When a regular customer feels he is only one step away from getting a favorite dancer into bed, he may proposition her. In addition to regular customers who feel they have some investment in a particular dancer, strip clubs also attract men who proposition dancers immediately and repeatedly. Clients offer money, clothes, cars, and breast jobs in exchange for sexual favors. This constant propositioning forces dancers to set clear boundaries. Dana offers a standard comeback to propositions:

> There's a lot of them that come in and proposition you all the time. "Will you do this? Will you do this? My wife's out of town." And you're like, "How gross are you? You're married and you have a child, and you're still asking me to go home with you?" My whole thing is: I'm not about that. [I am] not a whore. Go to the street corner. Not about me. "Not a whore." They usually don't say anything when I say that. What can they say? I've never had anybody reply to that when I say, "Not a whore. I'm not for sale." They just look at you kind of dumbfounded.

Sarah and Vera, roommates I interviewed together who also work at the Lusty Lady, discussed the phenomenon of rude customers and their subsequent responses to this behavior in the following exchange:

> *Vera*: If men could be polite to sex workers and women, in general, the job would be absolutely perfect and there would be nothing wrong with it at all.
>
> *Sarah*: I don't know why they don't understand that, because a lot of repeat customers that will come in there will continue to be rude. I talked to this guy who had been coming to the club who said they were paying for the privilege to be rude to you. Like it's your job, you're being paid to take it. And they think it's the privilege of the customer to give that treatment because they can't give it anywhere else.
>
> *Vera*: And that goes along with what you were saying about what exactly is the woman's role. I think that it's a service and people should treat you with respect. You don't order a waitress around in a restaurant. You don't say, "Get my water, bitch, right now."
>
> *Sarah*: That's where I kind of think that's a little wrong, because some people do order the waitresses around. I think, in reality, a lot of the time, men are truly rude to women, and it's up to me to make them be polite to me because they want my pussy. And if they're going to get it, they're going to be polite and nice. Sometimes, I think of my job title as the Educator of the Men of San Francisco in Politeness and Kindness towards Women because I don't put up with their shit. And, hell, they're just

putting in twenty-five cents. They certainly aren't paying me to do so. If the guy wants to come in and says, "I want to be raunchy and call you dirty names," I'll be like, "Okay, this is how much you have to pay for it." But onstage, they are not paying for the privilege to treat me poorly. They are paying for the privilege to see my naked body. And I sometimes say to the other girls, "They can be disrespectful towards their mothers and wives and secretaries, but when they come in here, they are going to treat me well, damn it!" And that's the way I look at it.

Like Sarah expresses here, many of my informants, as well as first-person narratives by dancers, make the link between the sexual harassment and abuse they observed and experienced inside the sex industry and that in the world more generally.[12] Dancers endure a compressed version of culturally sanctioned misogyny. By choosing to take her clothes off for money, a woman steps outside the spoken and unspoken rules for appropriate gender behavior. The liberating part of this is that she does not have to conform to sexist double standards. The disturbing part is that she has given up the paternal protection that "good" girls supposedly receive from men. By unpacking this fantasy of protection dancers can develop a critical perspective on masculine privilege and female subordination and deconstruct existing power relations. The constant verbal abuse —especially combined with the physical violations detailed in the next section—can take a serious toll on dancers' attitudes toward their profession and toward men more generally.

Physical and Emotional Abuse

In addition to dealing with generally rude behavior, every dancer told me about fending off clients who tried to touch her. They all have had men kiss them. One dancer told me about having a client shove his tongue down her throat; another put his tongue inside her vagina when she was performing a naked dance. Darby and Dana both experienced the humiliation of customers pulling down their g-strings while they were dancing, each responding the best she could. Darby shared the following:

> I've had bad things happen at strip clubs. I've had dudes come up and throw change at me. I've seen other girls get it done to them too. Dudes get drunk and they don't like you, you know, they don't like you. They

go up and do something rude like throw change at you or, if you diss them—they'll want you to come over to their table and you're sitting with good money so you don't go—they'll have to come up and redeem theirself by making you look bad. I had a dude jerk my g-string off one time, and I broke his nose with a six-inch heel. And he tried to sue me. He didn't win. He pulled my g-string right off of me. I was butt naked onstage. Broke a thirty-dollar pair of bottoms, I'm going to break your nose.

Dana described an evening during which two separate clients assaulted her physically. After these incidents, she sat down and refused to give any private dances for the rest of her shift.

This guy yanked my bottoms down in the back. I turned around and smacked him, and then I went and got the bouncer afterwards. But that's just—that's horrendous. I hate that. I don't like people touching me or anything. The first time that happened was during a regular table dance, and prior to that this guy had had his hands all over me. The same night that my bottoms got pulled down, just a couple of hours before, this other guy had been in there with his hands all over me. He wouldn't stop touching me, and I kept trying to get the bouncer's attention. Finally I got it, and he watched. He warned him, and the guy did it again, and then he got all violent with the bouncer. Later on that night was when the other guy grabbed a hold of my bottoms and yanked them right down to my knees. It was a horrible night. After that, I literally quit working. I said, "That's enough, twice. I'm done!" I went up to the DJ, and I said, "I'll go onstage for you, but I'm not doing another single dance. I'm not doing any dollar dances. I'm not doing a thing." So that time, that was bad; that was really bad. After the dollar dance thing, I was just, "Throw him out. Get him out." Why even let him in here? That's crazy.

Each dancer also shared at least one story of a psychologically disturbing experience she had while working, an experience that irrevocably colored the way she perceived herself and men in general. April vividly recalled one such night:

I was onstage one night. I was at Lace and Lashes. Oh, it was such a bad night. It was terrible. And nobody had been there or anything. This guy comes up with a hundred-dollar bill. I was just like, "Thank heavens, my whatever's getting paid." And I go down to get it and say, "Thank you, thank you," and he just laughs and flips it away and walks away. I don't think I've ever felt so cheap and just awful in my entire life ever. And I went back there. And I don't have a temper. I did when I was smaller, but I don't lose my temper anymore. I did that night. I lost my temper really bad. I went down there, and I took my shoes off. I was getting ready to hit him with it, and I told him, "I'll have you know I'm a 4.0, I'm on the Dean's list." I went over there and said, "I just want to know why you did that. Tell me why you did that." And my bosses, which was a man and a woman, they started coming 'cause they knew, 'cause I'd never lost my temper before—never—and they could tell something was going to happen. So I went over there and said, "Why did you do that?" He said, "I wouldn't let my daughter do this. You're a whore," and all this stuff. And I was like, "I'll have you know . . ." and I started going off. And he says, "Okay, okay, okay," and they come over and they grab me, and they take me back to the dressing room. I'm beating down the paneling. I'm just screaming and just crying at the top of my lungs, and that was a really negative moment.

April is kind, generous, and easygoing. About a year after our initial interview, she quit dancing, finished her M.A. in counseling psychology, and now works as a counselor for rape victims. She doesn't get angry. She doesn't threaten people. But this experience—being offered a huge sum for very little—raised her expectations so greatly that when the customer withdrew the money and insulted her, he triggered a vast wellspring of rage. She ripped off her shoe and raised the spike heel daggerlike—among the most menacing moves a dancer can make, threatening him with this emblem of her own sexual servitude.

Similarly, Morgan described an episode in which a client seriously disturbed her emotional well-being:

I had a guy tell me I reminded him of his daughter. This was at the Cherry Pit during a couch dance. He was like from Cleveland or something, and I was dancing for him and he was like, "You remind me of my daughter," blah, blah. He was talking about details: "She's got pretty blue eyes like yours and long brown hair like yours." And I'm like, okay, when people start talking about their kids I'm usually like, "You got any pictures?" whatever. But we're on the couch. I'm like, "Really, how old is she?" He looks me right in the eye and gets this big grin on his face and goes, "Ten." I was like, okay, "That's it. Get up. Out, out. Pay me and get out!" That absolutely—that's the absolute worst, creepiest, grossest thing I've ever had happen to me in a club.

The client left when Morgan demanded that he go, but the experience continues to haunt her. She still thinks about the little girl this man may or may not have in Cleveland and what her life is like. Episodes like the ones that April and Morgan vividly describe here contribute to the long-term toll of stripping.

Rejection

In addition to physical demands and abuse, dancers cope daily with the emotional issues raised by constant rejection. As I explained earlier, most dancers make the bulk of their income from private dances: table, lap, and couch dances. This means that unless they have one or more regular customers present on whom they can count to supply them with money, dancers must circle the room soliciting dances from strangers. In Honolulu, dancers listlessly sit on foam mats waiting for clients to approach them for semiprivate shows on the main stage. Like employees selling anything from wireless service to timeshare rentals, dancers experience frequent rejection. Anyone who has ever done sales work understands how exhausting and debilitating it is to be perky, pleasant, and positive when the phone is slammed down in your ear or when someone closes a door in your face. Imagine how much more of a strain it might be to maintain a friendly, seductive demeanor and high self-confidence when the product the customer refuses to buy is you.

The constant necessity to maintain a cheerful front in the face of rejection is a particularly painful form of what sociologist Arlie Hochschild describes as emotional labor in her book *The Managed Heart*. Hochschild defines emotional labor as face-to-face or voice-to-voice contact that "requires one to induce or suppress feelings in order to sustain the outward countenance that produces the proper state of mind in others."[13] Hochschild theorizes that this form of labor exacts a high cost from the worker. Constantly reminded that a woman's worth in the world is tied to how beautiful and desirable she is, a stripper must also learn to dissociate from the full personal implications of that knowledge.[14] Basking in the glow of a great tip, a dancer may feel like a queen. But she has to be ready at a moment's notice to don her protective armor against abuse and rejection. Hence, dancers experience both positive reinforcement and rejection daily for the same reason: their sexual bodies. Managing the conflicting combination of compliments and abuse on her physical form requires a tremendous amount of emotional energy.

Many dancers described humiliating moments on the main stage during which they felt rejected and unattractive. The night before our first interview, April had participated in a contest called the Tiniest Tan Line, which was a special feature the club organized to attract clientele. Clubs often host special events to maintain a feeling of novelty in the environment. The Tiniest Tan Line competition was similar to a beauty contest in that all the dancers lined up to be judged not only on their tan lines but also, of course, on their bodies. Each dancer wrote an introduction for herself that the DJ was instructed to read over the microphone. Because April finished in last place, the contest destroyed her self-confidence for the evening:

> It ended up ruining my whole night because I got the worst of the worst. I was the first one to be eliminated. I mean, they didn't even let me do anything. And they ad-libbed what I'd written. They didn't even read what I'd wrote down. So it just ruined my confidence for the whole night, and I didn't make any money at all. It didn't really have a good impact. I mean, I wasn't even caring, I wasn't even planning on getting first or even third, but to be the only one knocked out, to have everyone's name read off but yours . . . It's very, very humiliating, very humiliating.

Mandy, forty-two years old, faces rejection more often than many dancers. She worries that the clients find her ugly, that she's too skinny, that she doesn't measure up to the other dancers when no one tips her or buys a private dance from her:

> Mentally, you think like, "Today, I had to pull teeth to try to make a dollar." You're up there and you're dancing, and you're either getting into it or you're not, whatever. You're doing what you're supposed to be doing, and then you get rejection. A lot of women say, "Don't think about them." But, I'm sorry, if you get rejected so many times consistent, it's going to get to you: "God, is there something wrong with me?" You go

back to the men, keep checking, and so mentally sometimes you don't feel up to what they expect. You don't perform well enough for them. It's hard on my self-esteem. Especially starting at my age. You go in at my age, no breasts, very tiny, and you go up there. It's hard on me.

It's difficult for dancers to externalize this kind of daily rejection—to believe that even if no man wants a dance from them, they are still worthwhile and attractive. Instead, they tend to make sense of the experience by deciding that they are not pretty or sexy enough. I expected that, of all women, dancers would be adept at managing rejection. That even dancers struggle with maintaining their self-worth when rejected by men, many of whom themselves are unattractive, is evidence of the power cultural messages and gender socialization wield over women's perceptions of their bodies. So how do dancers manage an environment in which they are subject to insults, rejection, and physical assaults? One of the few successful techniques dancers shared for dealing with rejection and abuse was setting boundaries.

Surviving Stripping by Setting Boundaries

Violations of their bodies through uninvited touch and cruel insults about their bodies and character were among the worst abuses dancers described. Lisa shared that she believed exotic dancing had been emotionally destructive to both April and her previous girlfriend:

Dancers are emotionally abused, and they have to take it night after night. They have to listen to these men speak of their kinky fantasies or what they would like to do to them. Or how much money would it take for them to have them? That is not something that makes you feel really good about yourself. I can go home at the end of the day, after doing my job, and I can say I feel like I accomplished something. A dancer goes home and the only thing she feels good about is the money she made. You don't feel good that you had umpteen men grab your breasts or your ass or make a nasty comment to you.

The sex industry can be especially harmful to the woman too shy, insecure, or confused to draw lines and say, "I won't do that." On a daily basis, dancers battle the stigma of stripping, as well as aggressive clients trying to get them to do more, say more, take more off, and give them more. Dancers survive the sex industry by setting clear boundaries between the sex acts they allow and those they do not. Every woman I spoke with, and every stripper narrative I've read, emphasized setting boundaries.[15]

For example, a dancer might establish the following personal boundary: "I don't let customers touch me." Doing this, she imagines a tangible boundary separating herself from the client. This not only provides a clear guideline to which customers are instructed to adhere but also allows the performer to maintain a self-perception of respectability—she is a nice girl, providing a service; she is not a slut or a whore—and she has control over the interaction. Moreover, should this boundary become inconveniently constricting to a dancer's income or level of intoxication, she can always expand its horizons. She may decide, "It's okay if I let my regulars touch me sometimes, but I would never go out on a date with any of them." Setting boundaries is crucial to surviving an environment in which men continually and repeatedly attempt to solicit unsupervised sexual favors.

Significantly, the women shared that working in the sex industry taught them how to say no to the worst of men's suggestions and behaviors, a skill that they suggested they would not have easily learned otherwise and that improved the overall quality of their lives. In a male-dominated society, women are socialized to be available for men's sexual gaze[16] and to accept a certain amount of harassment as normal, even desirable.[17] Morgan realized that dancing gave her the tools to demand respect in her personal relationships:

The more I dance, I think in an odd way it's almost a self-esteem boost. The more lines I feel comfortable, the more respect I feel comfortable demanding. This is how it is. If you don't like it, well here's the door. I think that a lot of women are raised in a climate that makes you uncomfortable with saying no, but I think a lot of women don't know when to say no and how to say no. And this is something that dancing absolutely teaches you how to say. It teaches you how to say—to look someone right in the eye no matter how intimidating they're being or how much money they're giving you, whatever, say, "Fuck you, no!" It teaches you how to be very emphatic. I sort of turn into a bitch in a way. I'm very demanding now as far as my personal relationships go, very demanding of respect. It's definitely boot camp in more ways than one; its fairly psychologically traumatizing. It's one of those things that either kills you or makes you stronger. If it doesn't kill you, it makes you stronger a person. I mean, kill you spiritually, emotionally.

Like Morgan, Janeen expressed that dancing taught her how to say, "Stop, you can't treat me this way":

Before I started working at the Lusty Lady, I'd let people talk to me however they wanted, following me for blocks and sexually harass me. But when I started working there, someone followed me from the bar, and I told the management and asked to work during the day. The manager asked what I did when they followed me. I told her, "Nothing." And she said, "If someone's following you, you tell them to stop." I told her, "I couldn't tell them to stop." Then, I saw the girls onstage, and they were saying, "Don't tell me what to do. This is my show, leave me alone." I was able to take that from behind the glass to the street, in real life. And that was the first time in my life I was able to have boundaries with people, and the Lusty Lady helped me to have those boundaries. It really did.

Dancers shared that clients regularly pressure them to perform sex labor in violation of club rules and their personal boundaries. Some make a game out of challenging a dancer's boundaries. They might repeatedly ask her to pull her g-string aside so they can see her genitals, touch her inappropriately, or proposition her for sex. These episodes are upsetting for the performer not just because they involve a physical or verbal assault but also because they are a measure of clients' level of respect for dancers and they underline the lack of control a dancer has over her body. Furthermore, with each accumulated violation of her boundaries, dancers may wonder, like April, "Maybe I am a slut. Maybe they know the truth." Thus, if after firmly setting her boundaries with a client, he continues to disrespect her, even a trivial action can push a dancer to respond violently. Melinda illustrated this cycle with a fairly typical club incident:

The worst things that happen to you are the real grabby people that you usually end up clocking by the end of the night. I can't tell you how many dancers I've seen haul out and knock somebody out. The only violence you see in clubs doesn't usually come from the men. It comes from the women. Men, I understand that it's a terrible thing that we do. It's like telling a dog to sit and holding a raw steak in front of them. Usually, it's not a one-time incident that makes a girl finally hit the guy. Usually it's been, "No stop, don't do that. Stop," over and over and over again until the girl just finally hauls out and knocks him. I've seen a girl get off the stage. This guy walks up to the stage to tip her and said something rude—like he called her a tramp or a slut or something—and didn't tip her. He had the money in his hand and walked away. It was just a dollar. It's not like the dollar was the big deal, but the girl was mad. She got off the stage. The song wasn't over, and she just walked over and knocked him out. She was just so mad. She walked up, touched him on the shoulder, he turned around, and she was like, "Now who's your slut?" and knocked him out.

In this instance, the dancer physically reasserted her control over her own, and others', perceptions of her body, sexuality, and self-worth with a decisive response.

Sex work forces women to establish boundaries to help them manage societal expectations about proper femininity, as well as male lust. Dancers and customers experience and express primal emotions in strip bars. Jealousy, rage, betrayal, lust, and disgust simmer beneath the surface of the strip bar, ready to erupt from what might appear to an outsider to be little provocation. Women learn from an early age that it is dangerous to excite a man and disappear without satisfying his lust: this is an instigation to rape. The stripper juggles a complicated set of conditions then: arousing men, coping with abuse and contempt, deflecting and neutralizing potentially dangerous situations, and, meanwhile, extracting as much money from them as she possibly can.

The Möbius Strip

When women begin dancing, many enjoy it immensely.[18] Those who do not tend to last only a few nights. They bathe in male attention, they display their bodies proudly, they collect quick cash, the lights flash, the music pounds, they are heady with alcohol, drugs, and a sudden ego boost. Almost every dancer I interviewed confided that, in the beginning, she loved dancing.[19] More than one woman expressed that it was delightful to be paid for partying, listening to a great stereo, and receiving compliments from hordes of men.

Unfortunately, this ego gratification is unstable. In the world of the strip bar, the dancer's pride and pleasure in her self-display is just one nasty comment away from either the sting of rejection or the humiliation of being treated like a piece of meat. During a typical shift, a dancer's experience of the strip bar may vacillate between exciting financial rewards and degrading comments, with the threat of physical abuse and societal stigma a constant backdrop. One moment she may be center stage performing when someone throws fifty one-dollar bills at her. Feeling money rush all over her naked body, the dancer may perceive herself as having what men want: beauty, sexual desirability, and the ability to attract attention. The next instant, propositioned for a fifty-dollar blow job in the parking lot, she is roughly thrust off her imagined pedestal and treated like a prostitute.

April shared a story illustrating the unpredictable male behavior she experienced at the Velvet Lounge. She described the time a patron approached her and said, "I have two words for you: 'nice ass.' " When I asked her how she handled comments like that, she replied,

> I'm just like, "Thanks." You know, that's all you're supposed to be, because that, to them, is a compliment. You know, them coming up to you, because it's a skin bar; it's like them coming up and saying, "nice lamp." It's the equivalency. It's not like you're working at a doctor's office and a guy comes over and says, "nice ass"; it's totally different. It still just makes you want to puke on them, shoot. You never like to hear it, but that's—that doesn't happen that often. It really doesn't. I mean, you probably may hear it once a night from somebody, you know, if that. I'll go a week without hearing one negative comment from one person, you know. So it's not as degrading as people think it is. Not at all. It's actually quite the opposite. 'Cause, I mean, you know, women, they are— they're the power figures in there. They can't touch you. They can't say nothing bad to you. They can't do nothing to you. If they do, they're going to get physically beat up, you know. Or get thrown out.

In this excerpt, April depicts dancers as the power figures at the same time that she explains her strategy for dealing with men who do not respect her. Hence, the metaphor of the Möbius strip: wearing six-inch heels, drinking shots of Cuervo, dancers delicately traverse a spiral of customer reactions in which each emotion or behavior may become its opposite in an instant. Over the course of a career, however, the dancer's trajectory is almost exclusively unidirectional, as the emotional labor of putting on a male-friendly, sexy, confident front, despite the everyday vicissitudes of abuse and rejection, drain her energy and erode her confidence.[20]

Colored by my own love of dancing, I expected to find that the dancing itself would be a renewable source of pleasure for the women. I was surprised to find that few women actually performed anything resembling dance movements or even liked to dance. Obviously, these women derived satisfaction from other areas of the work. I also learned that even for those who love to dance, the power rush they feel when performing on the main stage is precarious. This is because the dancers encounter in their work environments a compressed experience of both the pleasure and pain women feel more generally about displaying their bodies. Clearly, the dancers' comments in this chapter reveal that they sometimes feel an intoxication and pride in their performance, as well as intense humiliation, rejection, and low self-esteem. For some, the sense of adventure that encouraged them to decide to dance remains gratifying for a period of time. Most dancers learn over time, however, that the pleasure they experience working in strip bars is transitory and may easily change into disgust, anger, and hurt as clients' crude propositions continue shift after shift.

Depending on when you question a woman about stripping—as an early- or late-career dancer—you are likely to get a different self-assessment of her "power" or "oppression," since what dancers initially experience as pleasurable becomes increasingly fraught with problems. That "power" (or lack of it) is, however, neither as seamless nor as static as partisans in the sex wars portray it. Using the metaphor of the Möbius strip, one might say that each side of the sex-wars debate focuses on a different exposed surface of the strip while ignoring its underside. It's easy to make a Möbius strip; simply twist a single strip of paper and glue the ends together to form a ring. Once in place, though, it's perhaps harder to understand the optical illusion of the seemingly twisting movement. A closer look, however, reveals that the surface and the underside are actually the same—it's impossible to paint the strip with more than one continuous color. The early-career dancer too often finds, sometimes the hard way, that the surface or daily tasks of her job are inseparable from the underside of the sex industry and that it is impossible for her not to be part of both sides, often to her detriment.

3

Bad Girls

I guess the one thing I disliked the most is that, at the time when I
was dancing and people asked me what I do for a living, I wouldn't
just come out and say, "I'm a dancer." As soon as you mention the
word "dancer," or "stripper," or "exotic dancer," people automatically have this thought in their mind that "she's a prostitute, and
she sells her body for money." It's not even like that. I look at it as
there are girls that go to these nightclubs, and they are dancing on
the dance floor practically half naked, and they are bumping and
grinding with guys they just met. I look at it as if girls are doing it
every night, and doing it for free. What is so bad about me getting
up onstage and taking my top off and getting paid for it? People
don't look at it that way, They think because you take your clothes
off for a living you are a bad person. Some of the best people I have
ever met are dancers or were dancers, and a lot of them go into
dancing for good reasons—like they are trying to put themselves
through college or they are raising a family because they are single
mothers. I know girls that are dancers that were going to school to
become lawyers and doctors. Not all of them are bad people.
                     —Tara, a single mother and former dancer

Dancers dislike the physical wear and tear on their bodies, the
daily rejection that damages their self-esteem, and the verbal and sometimes physical abuse they experience inside the clubs. But some dancers,
like Tara, explained that the hardest part of dancing happened outside the
club: confronting the constellation of assumptions about who they are because they work in a strip bar. These stereotypes range from depicting her
sexual character as victimized martyr or conniving slut to judgments
about her education level (high school dropout)or her class background
("dancers are trailer trash"). If she is a woman of color, her race is another

potential site for cultural assumptions, for example, that she is the Asian "lotus blossom," African American "hoochie," or Latina "hot babe." Furthermore, patriarchal anxiety, and desire, paint sex workers as bisexual or lesbian: "they're all really dykes." Stereotypes also depict dancers as stupid, lazy, sex starved, addicted to crack, psychologically disturbed, and hookers for the right price—and overall, as Tara expresses in the epigraph, that being an exotic dancer means you are a "bad" person.

This chapter explores the difficulties dancers endure outside the clubs. Stripping is a stigma-laden profession; here I explore how the dancers manage that stigma. The stigma of stripping plays an important role in determining how long a woman remains in the profession. Although the work itself involves both empowering and oppressive aspects—much like many professions—there is nothing empowering about the stigma dancers shoulder. More than any other single element of sex work, the stigma of stripping effects every area of a woman's life. She can't leave it at the office, put it on the back burner, or take a vacation from it. The only way to rid oneself of stripper stigma is to quit stripping. (And, even then, one is always an ex-stripper, forever haunted by the attendant cultural stereotypes.) Thus, a woman's success in managing this stigma is key to both her longevity in the sex industry and her understanding of the toll of the profession.

How Are Women Supposed to Be Sexy?

Women's understanding of sexuality is distorted in this male-dominated society. Radical feminists theorize that individual men and the male-dominated state exert a variety of coercive and manipulative controls over women, such as the threat of rape, domestic abuse, and unrealistic beauty standards, to convince women, as well as men, that a woman's sexuality is the exclusive province of men.[1] Very few of us are immune to the potent socialization processes that occur in the family, schools, the workplace, religious institutions, and the media about women's virtue. We absorb the following kinds of contradictory messages about sex: *Sex is dirty and shameful but also fabulous and life altering. Everyone is doing it, and everyone doing it is gorgeous and thin. It all happens in a passionate embrace, under the sheets. It's magic, but you should wait until you're married or become a born-again virgin. If you do it you're a slut, and if you don't you're a prude.*

No wonder we are confused.

It's difficult for young women to sort out these messages. Girls are supposed to be sexy—for boys—but not too sexy, because to be labeled a slut is a terrible fate. Leora Tanenbaum explored the widespread sexual harassment and policing of young women's sexuality in her poignant book *Slut! Growing Up Female with a Bad Reputation.* The book is brimming with gruesome, if commonplace, tales of the teenage torture of young women. Indeed, Tanenbaum shares the disturbing statistic that two out of five girls nationwide have had sexual rumors spread about them.[2] Hence, young women in particular tend not to explore or to articulate their own sexual desires because doing so increases the possibility of their being labeled a slut. Unfortunately, a young woman's sexual ignorance means that she often learns about her sexual self with the worst possible candidates: fumbling, poorly educated, ill-prepared, overeager young men.

For a dancer, issues with sexuality may be even more confusing. While she is explicitly selling her sexuality to men, she may also feel that at least she owns her sexuality enough to charge a price for it. She's not giving it away for free. And, as I discussed earlier, dancers are hardly unique in their immersion in a media-driven climate that encourages them to provide sexual services for men. The kinds of flirtatious behaviors expected of women who work in strip bars replicate the behaviors women learn throughout their lives. Many women who are not sex workers learn how to be sexual to please men, and often without receiving physical pleasure, or financial compensation, in return. They may have sex with men for many of the same reasons dancers dance—for the attention, to feel powerful, to feel beautiful—or simply because they feel, like many of the undergraduates I teach, that they are expected to. When questioned about what it was like to have sex for money the very first time, author and self-described "holy whore"[3] Cosi Fabian explained in a *20/20* interview that as she completed her first act of prostitution, she walked away realizing, "I have done *that* many, many times before." By "*that*" Fabian implied that having sex with a stranger was hardly a new experience for her. The new part was getting paid for it.

Sociologist Erving Goffman explored the experiences of stigmatized individuals including sex workers in his classic book *Stigma: Notes on the Management of a Spoiled Identity.* "Normals," as Goffman described the unstigmatized, feel uneasy around those who bear a stigma, those Simone de Beauvoir described as the "other."[4] The stigma may be visual, what Goffman calls "discredited"—a scar or limp, or skin color—or the stigma may be "discreditable," behaviors an individual engages in such as sexual practices, criminal activities, or sex work. Exotic dancers could fall into either category but are more likely to be perceived as discreditable. Because stigma makes us uncomfortable, because we are scared that it is contagious, we "normals" have historically gone to elaborate lengths to protect our privileged status and contain the stigmatized others. We have put people in jails, hospitals, and nursing homes. We have detained them in concentration camps. We bus them to separate schools. We make them hide who they sleep with or where they work. We encourage blind people to wear sunglasses, and the homeless to stay away from affluent neighborhoods. We don't even *have* public transportation to many affluent neighborhoods; some are now protected by security guards and gates.

Contemporary teenagers use slang phrases like "that's gay" or "she's retarded" to illustrate that an act or a person is bad. *Whore, slut, cunt, skank, hoochie, ho*—words that reinforce the idea that women and women's genitals are dirty and disgusting—are just the beginning of a rich vocabulary of slurs used interchangeably as casual comments or stinging insults. Goffman explained how these insults both create and reinforce a stigmatized identity:

> By definition, of course, we believe the person with a stigma is not quite human. On this assumption we exercise varieties of discrimination, through which we effectively, if often unthinkingly, reduce his life chances. We construct a stigma-theory, an ideology to explain his inferiority and account for the danger he represents, sometimes rationalizing an animosity based on other differences, such as those of social class. We use specific stigma terms such as cripple, bastard, moron, in our daily discourse as a source of metaphor and imagery, typically without giving thought to the original meaning.[5]

To survive the stigma of being a stripper, dancers develop strategies to deal with the most egregious insults from strangers and from family and friends, or they suffer the emotional burden of hiding what they do. And managing stripper stigma only gets more burdensome with time.

"Coming Out"

In their own eyes, dancers are regular people, "nice girls," struggling to make ends meet the best way they can. Dancers cope with other people's judgments, and potential judgments, in a variety of ways: some hide their work from others; some openly share what they do; some confess their job to certain friends but do not tell their families. Julie strongly expressed that she did not like the way people treated her when they learned she danced. To avoid this, she chooses to be deliberately vague about her work:

> I hate the judgmental part of it. I hate going into a place and interviewing for a job and trying to do something else, applying for a loan and that kind of thing, and you have to write down where you work. And right off the bat you're judged. I don't like socializing and have that question asked, because it's not my character to say I strip for a living. I don't say that. That's stereotyping. I'm doing it myself, but I don't come out and say that. I'll say I work in a club. I don't like that about it. I don't like having to deal in that manner with it.

During our first interview, when she was still dancing, Morgan explained that she preferred to be open about stripping but was careful when she disclosed her work to others. Morgan learned that people are more accepting and less judgmental when they have the opportunity to first know other things about her than that she strips for a living. Morgan explained:

> There's definitely a stigma attached, absolutely. I think that I make it a point not to lie and to not hide what I do. If someone asks, I'll tell them, and sometimes if they don't ask. But I do try to avoid the subject until they've known me for a while so that's not the first thing. Because if that's the first thing, that tends to be the thing. It affects how you're being judged. If that's the first thing people know about you, you're judged by that stereotype. I don't think it's right. If you're an attorney or a doctor you can walk up to somebody, "Hi, I'm Dr. So-and-So and I'm a chiropractor." But I don't just walk up to people, "Hi, you know, how are you, I'm Morgan and I get naked for five bucks a pop for strangers. Great, great to meet you." If I choose to use something that I do as a

way of defining myself right off, I might say, "I'm a student, a pre-med major," or something, rather than a dancer.

Now that Morgan has stopped dancing and entered medical school, she makes no effort to hide the fact that she danced for seven years. Rather than let her past define her identity, Morgan chooses to be open about her history. By controlling her story, by being the one to present it, she hopes to prevent anyone from using her time spent dancing as a way to stigmatize her. Moreover, now that she's quit dancing, Morgan acknowledged that it's much easier to be forthcoming about it. Our culture is more forgiving of young women who have had a "stripper phase," especially someone like Morgan who shot from the bottom rung of the occupational ladder to the top. The notion of the "stripper phase" is a convenient, stigma-reducing concept I use here to describe how family and friends, and even dancers themselves, prefer to interpret their beloved daughter, sister, friend, wife, or self taking off her clothes for money. The story might go: "It was a crazy job she had when she was in art school, or living in San Francisco, when she was dating that motorcycle guy and living in a vegan commune. She was rebelling against everything."

Beatrice, twenty-one and a recent UC Berkeley graduate at the time of our interview, felt that she was nearing the end of her stripper phase. She explained that exotic dancing was an acceptable job to have done for a time, while she was in school, but now that she had graduated, she needed to move on.

> I think that, overall, I've come to kind of see my job in a different light. I used to like it when I first started and I was young and stuff. But since then, I've started to feel bad about it, almost guilty like, "Gosh, in the future, if people find out about my job, what are they going to think of me?!" They're going to think that I'm a lewd woman or—a lot of people see it as a degrading job. Especially people who don't know about it. It just builds up over time.

A middle-class woman who has quit exotic dancing and turned respectable is the most acceptable version of the stripper phase. It's titillating but not ruinous. "Marrying the job," as an informant described a once close friend who went from exotic dancing to marrying the owner of the strip club, "is something else." Presumably, something foreign and scary. Something that permanently stains the stigmatized individual.

"Once she married him, I effectively divorced her." Morgan reflected on this phenomenon in our second interview:

> It's okay to say, "I used to be a stripper, but I got out of it." It's not okay to say, "I was a stripper for seven years. I fucking loved it. I had a blast, and I still miss it today." I think the thing about moving from that to this, particularly, is that this gives me a lot of social leeway. I've gone from the bottom of the social heap to the top of the social heap. I'm probably unique in that just because I have the social leeway to be able to say that. I had a blast, and you can kiss my ass if you don't like it because I can validate myself.

As Morgan describes, the dancer and ex-dancer are often discouraged from talking about how the experience of dancing shaped her, let alone that she enjoyed it. The "don't ask, don't tell" philosophy polices the lives of strippers, and ex-strippers, much as it does with other sexual minorities, such as gays in the military. This silencing of one's experience creates a lasting psychological imprint: it reinforces the dominant perspective that stripping is bad and that you are a bad person for doing it. Few other parts of our individual biographies are as off-limits for discussion, reminiscing, and processing as a woman's experiences working in the sex industry. So the stripper or ex-stripper hides the stigmatized behavior, thus colluding in and reinforcing dominant stereotypes about women who work in the sex industry.[6]

Discrimination

Dancers not only face rude questions and sudden rejection in their personal lives when others learn that they strip, they may also experience discrimination finding housing or new employment and obtaining medical care. Maureen spent six months trying to find an apartment in Silverton when she first moved to town. She confided:

> It took me six months to find an apartment. I stayed in a motel for six months. I tried to get an apartment. I had this one lady down here on N. Broadway, cute little second-floor apartment, four hundred something a month. I put down where I work, and she called me back and asked me, "Was it a strip club?" And I said, "Yes." And she goes, "Well I just can't

rent to you." I said, "Why?" "You guys party a lot." I said, "I don't."
That's discrimination.

Maureen is a quiet, shy woman who purposely worked the day shift so
she could go to bed and get up early, ensuring her enough time to take
care of her children. Her dream is to settle on a small piece of land with
a trailer. The money that she spent on a motel, and eating every meal out,
could have been far better spent investing in her future.

Sarah will tell most people she dances, except those who directly have
power over her body, such as hospital workers. It is one thing to risk rejection from a potential acquaintance; it's another to take chances with
poor medical care. Sarah explained:

> The one time I went to the ER after a genital piercing, they asked me
> what I did for my job. I don't feel like telling an ER nurse what I do. Or
> if I go to the doctor. But when I meet new people, I'll tell them. I used to
> worry about people challenging me or picking fights; but, if they don't
> like me or sex work, that's their prerogative. They can enjoy that per-
> spective far, far away from me.

Dancers worry not only that potential friends and partners will reject
them but also that they might experience discrimination in housing or
medical care. If they do other kinds of work, they also fear losing those
jobs or internships should someone find out they dance. As part of her
schooling as a pre-med psychology and biology major, Morgan worked
with autistic children. She did not reveal to the people she worked with
at her internship that she danced, for fear that they would then assume
she was a pervert and child molester. Morgan explained:

> And that's what bothers me about the way that people are about the
> dancing is that I always have to be ready to field those damn questions
> when I say what I do. I have to be ready to be prepared for people to de-
> cide that they don't like me. Especially women. Somebody who liked me
> and was getting along with me just fine five minutes ago to, when that
> comes out, to not like me and not want to associate with me anymore.
> To not want me to be around their kids. And I hate having to lie. But the
> families whose children I work with, I can't tell them until or unless I
> know them well enough to know that they aren't going to all of a sud-
> den decide that I'm some kind of sexual pervert and start suing me for

touching their kids the wrong way or something freakish like that. I have to worry about things like that. That therapy is so very, very difficult because all the reinforcement are typically tickling or hugging or picking the kid up and swooping him through the air. I mean even just being accused of something like that never goes away. That follows you for the rest of your life. I just can't imagine. Some woman decides that I must be a freak since I do that.

Like Morgan, several dancers spoke about how difficult it is to make friends, or sustain friendships, with people unfamiliar with the mores of the sex industry.

Telling the Kids?

Of all the relationships that women worry about their dancing affecting negatively, the one that causes them the most anguish is with their children. Dancers fear that their children will suffer: they might be teased by classmates, ostracized from peer activities, or simply feel ashamed of their mothers for stripping. Dana shared that she planned to stop dancing before her daughter started school so that it would never become an issue for her:

> I hope to be out of this by next year. It's a big hope, but my daughter will be starting school. She'll be going to kindergarten, and I don't want to be doing this while she's in school. I hope to be out of it by then, by August. I'm really concerned for her. I would hate it if someone was picking on her because "your mommy's a dancer" or whatever. Because the parents may say something if the kid goes home and says something, and the kid comes back and calls me a name. Kids are so cruel anyway.

Unfortunately, not all dancers have the option to quit dancing when their children reach school age. Indeed, this is often the time that the child's material needs increase. Marcy, Susan, Carol, and Tracy discussed their children and dancing with me while they were getting ready in the dressing room of Vixens.

> *Carol*: I worry about my kids.
> *Tracy*: What kind of stigma they're going to have.

Marcy: I don't mind 'cause I don't feel like I'm doing anything wrong, and my kids have always been older.
Tracy: My kids know.
Carol: Yeah, but you still worry about it.
Marcy: Yeah, you always worry about it.
Tracy: You worry that they're going to get it at school.

In our increasingly materialistic world, this worry is tempered by the pressure to buy Tommy Hilfiger jeans and a laptop computer.

Othering

Managing stripper stigma requires employing a variety of psychological strategies. In addition to setting boundaries with clients in the clubs, hiding their work from family and friends, and constructing their time spent dancing as a "stripper phase," several of the women I interviewed distanced themselves from what they perceived as the negative stereotype of dancers by condemning the actions of their fellow dancers. To illustrate, dancers followed boundary-setting comments such as "I don't let customers touch me" with a statement like "The girls who let them do that kind of stuff make it harder for the rest of us." Imagining herself in relation to a "straw" dancer, a performer creates another kind of boundary: a mental cushion between herself and other dancers who she imagines allow the customers to touch them.[7] *Those* girls then become what Simone de Beauvoir describes in *The Second Sex* as the "other": individuals and groups who do not belong, who are different and inferior.

Othering is, obviously, a problematic strategy. By condemning other dancers who commit "inappropriate" acts, a woman reinforces negative stereotypes about dancers which, in turn, contribute to her own marginalization. At the same time, this strategy of "othering" is a means of surviving painful circumstances and, as such, is eminently understandable. Dana's comment is typical:

> Customers are trained to come in and spend money, but you've got girls that aren't playing the game quite correctly. And they do things out of the ordinary. So it hurts it for a lot of other people. I've heard too many people talking. Too many people know too many details. Then the customers will run their mouth about stuff.

Similarly, Beatrice shared that she felt the women working at Mitchell Brothers were not your "stereotypical" strippers in comparison to dancers at other clubs. Beatrice described the types of dancers she encountered other places:

> I've seen a lot of very smart women, some putting themselves through school. A lot of girls see dancing as a way to have leisure time to pursue other interests. But I also saw what society thinks of strippers when I was in Florida and Las Vegas. The girls weren't as smart. They weren't students; they were more in it for careers. At Mitchell Brothers, there are a few girls that are career strippers, but for the most part, I think it is a transition for a lot of women, something they do until they figure out what they really want to do or just for the experience, temporarily, for a few years. There are a lot of very smart, talented women here. That may be something they look for in the audition. Maybe somehow that's advantageous to the business. Maybe it sells better. Maybe they don't get burnt out so quickly.

In this discussion of cultural stereotypes about dancers, Beatrice separates herself and the women working at Mitchell Brothers from dancers she worked with in Florida and Las Vegas. They were examples of "what society thinks of strippers," whereas the women working the O'Farrell Theater are "students" or, as Jenna, another Mitchell Brothers dancer characterized them, "property owners and world travelers." In interviews, dancers frequently contrasted themselves with other dancers—those working in a certain part of the United States, those older, less educated, in terrible relationships, and so on. Again, this separation of self from other is a defense mechanism dancers use to manage stripper sigma.

Julie demonstrated this "othering" technique the most among my informants. She managed stripper stigma by holding others—those who get naked and have sex with clients, for example—responsible for the stigma they all shoulder. Julie accused the "girls who take it a step further" as giving all dancers a "bad name":

> When you go into it, you realize it's really no big deal. If it's the kind of club where it's just topless, there is no touching, there are no lap dances, and it's kind of just a bar, respectful atmosphere, it's really no big deal. But the girls that take it a step further and do prostitution in it and do those little extras for a little extra money. Then, I think they

give it a bad name. And no wonder we feel exploited sometimes, because a lot of women don't take it seriously. They use it as a place where you can make as much money as you can, when actually it should just be something to make money, but respectfully. Actually, it's no big deal. It's really not. I mean, it might sound a little cliché but I think it's an art form in our club to a point. Because it's not just nasty. I think a woman going totally nude onstage and crawling around is kind of nasty. I wouldn't want to do that. I think, if anything, women give it a bad name.

Julie locates the site of her exploitation not with the customers, the club, or patriarchy in general but with other dancers who do "nasty" things. In her mind, if women took dancing "more seriously," people would not think badly of her. And by "seriously," Julie means establishing and maintaining the same boundaries that she defines as appropriate.

To illustrate her point, Julie described feeling extremely uncomfortable watching the Velvet Lounge's feature dancer perform nude. Feature dancers travel from club to club for a set payment and perform from one day to a week during a special matinee. Hence, their money is not entirely dependent on tips. Generally, feature dancers are women with "perfect," probably surgically enhanced, stripper bodies who have credentials that attract more business into the club. They may have won a number of contest, such as Best Behind Miss Hawaii or cover girl and centerfold of the year for *Hustler*'s Best of Beauty. Usually, they have starred in porn movies as well. Julie shared her thoughts:

> I told you I went to the Velvet Lounge one night when they had a "feature." I was embarrassed. I went with a bouncer from work, and we sat on the stage area—and you know how close up that stage is. And I've never ever seen a woman get completely nude onstage. She's crawling around onstage, and I had to turn my head. I was so embarrassed. I don't know why I felt that way. It was just weird for me.

Julie repeatedly expressed discomfort with dancing throughout our interview. She made statements like the following: "I hate it when the customers touch me," "I would never dance nude," "There is nothing good about taking your clothes off and dancing for strangers." In describing her experience watching the feature dancer crawl around onstage, Julie felt "weird" because the boundaries separating her from the feature dancer—a woman writhing on the ground naked—blurred. On some level perhaps Julie registered that there was really very little to distinguish her actions from those of the feature dancer. Such an explicit scene vividly illustrated to her how powerless and vulnerable women can be in strip clubs. Watching a woman's naked crotch inches from her face—or as Susan so eloquently expressed, "You got these nude bars sticking their shit right up in a man's face"—the illusion that exotic dancing is "no big deal," or a fantasy and an art form, falters.

Establishing a psychological distance from other dancers may enable a woman, like Julie, to continue dancing for a length of time. Asserting that she is better, different, not like those other girls helps a woman manage stripper stigma. Dancers are not unique in this behavior. Members of stigmatized groups marginalize each other frequently.[8] For example, a gay or lesbian accountant might say, "I'm not like those other queer people; I would never dress in drag." A middle-class African American may be especially critical of those who dress as "rappers" or "hoochies." Unfortunately, by "othering" sex workers who do not conform to their standards of appropriate behavior, the stripper reproduces in her own world what the "morally correct" society does vis-à-vis the stripper world. Othering cyclically reinforces destructive and one-dimensional stereotypes about exotic dancers. Although this coping mechanism may temporarily alleviate the toll of stripping, it is a problematic long-term strategy because it reinforces, rather than deconstructs, the cultural stereotypes that burden all dancers. Ultimately, "othering" one's peers inhibits women from recognizing the oppression exotic dancers share in common; it hinders collective resistance and collective feminist consciousness.

Furthermore, othering fellow dancers has no positive impact on general public perceptions of strippers. Most people do not perceive exotic dancing to be a reputable profession regardless of whether the club is totally nude, topless only, located in a good section of town, or a front for prostitution. Most citizens are ignorant of the finer distinctions between strip clubs and do not care how any dancer constructs herself. It is highly unlikely that the public face of topless dancers would change overnight were no dancer ever to prostitute herself with a client. The vast majority of dancers do not sleep with their clients, but that has not changed the popular stereotype that strippers are also whores and hookers. To many people, just exposing one's breasts for money is a kind of prostitution in itself. Hence, no matter how hard a woman works to define her status of exotic dancer as something positive and worthwhile, and herself as unlike "those other slutty dancers," she has little control over how the media, churches, parents, teachers, and friends interpret her work.

The Dancer Persona

Another psychological tool dancers employ to manage the toll of stripping, and stripper stigma, is to develop a "dancer persona," a self that exists in the clubs who has a different name and personality.[9] Every dancer I interviewed separated out what she thought of as her "real" self from her stripper self partly through the use of a stage name. Indeed, most clubs prefer that the dancers choose stage names, insisting on this as a condition of employment and telling their employees that it is not safe to let customers know their real names. (Management at most clubs will not hesitate to play on an individual's fears if it suits their interest; they will minimize the risk of harm to the dancers for the same reason.) In most instances, dancers prefer to use a stage name regardless of management policy because it facilitates a separation between the self who plays soccer, picks up the kids at school, and feeds the cat from the self that takes her clothes off for money.

The act of dancing is an elaborate charade. A dancer must meet her customer's desires to keep the money flowing. Over the course of a single shift, she will make conversation with men ranging from bikers to corporate executives to professors. To do this, Darby explained, a dancer must be adept at reading people and performing what they expect. Darby confided that she has no scruples about lying to customers when she is working:

> I've told people I was in school. I've told people I was married with kids. There ain't much I ain't told people. If it makes me money, I'll tell you. I don't believe in lying, but when it comes to my job, it's not me. That's a complete other person. I am not me one bit, 'cause if I'm not myself, it's kind of like I ain't really the one doing it, I ain't doing it, you know.

Darby distinguishes the person she really is—honest—from the dancer self who not only lies freely but also feels comfortable doing so. The dancer persona allows a woman to do and say things at work that would otherwise violate her moral boundaries. She is not Mary or Stacy or Carol on stage. She is Savannah or Desiree or Vanessa. This means that sometimes the dancer is not only performing a fantasy for her customers but also performing a fantasy for herself. The specific nature of the fantasy— sex goddess, most popular girl in school, avenging warrior woman—is less significant than its purpose: to enable a woman to act in ways she normally would not and preserve her self-respect. Indeed, management at the Lusty Lady encouraged the performers to explore their sexuality at work, so long as this sexuality conformed to the range of behaviors most men find desirable. Like getting to eat meals for half price if you serve in a restaurant or exercise for free if you work at a gym, some management advertise the opportunity to explore your sexual fantasies on the job as one of the perks of stripping.

April agreed to a second interview with me after she had stopped dancing for a few months. During this follow-up interview, April explored the role "Ariel," her dancer persona, had played in her decision to stop stripping. In April's mind, Ariel was a separate personality that brought both positive and negative elements into April's life. She explained that she was able to set better boundaries, to protect herself, and to be more aggressive and emotionally distant as Ariel. But as she became a late-career dancer, she worried that April was slipping away and that Ariel was becoming more dominant—not only when she was stripping but in the rest of her life as well:

> I think Ariel did the first interview. You could probably play the two tapes together and even see a significant voice change. I was having a character conflict because April had just about disappeared, and then, all at once, Ariel was the only person I was dealing with. I was two separate people. I had to learn to integrate the good qualities of Ariel into my life, the good things about her—having self-esteem, feeling good about myself, feeling intelligent, smart, beautiful.

At the same time, Ariel had many qualities April did not like:

> I was, I felt, manipulative. My whole job was psychological gain. You know, taking your clothes off has always been the smallest thing of what I do. Somebody is sitting there, holding their money in two fists, and you got to figure out how to pry each finger back and get it.

Lisa, April's partner, observed this personality split firsthand:

> Living with dancers, I hear them talk about having another personality when they dance that's not really them. That personality is a lot of the nasty things about themselves that they don't really like to face. Dancing allows her to come out and do those things to men and say those things and manipulate them. That personality takes over and does that for them.

Fortunately, April felt that after leaving the profession she was able to wrest the best parts of Ariel out of the strip bar and into herself and leave the worst behind. Like "othering" fellow performers, as April realized, adopting a dancer persona is not a long-term solution to the problem of managing the toll of stripping because doing so created a core of self-deception and dissociation ("This isn't me on stage"). Nonetheless, the coping strategy had served its purpose.

Media images of women who strip socialize us to read dancers as one-dimensional stigmatized others. There are few texts that describe dancers as fully fleshed-out individuals with families, hobbies, and friends, as people who buy tomato sauce and milk at the grocery store and grumble about traffic. Like lesbians and gays whose choice of a partner shadows every aspect of their lives, the stripper embodies an all-encompassing stigmatized identity. Even if she has only danced for a short time, the shadow of the strip bar obscures the rest of her life. We do not see her as a student, an activist, a daughter, a mother, a gardener, a *Star Trek* fan, or a master carpenter. Because she works as a stripper, she is a stripper, twenty-four hours a day. This means that she is, above all else, an easy lay. A large part of the toll of exotic dancing is managing this stripper stigma. Strategies my informants used to manage stripper stigma included hiding their work, othering fellow dancers, and creating a dancer persona. Dancers employed these psychological tools to bolster their self-perceptions and avoid internalizing the negative stereotypes about strippers. The more successful a woman is in externalizing stripper stigma, the happier she will feel about herself and the longer she will last in the sex industry. Unfortunately, maintaining one's self-esteem as a stripper is often an uphill battle. And like most aspects of the sex industry, managing stripper stigma becomes more trying over time.

4

The Toll

All you see in dancers is nothing ever comes of them. They never
make anything. Very few do. And the ones that do are like real
rare, like a unicorn. You don't see them things every day. You don't
see one that actually goes to school and does something with their
life. 'Cause the lifestyle is so different, you never have time for
sleep. By the time you get off work, you're always smashed. You
sleep all day. You can't get nothing done.

—Darby

What are the effects of dancing over time? After close to ten
years studying the sex industry, interviewing dancers, reading narratives
of sex workers, spending time in strip bars, and perusing the findings of
my colleagues, I have observed a common theme linking most of these
texts, environments, and stories: working in the sex industry exacts a toll
on sex workers the longer they remain a part of this morally ambivalent
world. The toll of stripping is a complex accumulation of experiences and
emotions that taxes the energy and self-esteem of late-career sex workers.
Darby's comments demonstrate some of the effects of this toll:

The money gets so addictive and you get so used to having the money,
you spend the money like crazy and you don't save it. You don't think
about it. Easy money spends easy. And nothing ever really comes from it.
I've got nothing to show for all the money I've made. I've made tons of
money. I've had a lot of things. I had a 'Vette. I wrecked it. Everything
nice I've ever bought, something's always happened to it. And dancers
say they'll quit. And then you quit and go to a job, and you might be having benefits, and you might be making seven or eight dollars an hour. You
might have a good job, but you're sitting there thinking, "I could have

made four hundred dollars a night instead of eighty dollars. And you watch all that money go by. And dancers, they get so tired of dancing. Dancers always do it. They get real tired of dancing so they'll quit for like three weeks, a month, something like that, and then they come back because the money is so addictive. Oh god, the money, I could give up anything; I could quit smoking cigarettes before I could give up my money.

Darby is not alone in her expressed addiction to money. Indeed, it is the most logical response to living in a society in which we are exhorted to consume at every turn. Moreover, unlike cigarettes, we require money to survive, and the more money we have, the safer we may feel. Many sex workers find it difficult to exit the sex industry—even when it is destructive to them—because they need the money. And stripping over a number of years colors a woman's perception about the career options available to her. She feels, like sociologist Jennifer Johnson's working-class subjects in her aptly titled book *Getting By on the Minimum,* trapped by economic need and by her own low expectations. Johnson analyzes the way working in unskilled jobs shaped the expectations of the working-class women she interviewed:

> Women in unskilled jobs occupied a distinctive work world with distinctive conditions; they had not just a little less autonomy, but a lot less, not just a little less pay, but a lot less. And many of these same women had also occupied a distinctive world outside the workplace, a world in which money was scarce, conditions were hard, and jobs offered few rewards. They were offered a minuscule fraction of the monetary and nonmonetary rewards available to middle-class women, but by the time they had entered the workplace, this was what they had learned to expect.[1]

In the case of exotic dancers, the more the stripper is treated poorly, the more she learns to expect such treatment; the more she believes she deserves it, the harder it is for her to create positive changes in her life. This is part of the psychological toll of oppression.[2]

Many of the women I interviewed spoke about exactly this psychological toll, specifically, that the longer they danced, the more the negative aspects of sex work began to outweigh the positive and the lower their self-esteems sank. Their stories charted a similar course. Most dancers found that no matter how much they made in a shift—two hundred, six hundred, twelve hundred dollars—no amount of money compensated them for sex labor. Paradoxically, dancers also observed that they began to value their sexual desirability and overall worth in the world as late-career dancers by the daily, unpredictable income of stripping.

Approximately 50 percent of my sample described experiencing an aversive response—fatigue and nausea—to thinking about and preparing to go to work. April and Kelly interpreted these flulike symptoms to mean that the strip-bar environment itself was growing psychologically toxic to them. In their personal lives, the women I interviewed shared that stripping created tension in their intimate relationships—most often jealous partners and reduced sex drives. Moreover, many of the women I spoke with began to develop a deep disdain for men in general. The more men treated them disrespectfully, the more they were ostracized by mainstream society, the more their bodies aged, the more monotonous the strip bar became, and the more dancing cumulatively debilitated the dancers. This is the toll of sex work, briefly fractured and then reinforced by the unending loop of the Möbius strip.

A Distorted Sense of Self and Money

Sitting cross-legged in a windy park in the Castro in San Francisco, Kelly shared that her feelings about stripping had radically changed over the five years she had worked in the sex industry. When she first began stripping, Kelly experienced dancing with a kind of subversive feminism. But she explained that she noticed she was becoming increasingly insecure, resentful, embittered, and confused about how she perceived herself the longer she stripped.

> Well, my self-esteem became tied to how much money I made. And my emotional state as well. So, on days where I wouldn't make money, I felt really bad about myself and I got depressed. On days I made a lot of money, I felt really powerful and on top of the world. That sucked. My worth was tied into being how sexually desirable I am. I find that reflected in my life and my personal relationships. I think that that happened outside of sex work context. But it becomes so much more ingrained in my psyche because I had to encounter it every day I went to work. My rent was dependent on my being sexually desirable. And I noticed a lot of the same things happening in dating. I tried to keep the separation, but it's too personal.

When money is the means through which a person measures her desirability, she may develop a warped self-image. She might feel, as Kelly expressed, that being paid to be sexually desirable changes one's relationship to one's body. Not that women have uncomplicated relationships
with their bodies regardless of whether they support themselves by being
sexy. No matter what her body shape or size—large, small, chubby,
skinny, curved, or perfectly conforming to contemporary ideals—women
often feel conflicted about their bodies.[3] They feel not only that their
physical forms are flawed, although that is, of course, what almost every
woman feels, but also that their bodies do not belong to them. Instead,
women experience their bodies when they are reflected back, distorted by
the glare of culture, religion, parents, peers, and, most especially, men.
For example, after Trina learned that other performers made over a thousand dollars a night at her club, she felt that, because she did not make as
much money, it meant that she wasn't as attractive as the other dancers.
Also, significantly, she felt dissatisfied with her income:

> But for some girls, the more attractive you are, you should be able to
> make more money. Some girls should be able to take home a thousand
> dollars a night. So for a long time I never felt like I had a good night be-
> cause I never took that much home. And when I would take six and
> seven hundred dollars home, I would feel like it wasn't enough because I
> hadn't taken a thousand dollars home. A good night for me I would say
> is anywhere from three hundred and fifty and above. The most I ever got
> to take home was eight seventy-five. I made like twelve hundred dollars
> that night, but the club takes so much money. My concept of money is
> distorted and part of that might be due to that. This may be why I am
> not able to save that much.

Strippers, then, like Kelly and Trina, experience their bodies as
uniquely contradictory. The U.S. cultural preoccupation with slender,
toned, provocatively posed female (and recently male) bodies spawns a
wide range of personal and social problems from body dysmorphia to
eating disorders to overwhelming feelings of inadequacy in women.
These problems have been well researched by feminists such as Susan
Bordo, Jean Kilbourne, and Naomi Wolf.[4] But women's sexuality is also
a site of power, as the women I interviewed elaborated. For some women,
exotic dancing may be the first time they actually experience their bodies
subjectively, and this is liberating.[5] Moreover, stripping encouraged some

of my informants, including Kelly, April, Trina, Beatrice, Morgan, Janeen, and Joscelyn, to consciously explore a sexual side of their personalities. The paradox is that this potentially transformative sexual exploration is largely limited to the confines of the strip bar, arguably the gut of patriarchy. So while stripping will push a woman back into her own skin, claiming that alien territory as her own, over time the structure of the sex industry with its overwhelmingly objectifying male gaze forces her to "numb out" and dissociate all over again. And the stripper not only engages in the ordinary evaluation and self-scrutiny of any American woman, if she doesn't look good and act sexy enough, she also may not be able to pay her electricity bill.

Furthermore, making money as a stripper, even fabulously huge amounts of money, creates not only the psychological tension Kelly and Trina described previously but also unanticipated material obligations. Ellen, a ten-year veteran of the Pink Cave, an upscale club near Silverton, expressed deep unhappiness with dancing to me in a quick conversation at the bar while she was getting her before-shift drink. Dressed in a black bunny costume, ears drooping, mascara already running, Ellen cautioned with quiet desperation, "Don't ever start dancing. The money will trap you forever." With children to support and family members depending on her, she could not give up a job making two hundred to three hundred dollars a day to take one that paid just ten dollars an hour. Ellen offered me her hand, palm up, and sighed, "When they find out you dance, everyone wants a handout."

Again, dancers are not uniquely troubled by problems that stem from tying self-esteem to money, nor in performing physically and psychologically stressful work to achieve a certain level of income. Many people find themselves in unsatisfying jobs: funneled into a business or accounting major because their parents didn't know what on earth they could do with an English or theater degree or working at the mill, the mine, the shop because those are the only jobs available, and they need to stay nearby to take care of a sick mother. Or as Darby explained in the opening epigraph to this chapter, and as sociologist William Thompson theorized in his study on assembly workers at a slaughterhouse, the more money a person has, the more likely he or she is to spend it, particularly if one works in a low-status profession. Consumer capitalism socializes us to perceive big-ticket, high-status material items like luxury vacations, expensive electronics, and sports cars as compensation for hard work and as a measure of one's success in the world. Then, the debt accrued buying these things traps individuals in jobs they dislike. Thompson explores this cycle among the workers in the slaughterhouse:

> Consuming spending patterns among the beefers seemed to "seal their fate" and make leaving the beef plant almost impossible. A reasonable interpretation is that having a high income/low status job encourages a person to consume conspicuously. The prevailing attitude seems to be "I may not have a nice job, but I have a nice home, a nice car, etc." This conspicuous consumption enabled workers to indirect pride in their occupations. One of the ways of overcoming drudgery and humiliation on the job was to surround oneself with as many desirable material things as possible off the job. These items (cars, boats, motorcycles, etc.) became tangible rewards for the sacrifices endured at work.[6]

Darby bought herself a corvette. Beatrice vacationed in Hawaii. In *Strip City,* Lily Burana narrates her experience of purchasing a fur coat for herself for her birthday. Doing any job you loathe creates internal tension and a battered self-worth. Marx called this alienation from one's labor.[7] We are socialized to soothe this alienation in the profit-driven and profit-drenched United States by constantly consuming new things.[8] The equation we learn, and blindly ape, is that money and things equal success. Consequently, many Americans "prostitute" themselves by performing work that leaves them feeling dull, unsatisfied, and unhappy, like the slaughterhouse assembly workers in Thompson's study, to maintain a certain material standing in the world. What distinguishes strippers from other workers in low-status jobs is, one, the unique stigma associated with sex labor and, two, that their bodies are the tools, products, and currency of this labor.

Blurry Boundaries

As I discussed previously, dancers must set boundaries to survive the sex industry. Part of the toll of dancing for many late-career dancers is watching those boundaries erode. There are many reasons why dancers expand their boundaries past their comfort zone. Some women begin to dissociate while dancing so that what they are doing seems less and less real to them. For instance, Julie, an early-career dancer with a late-career perception, explained why she tuned out when dancing:

I don't want anyone to touch me, and I don't particularly want to touch anyone else. You kind of disassociate yourself from the work you're doing. You get used to it. It becomes a habit. It's not something you consciously think about while you're doing. With men that are rude and obnoxious with a lot of sexual innuendoes, it's kind of degrading in a sense, so you really want to, really disassociate yourself from it.

Some women find that they must perform more sexually graphic acts to make the money they desire. In her article " 'Where Am I Going to Stop?': Exotic Dancing, Fluid Body Boundaries, and the Effects on Identity," sociologist Jennifer Wesley observed this phenomenon among her subjects. Wesley described a continual "upping the ante" of stripping income as her informants made moment-to-moment decisions about where to draw their boundaries. The more money clients offer a dancer, the more tempting it is to stretch her boundaries. Tyler, a Honolulu dancer, illustrated this:

Money does things to certain people, but you still have to keep your pride and stuff. That's what it all boils down to, because if you don't, you are just losing yourself. You're money; you're not anybody but money. I could see how it could be easy to get greedy like getting propositions by men and stuff. I could see how some people turn to outside activities. If you are propositioned by the right person who says, "Name your price," a lot of people will just go for it, because everything has its price like they say; but your pride doesn't. A lot of people when you are in a certain situation will turn to outside activities.

So the dancer who blurs her boundaries, and names her price, has then monetarily valued an aspect of herself—her pride, her sexuality, her character—that culturally we learn is priceless. The more a dancer values her self-esteem and beauty at a certain figure, like Trina explained earlier, the more important it becomes to make that much money—no matter what it takes. Then, to make this arbitrarily determined amount, the dancer finds she needs to blur her boundaries further.

In addition, some dancers, like Kelly and Janeen, experienced workplace pressures to expand their boundaries. Kelly partly ascribed her negative feelings about stripping to the degree she blurred her boundaries while working at the Market Street Cinema, a topless theater in San Francisco:

During the time I worked at the Cinema a lot of changes occurred in the clientele and workers. The prostitution became rampant, and in the end, it was almost impossible to make money without doing more. The Cinema pushed my limits as far as what I would do. And I'm a prude compared to most of the girls that work there. I was doing things I never could have pictured myself doing, including naked lap dances. For me, that was really pushing my limits. But to most dancers, that was nothing.

A lot of the reason for this is that the city cracked down really hard on street prostitution, which pushed them into the clubs. They raided the massage parlors and escort agencies, too. So if you are a prostitute, it's the safest place to work. The men come to you. You only have to pay your pimp a hundred dollars a shift. I can understand it, but if you're a dancer who doesn't want to do that but just wants to lap dance, it became increasingly difficult to make money.

Within a year, the amount of money I made in a shift was cut in half, which was still pretty decent, but I also had to work a lot harder for the money. I was constantly propositioned—like every two seconds. And the men became more aggressive as far as grabbing my ass and my pussy and my tits. And some people would say, "that's part of your job," but I don't think it is. I think they should have to pay me if they want to do that.

The influx of prostitutes into the Cinema meant that customers had the opportunity to choose from women willing to engage in a variety of sexual acts, including manual manipulation, oral sex, and intercourse, in addition to the usual lap dancing. This drove down all the dancers' incomes, and Kelly, consequently, could not make the money she was accustomed to from just performing lap dances. Furthermore, customers' expectations about how much sexual contact they deserved for their money encouraged them to make increasingly aggressive sexual demands.

Like Kelly, Janeen struggled with maintaining her boundaries. Janeen, first a phone sex worker then a dancer, explained that phone sex completely eroded her boundaries. Phone sex is grueling. The advantage for the phone-sex worker is that there is no possibility of physical contact with clients. Unfortunately, the lack of face-to-face contact has a hidden cost, as the anonymity of the telephone enables some callers to act out more socially deviant fantasies, like rape, bestiality, violent sex, and incest. Janeen's employers expected her to respond encouragingly to every kind of sexual demand from the customers, no matter how overtly violent and abusive they were. This left her feeling both emotionally violated and extremely drained. Janeen explained:

Well, the phone-sex situation was like eight hours of men yelling in your ear. I worked for a really fucked up company. There are a lot of companies that say you can't do any bestiality, child stuff, no extreme violence to women, etc. My company was like, "If the caller calls and he wants you to be a German Shepherd, you better start barking." There was a soft-porn line and a hard-porn line. On the soft porn, you weren't allowed to say "dick"; you had to use a metaphor, because kids could call in on that line. If you got good on the soft-porn line, you went over to the hard-porn line, which was more money, but then you were forced to do anything. Any scenario. Ninety percent of the girls would unplug the phone, and we'd get written up. Just eight hours of that foolishness. "I'm going to chop your legs off and shove them up your cunt." "I'm going to take your tits and boil them and give them back to you." And you're supposed to be like, "Yeah, thanks. That's so totally nice of you to give them back." Affirmation is the same thing over and over; it must work the opposite way. So eight hours of "Fuck you, fuck you, you bitch. I want to put pencils through your labia." And you're talking to hundreds of men, and they're all giving you their worst thoughts. Some of them might be cool people, but when they call, whatever issues they have, that's what you get.

By affirmation, Janeen is referring to the pop-psychology, New Age concept that our bodies and minds record the messages that we hear over and over. These can be either positive or negative imprints on our psyches. For Janeen, doing phone sex forced her into a situation where she had to engage with undiluted negative messages about her sexual self. Janeen said she finally quit phone sex when one night, woken out of a dead sleep, she automatically started having phone sex with a wrong number:

When I was stripping, I'd wash it off. But with phone sex, I didn't do anything. I got to the point where someone called my house in the middle of the night as a wrong number, and I was so out of it I talked phone sex to this wrong number. That's when I quit. I didn't even realize what was going on. It was unbelievable that I did that.

In this case, Janeen recognized that she was losing her ability to distinguish appropriate from inappropriate sexual acts the longer she performed phone sex.

Traditional gender socialization and rape myths teach us that it is dangerous to excite a man without satisfying his lust. Such behavior can incite sexual assault.[9] Acting sexually aroused and available is also, paradoxically, one avenue to male attention and adoration for women. Strippers establish boundaries to manage this paradox while working. And a dancer's complicated job responsibilities—arousing men, coping with abuse and contempt, deflecting and neutralizing potentially dangerous situations while extracting as much money as possible—along with pressure from clients and management, drug and alcohol use, and money worries all tempt dancers to blur their boundaries.

Disdain for Men

I heard it from many of my subjects: "men are pigs," "men are assholes," "men are bastards," "but Bernadette, that's what men are *like*." You can see this sentiment expressed in dancers' comments sprinkled throughout this book: "Men are such takers of sexual energy," "If it weren't for the clients it would be an excellent job," "Men are horny assholes." The longer my subjects worked in the sex industry, the more likely they were to express that they perceived the clients, and sometimes men in general, negatively. A dancer develops disdain for men after enduring a variety of abusive behaviors from them: one client throws quarters at her on stage, another grabs her breast, one drunk pulls down her g-string, a customer who smells like he hasn't bathed in a month calls her a "dirty cunt." Perhaps a dancer experiences only one of these really bad incidents with a client per month (and this is a low estimate). After six months, that's six bad things that men have said and done to our hypothetical dancer in the club; after two years, twenty-four. The glamour of stripping—the makeup, music, lights, money, and attention—dissipates with familiarity. Direct insults and assaults from clients, along with feigning sexual arousal for men they find physically repulsive, encourage late-career dancers to hold men in contempt.

Because men are literally buying the company of a nude or seminude woman performing sexual interest, this exchange invites them, even those who do not intend to be rude, to have unrealistic ideas about dancers' sexual availability. Most stereotypes of dancers in mainstream society characterize them as sexually promiscuous. Inside the clubs and peep shows, a certain percentage of clients (dancers cited on average about 20 percent) treats them like sexual objects. Over time, the late-career dancer has endured individuals both within and without the sex industry inferring, or insulting outright, that she will have sex with any man for the right price. This would not be so terrible if our culture did not classify women who have sex for money as worthless, dirty, and stupid. In response, to bolster their wilting egos, some dancers project these character assassinations back onto their customers. Put simply, sex workers tend to develop an increasing disdain and hostility for men the longer they work in the sex industry. Beatrice illustrated this in the following comment:

> I'm constantly turning men down to sleep with them. I'm always subjected to that side of men wanting me in that way. It's tiring to always think that that's all men want. I know that's not all men want, but when I'm at work, it seems like it is. So when I go to the grocery store and a guy looks at me, I'm just disgusted, and I'm like, "I know what he's thinking!" And even when my boyfriend wants to get sexual with me, I feel like, "Oh, gosh, that's all you want!" Because I am so subjected to that at work.

Beatrice concluded our interview by confiding, "I'm really bitter toward men. Maybe I'll grow out of that after I stop doing it. But it's made me smarter and wiser."

Hence, the dancer, perceived and interacted with as a willing and eager sexual partner to men she finds unattractive, begins to develop disgust for her customers. She thinks, "How can they be so stupid as to imagine I would really desire them?" To many dancers, as Darby shared,

> Men are just big wallets; they either got hair on them or they're bald. All you see is wallets with feet walking around a club, some of them fatter than the others. You go for the fattest wallets you can find. Everybody runs for the biggest wallet.

Some dancers cope with the cognitive dissonance of pretending arousal for someone physically repulsive by expressing frustration for, and contempt with, if not all men, a certain subgroup of men who represent "the bad ones." Although experiencing such abuse has the potential to awaken a woman's consciousness about the institutional effects of patriarchy, generalizing from the behavior of a few men to all men compromises a woman's ability to maintain healthy relationships with men. Indeed, dancers reported a variety of problems in their intimate, romantic relationships, particularly jealousy.

Problems in Partnerships: Jealousy

Whether a dancer is straight or gay, she will probably experience difficulties in finding and maintaining a healthy partnership. Although most dancers do not have sex with their clients, their job regularly consists of arousing any number of random men, and occasionally women. Because of this, few people feel comfortable and secure enough with themselves to be involved in a steady relationship with a dancer. Melinda described what she observed of some dancers' primary relationships at Vixens:

> I'll run into a lot of guys at the club who will be like, "If you were my woman, you wouldn't have to work here," thinking that we have to do it. I don't have to be a dancer. I choose to be a dancer. There are a lot of men who wouldn't be able to handle their girlfriends working at the clubs.

Marcy, Susan, Carol, and Tracy explored some of the complications exotic dancing introduces into their partnerships:

> *Tracy*: It puts a strain on them 'cause you live here more at work than you do at home.
> *Carol*: And you'll hear, "You like it."
> *Marcy*: Or "You don't act like that at home."
> *Susan*: "You're up there bumping and grinding."
> *Carol*: Or "I see you dancing; you look at him like you look at me."
> *Tracy*: Or "You wanting that guy the way you danced for him."
> *Marcy*: I wanted what was in his pocket baby.
> *Tracy*: I have to explain to mine all the time, "Hey, when you see me, it's not all bebopping around and having a wonderful time. I have the dollar signs in my eyes. That is the sparkle that you see, the romance, that the movement of my body is making across the floor."

The Vixens dancers explained that it was extremely difficult to find men who understand the nature of exotic dancing—primarily that it is work and not a real expression of their sexual selves—and who also do not feel threatened by the sexual gaze of another man on "his" woman.

When the glow of new love fades, most men (and women) make demands on strippers that are incompatible with working in the sex industry. Susan explained that one of her boyfriends began to express jealousy and act possessively over the same behavior that initially attracted him to her. For example, he was first drawn to the way she projected her sexuality and how comfortable she seemed naked or virtually naked. As time passed, her nudity and sexual performances—unavoidable aspects of her job—became qualities that incited jealousy. Marcy, Susan, Carol, and Tracy thought this especially ironic because the boyfriend originally met her dancing in Vixens.

Martin, a client I interviewed, shared an experience he had in a club in which a dancer's boyfriend became jealous of the attention he was paying the performer:

> In fact, I was in a place several months ago. I found this interesting because the boyfriend was there and his girlfriend was onstage dancing. I was sitting across from him. She was beautiful, and we're looking at her. And her boyfriend really got mad, and said, "What are you looking at?" I tipped her. I was very dignified, and I was very nice. I tipped her very well. I didn't do anything out of the ordinary. You could take the top off but not the pants. But he asked me, "What are you looking at?" I go, "Well, she's here, this is her job. I'm not being rude by looking at her. That's what I came in here to see." And he wanted to fight me. He got across the stage and started cursing at me.

Thus, many partners of strippers, insecure about their girlfriend's fidelity, or perhaps concerned about her safety, try to persuade her to quit dancing altogether. If she refuses to stop dancing, some relationships disintegrate.[10]

Lesbian couples have their own set of issues to negotiate. Joscelyn explained that her partner was less jealous of the clients than the other dancers:

> It wasn't necessarily that she was jealous about the clients but jealous that I got to go and be with naked women all day and she didn't. And

for me it was like, yeah, that's definitely a bonus of the job, but it wasn't like I was sitting there groping all of these naked women while I was at work. We're all kind of doing our thing while we're there. She really sexualized it in that way, and I wasn't. I was like, "This is just what I happen to do, and I happen to work with a bunch of naked women." And I think that was hard for her.

Sex work introduces a unique set of problems into an intimate, monogamous relationship, problems that require complex, daily negotiation and feedback from both partners. This was particularly evident to me during my interview with two roommates, Sarah and Vera, who both worked at the Lusty Lady. In addition to the dancers, Sarah's partner, Mel, was present. Each woman was accustomed to perceiving herself, and being perceived, as a sexual maverick; each articulated a multifaceted experience of the sexual margins. Sarah and Mel are in a lesbian butch-femme relationship, and Vera identified as bisexual. They all openly explore fetishes and BDSM (bondage, discipline, sadomasochism), and Sarah and Vera work in a peep show. They gave me a copy of a zine they publish on alternative sexual practices including fetishes and sadomasochism. Each of the women discussed my questions with an attitude that demonstrated that they felt largely positive about what their alternative sexualities, including sex work, have provided them in their lives.

Mel clearly adored Sarah and seemed very supportive of her work at the Lusty Lady. When I questioned the dancers about how the work affected their intimate relationships, Sarah turned to Mel and invited her to share her thoughts. I asked Mel if she had any concerns about Sarah working in a peep show, especially the mental image of all those men looking at her. She responded:

It only bothers me when the few assholes at this place actually leave saying those girls are ugly or they're bitches. It's like, "Who are you trying to impress?!" They have their friends with them, and they act like it's no big deal. But, you know, they're the ones who just left a mess in the room two seconds earlier. And they're leaving saying, "The bitch wasn't worth it." What's the point? First, you could have waited 'til you were out the door to say it. They are deliberately saying it in front of the support staff. That's the only time that it really ever bothers me. That and when the guys grab you in the hallway when she's walking from the downstairs. They think it's okay to reach out and grab a cheek. It's like,

"You're lucky that time. Next time your fingers get broken." They do get escorted out rather quickly. But I don't like it when they get rude or grabby, which usually happens every time.

What was most striking to me about Mel's response here was the anger that abruptly emerged when I directly questioned her about how sex work affected their lives together. The rest of the interview Mel was self-consciously positive about the role sex work has played in their lives. Furthermore, Mel demonstrated affection for Sarah throughout the interview. She rubbed her shoulders, kissed her hair, stomped in and out of the room interjecting affirmative exclamations, and generally reinforced Sarah's and Vera's thoughts. Mel's comments and behaviors demonstrated that although she ideologically supports Sarah's choice to dance, and even enjoys living on the sexual margins partially because of it, she does not like her partner to be disrespected. Even queer sex workers who live in Berkeley and practice BDSM, whose identities are wrapped up in embracing the sexual margins, struggle with the toll of exotic dancing in their relationships.

"You Couldn't Put Enough Clothes Back On"

Dancers also spoke at length about how difficult it is to find a partner that can handle the secondary repercussions of dancing, such as a reduced sex drive and not wanting to be touched. April explained how pretending to be sexual and available in an artificial environment drained her:

> But you don't feel sexual. See, that's the thing. Not one time that I ever danced did I ever get even minutely turned on. It didn't matter if I was dancing for Miss America. I did not feel anything. You detached yourself from it. I think part of the reason is that you are hung over a lot, and you go home, and you are wore out, and you don't feel like moving. And people have been trying to pinch and pull at you all night, and you're tired of that. Your body is sore, and your mind is sore. We would laugh because we would all say we were going back to the nursing home. Because we'd all cover up in big ol' quilts and just sit around just like big grandmas. You couldn't put enough clothes back on.

Joscelyn elaborated:

It's hard when you're doing this type of work because it's sexualized and you're using your body in that capacity. For some people, they take their work home in that respect, and you're used to doing this performance for men. It's easier because I don't come home to a male partner right now, and I didn't necessarily while I was working either. So whatever I engaged in with the clients, that was work for me. And because you're using your physical body, you just don't feel like being touched. Someone gropes you in the wrong way, and you may have the reaction of slapping off someone's hand and not realizing it. And you don't realize that was a good touch, not a bad touch. That's where it gets hard. It has taken time and healing from some of those bad situations.

While they applied makeup, teased, sprayed, and curled their hair, and changed into their costumes, Vixens dancers Marcy, Carol, Susan, and Tracy explained that thinking about sex and being sexy all the time made them, like April, want to go home, put on an old robe and bedroom slippers, and watch a movie. Many dancers shared that they dislike it when their partners ask them to dance for them. They often outright refuse to do so. Dancers struggle to separate being sexy at work from being sexy at home. They also struggle with how tedious and exhausting it is to be sexy at work. In some cases, informants decided to give up the battle and turn off their sexual feelings altogether. Kelly shared that the numb feelings that sex work induced in her transferred into her personal life. Beatrice believed dancing depleted her overall sexual energy because she gave away more of her sexuality than clients financially compensated her for:

> Men are such takers of sexual energy. When I'm there, I expect that; that's what the job is about. I'm giving a side of my sexuality to these men. That's what they are paying me to do is to dance with them and be naked with them. They get some sort of fix or gratification, and I'm constantly giving that. Sometimes it's sexual, sometimes it's more motherly, but I always feel like I'm giving, giving, giving. I'm receiving money for it, but I wonder if it's worth the trade-off. I think I'm worth more than what I make there.

Kelly sadly concurred: "All these guys are touching me, but there's no touch that is for me. It's always something I'm giving to them or is being taken from me. But there is never anything for me." The more a woman performs simulated desire, the less connected to any real desire the act becomes. One consequence of this is a reduced sex drive. But this also means that stripping can become strangely disembodied, rote labor like factory work or running a cash register, to the dancer.

Unsurprisingly, romantic partners interpret dancers' lack of sexual desire in a variety of destructive, self-sabotaging, and overall threatened and threatening ways. Dancers confided that partners read their low sex drives to mean that the partner him- or herself had become unattractive to her, that dancing was bad for her, and that she was really interested in a customer. The woman's exotic dancing then becomes a weapon the affronted partner can wield during fights: "I told you your stripping was going to break us up," "You only want to have sex when you're getting paid," "You're really just a slut after all." Among the most destructive reactions intimate partners have to the problems that emerge from being involved with a dancer is to try to hurt a dancer by calling her a slut. Several of the women I interviewed spoke about both their fears that their romantic partners would believe this about them and their experiences of having significant others insult them like this in anger. April and Dana each articulated that being called a whore hurt them enormously and was completely intolerable in a relationship.

Because it can be so hard to find a partner who can handle his or her own jealousy and who understands the difficulties of exotic dancing, some of my subjects went years without a serious relationship. Some believed that it was easier just to be alone, as Dana expressed:

> With me, I push everybody away. I could have a relationship probably with several people, but I push everybody away. I think it's not that I don't want one. Because I think, I really think, that I would like to have a relationship with somebody. But I think a lot of people have the wrong idea of a dancer in the first place. And then with me, I'm really particular about what I want. However, if a man comes in, they think, "Oh wow, she's a dancer, this is great!" And I'm like, "That's not what I'm all about." I'm afraid of relationships because you never know if a guy you meet is genuine or not. Because so many men that I've met are so full of it that I tend to push people away. They may be a really great person but I would never find out. I don't give them a chance.

Thus, for many women, being single is part of the toll of stripping.

The Toxic Effects

April and Kelly both shared that, at a certain point, as late-career dancers, they began to feel physically ill when they had to go into work. April explained:

> At the very end, I was taking the vacations and being nauseous and just being doubled over in the tub—because you don't wanna go—and vomiting and actually getting sick. I mean, it's psychological. You actually feel like you're getting the flu on the days you have to work.

Kelly enjoyed her experiences working in a peep show in Chicago but began to feel poisoned by stripping when she danced in San Francisco. At the time of our interview, she had stopped lap dancing altogether and was going through a difficult personal and financial transition—she barely supported herself working sixteen hours a week at the Lusty Lady. She explained that she nonetheless felt less infected by the clients' "toxic" demands and, consequently, healthier when shielded from their touch by a glass partition. As Kelly became a late-career dancer, the sex industry became increasingly noxious to her body and psyche:

> What prompted me to get out was that I kept getting sick. I thought I would plan it all out—pay my bills, save up some money, etc.—but I kept getting sick. I was sick for about six months. I swear I had an allergic reaction to my job. Every time I went to work, I would get sick again. It was like the flu. It was an allergy, but it would really knock me down. And, one day, I just woke up and I said, "I'm never going there again." It was the wrong time. I had been sick for six months. I was totally broke. I owed people money. I was two months behind in my bills. It was the worst possible time to quit. It got to the point where it didn't matter. I just couldn't ever go there again. I had this nightmare about work which woke me up in the middle of the night, and it was so clear to me. I haven't regretted it. I'm broke as hell. The Lusty Lady is part-time and pays low. I'm not even covering my basics, but I need my sanity back. I was just burnt from doing it for so long, and I just couldn't do it anymore. I just don't want to be touched anymore. I felt like, energetically, it was toxic.

Like Kelly and April, Janeen explained that sex work made her sick. Both the personal abuse she experienced from clients and the traumas she watched other dancers endure made her feel powerless and poisoned. In the following excerpt, Janeen shares the disturbing story of a young dancer, Misha, who worked with her at the Market Street Cinema. Misha's plight, as well as Janeen's inability to help her, affected Janeen profoundly.

There was this woman named Misha who was a bulimic. She was a tennis player who was ranked No. 3 in the U.S. when she was twelve years old. And then she became a prostitute and a stripper at the Market Street Cinema. She was severely bulimic. When I met her, she was crazy, but she deteriorated even from that. She came up to me while I was sitting on someone's lap, and said, "They're putting drugs in the candy machine, so don't eat any of the Snickers bars." She was just really delusional.

Her mom owned these exercise studios that were really massage parlors in the back. So I think the kids were really raped a lot by the tricks that were there. So she's going on in the dressing room, screaming that her mother raped her, and I go down to the bathroom—and again there are no fucking doors on the thing because someone OD'd, and so we lost our door privileges—and I see these six bottles of coke, three on each side of the toilet. I was staring at them, and she came up behind me and said, "Get out. Get the fuck out!" So I ran upstairs and got the management: "You have to do something; she's totally lost it. This is not appropriate." The manager then said, "That's Tony's problem." Tony was the night manager, and he was having sex with her. So he was like, "That's not my problem." So I go back down and go into the other stall, and I can hear her guzzling soda and vomiting into the toilet, and she was saying, "I hate me! I hate my life! I wish I was dead!" I had been so numb for so long, and I thought, "Here I am in the fucking Cinema, in a bad wig, in a stall with no door, next to a woman who's saying 'I hate my life' and puking. And no one can hear us. No one is even listening. And nobody gave a goddamn!" And for those few minutes I thought, "I am really fucked! This is fucked up! This is not empowering! This isn't good! This is nothing! This is fucked up! This woman is dying, and nobody gives a shit!"

No one ever listened to her. No one ever heard her. She never got any fuckin' help. She bought five dollars' worth of gasoline, sat in the back of a pickup truck, and lit a fucking match to herself and went up in flames and died. Uck. I'm going to get upset. And still, nobody cared. There are a lot of empowering things I could talk about, but I always wind up talking about her because she went up in flames so that she could be heard, and nothing.

Janeen eventually left the Market Street Cinema. The experience with Misha disturbed her but did not permanently shake her from her numb state. She explained what happened after that horrible day in the bathroom stalls at the Cinema:

> I left that day. And then I came back the next day and was like, "I'm fine." Nothing happened. Misha disappeared for months, and I just went right back into being numb. And I went, "You know what, I'm not going to work at the Cinema anymore." It was one of those utterly horrible moments where I looked in the mirror and caught a glimpse of myself, and my wig was not even on straight, it was to the side, and the wig looked just like Rick James. I was like, "Oh my God, I look like Rick fucking James! Not even a good Rick James!" At least his wig was straight. It was a horrible sight to see yourself.

The nausea, flulike symptoms, dissociation, and avoidance propel some women, like Kelly, Janeen, and April, out of the sex industry sooner than they are financially ready and regardless of any conscious intent.[11] This is sometimes a blessing in disguise.

Dealing with the Toll

Nancy, an eleven-year dancing veteran, succinctly summed up the toll of the sex industry over a beer with me in the dressing room of Risque:

> I think I got older and got sick of it. I was tired of degrading myself all of the time because I started realizing how degrading it was. I saw some bad things happen, like my friends getting messed up on drugs and stuff. One of them got murdered, and all sorts of weird shit. I would attract guys that did not respect me at all. I would get real sick of that too. I'm like, "I'm never going to get a decent guy as long as I'm a stripper." They are always going to have this thought that I'm some kind of a slut or

something like that. I have been in the past, but that doesn't mean I am now. It's really hard to explain. Because you grow up and see that things aren't the same anymore and I have to change. Even the ones that are okay with it still look at you that way and don't even realize it. A boyfriend I had before the guy I'm going out with now, his mom was a stripper. So he expected so much because his mom did this and that for them. I was like, "I'm not here to support you." I've had so many boyfriends that didn't work, who just sat on their ass and played video games all day and did nothing to make money. It was pathetic; I had to keep paying for everything.

What is the toll of sex work? The dancers I interviewed invariably described a process of acculturation into the sex industry that involved them becoming increasingly cynical, jaded, and ill as time passed, both with the actual work and with the motivations of men.[12] In response, most subjects reported profound changes in their sexual libido and sexual identity. Moreover, women frequently disclosed that the sex work caused them problems in their partnerships, stemming from the partner's feelings of jealousy as well as their own reduced sex drive. Dancers articulated that taking in and processing the variety of sexual desires and issues customers bring to the club is emotionally exhausting. Tracy, a late-career Vixens dancer shared, "I think we've all at one time or another quit dancing for a while because it gets so stressful in your head. You feel like you're going nuts because you can't deal with everybody and everything." For several dancers, even those who originally loved dancing, the cost of sex work grew too high. Eight of the women I interviewed quit dancing, four of these after our interview. However, just experiencing the toll of stripping does not inevitably mean a woman will successfully exit the sex industry. Although all the women I interviewed experienced some aspects of the toll, many were not financially prepared to seek other employment. Hence, most of my informants, like members of marginalized groups everywhere, developed creative ways to resist the toll. In the following three chapters, I will explore a variety of dancers' responses to the toll of stripping.

5

"You Have to Be Sexually Open"

"If you don't like pussy, you shouldn't be working here," the management of the O'Farrell Theater in San Francisco frankly informs prospective dancers. Strikingly, in the strip bar, a microcosm designed for men's pleasure, sexual desire between women is not only condoned in many settings but actively encouraged. In San Francisco, at the Mitchell Brothers, it is not only hip to be queer, it is management policy to require live woman-on-woman shows of all the performers.[1] The presence of vast amounts of woman-on-woman pornography (which can be easily documented by entering any sex store or watching pornographic cable stations) surely attests to male fantasies about viewing expressions of lesbian desire, fantasies that the O'Farrell Theater does not hesitate to capitalize on. Moreover, the image of two feminine women sexually involved for the voyeuristic pleasure of the (usually male) viewer is also reflected in mainstream media images of sex workers, as seen in films such as *Showgirls*.

"They are all lesbians anyway," is one of the stereotypes with which mainstream society labels sex workers. When I embarked on my field study of exotic dancers, I was curious about the possible truth inherent in this femme-on-femme stereotype, as well as the much more subversive manifestations of women desiring one another for their own sexual pleasure, not for the male gaze.[2] I wondered too how dancers felt about this stereotype. As I spoke with dancers about their sexuality, I observed a fascinating tension between the heterosexual desire that sex workers perform for their clients' viewing pleasure and the sexual desire some dancers feel for other women.

In response to the toll of stripping, a large percentage of the women I interviewed chose to explore their attractions to other women—often these were late-career dancers. As I have elaborated in previous chapters, among the facets of the toll of stripping women reported a reduced sex drive, problems maintaining partnerships, feelings of dissociation from their bodies, and difficulties separating the sexuality they express at work from some sort of "real" desire. Many of my informants creatively responded to the numbness of body and mind produced by the toll of stripping by exploring, or relying on, their romantic, emotional, and physical attractions to other women.

After extensive observation of and lengthy conversations with dancers, I learned that there was no single explanation for the slippery contradictions of sexual desire among dancers but, rather, three main channels women traverse to the pool of queer sexual subjectivity. Sometimes she floats blissfully down a gentle current, and other times she falls headlong over a waterfall. The environments of strip bars and peep shows offer women easy access to other women and invite them to break taboos; they attract lesbians because men are not their primary erotic partners; and, as I noted earlier, they encourage the performers to feel frustrated with men. Somewhat surprisingly, there is virtually no academic literature on the sex industry that researches the sexual subjectivity of strippers.

The Problems in Studying Sexual Identity

In the sex-work literature, some dancers identify themselves as queer.[3] Also, sex activists such as Carol Queen, Pat Califia, and Annie Sprinkle in their writing acknowledge the existence of queer sex workers and their relationship to the gay and lesbian community. Indeed, most of the pro-sex-work activist books lining my book shelves identify the writer as lesbian or bisexual. This list includes Queen, Califia, and Sprinkle, along with Susie Bright, Holly Hughes, Scarlot Harlot, Joan Nestle, and Amber Hollibaugh. Moreover, many autobiographical books and articles on stripping discuss the author's transformation from heterosexual to bisexual or lesbian.[4] In the anthology *Whores and Other Feminists*, edited by Jill Nagle, four out of five sex workers that wrote for the anthology reference a female partner at some point. Similarly, many of the anti-sex-work activists are lesbian as well—Andrea Dworkin, Kathleen Barry, Ann Russo, and Sonia Johnson, for example.[5] Although the number of lesbian and bisexual women studying, analyzing, and commenting on the sex industry is apparent, social science that addresses issues of sexual orientation is virtually nonexistent.[6] Why might this be the case? I have observed two general tendencies that contribute to the lack of research on the sexual identities of sex workers: reluctant dancers and reluctant researchers.

When questioned, my subjects had varying reactions to discussing sexual identity. Some said baldly that most dancers are queer. Some expressed that they hadn't thought about it before. Several suggested that the sex industry turns women into lesbians. Janeen, a bisexual woman in a lesbian relationship, felt uncomfortable even discussing the manifestations of lesbianism and bisexuality among sex workers. As you may recall, Janeen had labored as a phone-sex worker and exotic dancer and, at the time of our interview, had quit stripping to write and create performance art. Of all my informants, Janeen struck me as the most interested in exploring highly controversial subjects. She had already tackled the relationship between sexual abuse and the sex industry, a choice that caused her to be ostracized and ridiculed by other sex activists. I was surprised, then, when the very loquacious and articulate Janeen froze when I posed the following question:

> *Bernadette*: One thing that doesn't seem to be studied a lot is lesbians and bisexual women in sex work. A really high percentage of women in the sex industry are bisexual or lesbian, it seems to me. And in some ways, there are some contradictions there. Do you agree? Disagree? Why?
> *Janeen*: I agree. But it's hard for me, I feel like I can't answer that because . . . I don't want to answer that. Why don't I want to answer that? I don't feel comfortable answering that because I know what my theory is, but I don't feel comfortable talking about it.

Intensely curious why Janeen did not feel comfortable sharing her theory, I shared my own ideas about sexual identity and gently encouraged her to explore why this was such a difficult subject to pursue. She responded, "It's exhausting and it takes a lot of courage and emotional energy; and people just get on my nerves. So when you asked me that question, it triggered that."

My interaction with Janeen illustrates one of the problems researchers face studying the sexuality of sex workers: how do we talk about sexual identity without triggering any number of emotional land mines? If queer sex activists living in San Francisco respond poorly to exploring any idea that might reinforce negative stereotypes about dancers—for example, that all dancers are really lesbians who hate men—it is not surprising, then, that dancers in more homophobic parts of the country are hesitant to fully discuss sexual identity nor that researchers are reluctant to broach the topic. Our entire "don't ask, don't tell" culture conditions us that one's queer identity is "private," "nobody's business," something you just don't talk about. Working as a stripper already identifies such women as deviant in most people's eyes—why take on the "dyke" label as well?

Researchers have not been loathe to study the deviant identity of topless dancers and the ways sex workers manage to maintain their self-esteem when they face bigotry and abuse.[7] Indeed, it is difficult to write about sex work at all without at least some mention of the stigma women endure and negotiate in the industry. Unfortunately, some researchers have also reinforced homophobia directly or indirectly in their studies of sex workers.[8] Sociologist Kari Lerum proposes in her article "Twelve-Step Feminism Makes Sex Workers Sick" that most research on sex workers is dominated by a few perspectives (including the feminist perspectives of the sex wars) that conceptualize sex workers as "sick." She argues that

> the study of sex work has achieved social and scientific legitimacy at the expense of dehumanizing sex workers, and that this dehumanization is not an unfortunate coincidence, but a *requirement* for the production of contemporary institutionalized knowledge.[9]

Whether the sex worker is portrayed as a victim or a whore, in most studies she ceases, as Lerum notes, to be the subject of her own life. If dancers are so viciously "dehumanized" for the act of stripping, what are the consequences of adopting yet another socially stigmatized identity, that of lesbian or bisexual? Similarly, how much stigma can a feminist researcher unpack before her informants clam up or before she becomes tangled up in the layers of stereotypes she is trying to debunk?

As I have explained, dancers are sexually marginalized simply by virtue of their work. Strip bars are legal—but often just barely so—and dancers routinely experience discrimination. The more dimensions of discrimination a researcher attempts to illuminate, the more complicated and demanding the emotional and intellectual labor for both the researcher and subject. Others (both performers and the general population) tend to assume that anyone interested in exploring such a topic must be involved in both the sex industry and the gay community. Not every researcher is comfortable, or equipped, to deal with the burdens imposed by such assumptions, that is, that you yourself must be a queer stripper if you want to study them. This might especially be the case if the researcher is a lesbian who needs to remain closeted in certain settings. Moreover, in my experience, sex work has a sticky stigma. When I share my research in environments as diverse as radio talk shows, an Institutional Review meeting at my university, cocktail parties, and barbeques, people tend to assume that I am an exotic dancer. (My current age and appearance contribute to this assumption.) Hence, I often find myself in the awkward position of explaining that I do not dance without reinforcing the stigma associated with stripping.

For a male researcher, feminist or not, the fact that he is observing the dancers for "scientific reasons" does not erase the reality that, for the dancers, he is still a male client. Dancers are skilled at making men feel special and adored as long as the money continues to flow. This is the way all exotic dancing in mainstream clubs is performed: for the male spectator, as if his gaze, his needs, are at the center of the universe. Although the image of the glamorous lesbian erotically touching another woman continues to hold a special place in men's imagination, these images of beautiful femme women having sex with one another do not reflect subjective lesbian desire but, rather, at best, a bisexual expression of lust designed to arouse and satisfy men. A lesbian exotic dancer—a woman who receives no erotic charge from the presence of men—is thus an odd thing for the customer, or researcher, to wrap his mind around. It is counterintuitive.

Heterosexual men, then, even if they are researchers, face a unique struggle in unpacking the layers of sex workers' sexual subjectivity. Does the stripper exposing her breasts, spreading her legs, and rubbing her crotch on a phallic pole genuinely prefer to be sexually intimate with women? Are the women performing a live sex show under the black lights of a strip club just pretending to be aroused for men's pleasure or is it an expression of their own desire? Inevitably, exploring the sexual subjectivity of sex workers (assuming the informants even feel comfortable sharing their "real" sexual selves with a potential customer, and a man at that) destroys the illusion that all women, even lesbians, reserve their sexuality for men.[10] This may be something the male researcher does not want to explore too closely. Moreover, academia, for all the current emphasis on postmodern sensibilities, is still a conservative arena. At the very least, a man interested in studying the sexual identities of sex workers might reasonably fear that other academics will assume his research topic is motivated not by the pursuit of knowledge but, instead, by his own lecherous drives.

Finally, the researcher, female or male, who is already encouraging a woman to discuss intimate, potentially painful aspects of her life in the sex industry might logically fear that exploring the manifestations of queer desire in addition to the already loaded identity of sex worker could alienate the informant altogether. Sexual orientation, like race, is a frightening topic for many people to consider. For example, many white people tend to fear that any comment they make about race could potentially be perceived as racist. Thus, they say nothing. Similarly, some heterosexuals fear that any question they ask about sexual orientation could be construed as homophobic or offend their informants. This silence reinforces racism and homophobia better than any ill-chosen remark and, in the case of researching queer sex workers, further inhibits dialogue and understanding. This combination, then, of the multilayered discrimination queer sex workers endure, patriarchal assumptions about women's sexuality, homophobia, and the unique challenges female and male researcher face studying the sexual identities of sex workers all contribute to the lack of studies of lesbian and bisexual sex workers.

Defining Sexual Identity

About halfway into the research for this book, I took my male friend Jordyn on an admittedly slightly drunken whirlwind tour of some of the Silverton strip bars. We started in the afternoon at Enigma—considered the most "dangerous" and "sleazy" strip bar in town—moved on to Vixens, and finally ended our sojourn at the Velvet Lounge. Considering that we arrived at five o'clock, the Velvet Lounge was surprisingly empty of clients. Eventually, two dancers I did not know joined us. I bought them drinks. Both asked me if we would like a dance, a wise strategy since we might have been a couple and I might have been offended if they had asked my "boyfriend." I told them that I was a researcher and a lesbian. One of the dancers, Carrie, then happily proceeded to tell me that since she had started working at the club, she began to fantasize about sex with other women. She described sex shows she performed with a close girlfriend and their repeated jokes about some day doing it "for real." Both their boyfriends wanted to watch. This conversation illustrates the pattern I've heard in interviews and conversations with dancers: sex work is hard on her relationship with her boyfriend, her boyfriend doesn't like it, she's only doing it for the money, and yet the other women are great. If Carrie is typical, and my interviews indicate that she is, most dancers in Silverton have at least toyed with exploring their potential bisexuality.

When asked, "Of the dancers you know, how many are lesbian or bisexual?" most dancers provided information that leads me to believe that a higher than average proportion of dancers are lesbian or bisexual compared to the perceived number of gays (10 percent) and bisexuals (20 percent) in the general population.[11] I cannot, however, generalize my field work to the larger dancer population because this is an ethnographic study, not one involving descriptive statistics. Furthermore, I have not spoken with dancers from all parts of the United States. I am also a lesbian researcher, and I usually let the women I interview know this, so some of them may purposefully play up their lesbian encounters just to please me, especially since pleasing their customers with suggestive conversation is an important part of their work. Nonetheless, my field work suggests a great deal of lesbian and bisexual expression and identity construction among exotic dancers. This is striking and deserves further analysis.

With analysis, the real challenge begins. First, sexual orientation is hard to define. When does a woman qualify as bisexual or gay? If she's attracted to another woman? If she has sex with a woman? If she does a show with a woman? If she's in a committed lesbian relationship? Suppose she likes to have "three-ways" with her boyfriend and another woman? For me, however a woman chooses to define herself is the bottom line. But self-identification is complicated by the fact that sexual orientation is both fluid and changeable and differently defined by who's doing the defining. Many dancers who publicly identified as heterosexual but privately wondered if they were bisexual confessed to me the times they had had sex with women, the secret lesbian relationships they had years ago, stories about going out with a girlfriend to heterosexual bars to pick up men that turned into nights spent having sex with each other. Several women I interviewed were in committed relationships with other women while identifying as bisexual. Still other dancers were themselves not certain of their sexual orientation. In my own life, my sexual orientation has changed more than once. After coming out, I continued to identify as bisexual for a couple of years while I was seriously involved with a woman. At some point, however, I realized that it was unlikely I would ever romantically commit myself to a man again. It occurred to me, then, that I was probably a lesbian.

Clearly, sexual identity is a complicated category to measure. Statistics that describe the population are extremely difficult to generate when researchers are loathe to ask about sexual identity and dancers are confused about what to call themselves. Taking a crude average of all my data suggests that 50 percent of the exotic-dancer population is lesbian or bisexual.[12] Specifically, of the women I interviewed, fifteen identified as bisexual, seventeen as heterosexual, and four as lesbian. Of the fifteen women identifying as bisexual, seven had been or currently were in a relationship with a woman.

Because the women I interviewed interacted with more dancers than I did, I asked each a series of questions about their perceptions of the percentages of lesbian and bisexual women dancing. Their answers ranged from figures that are commensurate with the perceived gay population to estimates that as many as 80 percent of dancers are bisexual and lesbian. Throughout this process, my subjects and I struggled to come to a shared understanding of what kinds of behaviors distinguished lesbian, bisexual, and heterosexual women from one another. For instance, Morgan, who identified as bisexual, differentiated women who had had bisexual experiences while working in the sex industry from those who identified as bisexual or lesbian. She elaborated:

> I think a hell of a lot of them have had bisexual experience. A lot of guys want to see two women together, and a lot of the dancers who do private parties who aren't lesbian or bisexual will put on a show like that for money; but I don't think that really counts. It's probably about commensurate with 10 percent gay and 20 percent bi.

Maureen, heterosexual, believes the percentage is a little higher: 30 percent lesbian. Including bisexuals, she said it is 50 percent. Julie explained that it's difficult to know who is gay and who is bisexual. Although her co-workers think Julie is straight, she has had two relationships with women and considers herself bisexual. She just doesn't talk about these lesbian relationships with many people. She explained:

> I only know of one woman that is a full lesbian. I know about five girls that are bisexual. And the rest are mostly straight. But I'm looked at as straight in the club, but I've had experiences, so I don't know if you

would consider that straight or not. 'Cause I've been attracted to a lot of women, and I can say that openly, but I don't know if a lot of girls would say that in the club.

Predictably, Joscelyn, a bisexual San Francisco dancer, figured the percentage of queer dancers higher than most of the women working in Silverton:

I'd say at least 50 percent encompasses both lesbian and bisexuals. I think it's just sort of a natural process, because I was straight identified when I entered this industry. So, for me, I started becoming more aware of my attraction for women, and it was an easy place for me to do that because it was accessible and there were other lesbians and bisexual women. We weren't seen as abnormal in that respect.

Rachel, a San Francisco dancer, said frankly that "all my friends in the sex industry have had sex with women at some point or other."

Darby, a Silverton dancer, cited the highest percentage of lesbian and bisexual dancers in every part of the country she's worked. Darby is a lesbian and said that she has dated most of the dancers in Silverton. She explained that her figures were based on personal experience. Darby and I discussed dancers' sexual orientation in the following exchange:

Darby: I'd say about, in Silverton, I'd say for a fact 70 to 80 percent of the dancers are either bisexual or gay. And the rest of them are married. Married or got a steady, steady boyfriend. You never find a single woman hardly that dances. Most of them ain't single.

Bernadette: What about other parts of the country? Would you say the percentage was that high?

Darby: Actually it's worse further on down the line. God, in Memphis even licking pussy onstage is allowed.

Bernadette: But that doesn't mean they're queer; they could have been just performing.

Darby: Oh no, they was all [queer]. I sit with a customer and he was like, "Are you bi or gay? 'Cause there ain't a woman in here that don't like women." I lived in Florida for a little while. I don't know, it seems like the more populated towns you go to, the bigger it is, 'cause it's coming out more and more. It's kind of a real fad that's going around right now. It's hip to be queer. Like I told everybody, I was just in before my time.

Bernadette: Well, but do you think there's a difference between you and some of the women?

Darby: Yeah, no. A lot of the women like men too. Most of the women are bisexual. Most of them just screw women and have an old man. But there a lot of just straight-up gay women, but not as many as there are bi. There's a lot more bi women. I'd say only about 20 percent of them are straight gay. Most of them are bisexual.

Here, Darby may be accurately citing the sexual identities of her former paramours or embellishing her sexual experience. Regardless, most of the dancers' stories and experiences explored in *Stripped*, as well as those described by other women writing about their research and experiences in the sex industry, suggest a high percentage of lesbian and bisexual dancers.[13] Why is this so?

Breaking Taboos

Journeying from the Bible Belt to San Francisco, I visited the most famous clubs and peep shows in the Bay Area to conduct comparative research on dancers' lives. With the gift of a free pass from Jenna, I entered the Emerald City of sex clubs, the Mitchell Brothers O'Farrell Theater. I hoped not to see the Wizard but to meet and speak with the good witches who transform male lust into money. It was May and, of course, freezing cold in the city. I was a weary traveler, marching from sex club to dance bar to interview all day long and carting around a heavy backpack with notes and recording devices, three layers of clothing, and a jacket. I dragged myself into the theater lobby, lumpy and tired, after trudging fifteen blocks uphill in the icy wind. I offered my free pass to one of three large male bouncers (a thirty-dollar value) and made a beeline to the bathroom to shed some clothing. There was a used condom floating in the toilet, which did not want to flush even after three tries. After rearranging my layers of clothing and applying fresh lipstick onto chapped lips, I ventured into one of the performance spaces.

The space was so dark at first that all I could see was a dimly lit stage with a stunningly beautiful woman performing. When my eyes adjusted, I found the room cast in a dark burgundy glow. The seats were packed close together stadium style and so tightly spaced that I could barely fit my 130 pound self, burdened with backpack and jacket, in between the

rows. I was the only woman watching who was not a dancer. I shifted uncomfortably in my cramped seat for perhaps five minutes before Beatrice, a recent UC Berkeley graduate, approached me. We moved from the performance area to a quiet spot, and she generously spoke with me for over an hour. Like many of my research subjects, Beatrice is bisexual. She shared that she became interested in women romantically and sexually after working at the O'Farrell Theater. Beatrice's comments echoed those of many of the women I interviewed and served as yet another confirmation of the rambunctiously profuse queer desire in the sex industry.

Beatrice expressed that the close bonds dancers form with one another encourage them to experiment sexually with one another:

> For one, to be a dancer you have to be sexually open. Obviously, you're taking your clothes off, you're playing a role, you're doing this sexual thing, and you can't be judgmental of other things that are not sexually normal. Not that being bisexual or lesbian isn't sexually normal, but in society's eyes it isn't. If you're open to being a stripper, you may be open to other things. Mitchell Brothers is very unique in that way. The club started off being a film group, and they made one of the first pornos that has an actual "come" shot in it. So they kind of have a history of being on top of what's hot, and a lot of men think it is very arousing to see two women together. So a lot of the shows we have there are girl-girl shows. And if you're working there, you see girls having shows with each other, and it makes it more of the norm, more acceptable. And we all get to be good friends and are sympathetic to each other's emotional needs. We all talk a lot. We have an upstairs dressing room, and a lot of times we just sit up there and smoke and talk and complain about the customers and talk about our problems at home. And it is a very supportive environment. A lot of the girls are really friendly and nice. And a lot of girls end up being lovers. I think that might be unique to Mitchell Brothers.

Dancers are already sexually marginalized by virtue of their work. They have violated gender norms simply by taking off their clothes for money. Having broken this taboo and discovered that the world as they know it has not ceased functioning, they may be more inclined to break another taboo. Moreover, dancers work with beautiful, naked, or virtually naked, women daily. Many are encouraged to feign sexual interest in other women to titillate the customers—the policy of the O'Farrell Theater. This combination of easy access, job-related experiences, and the

pleasure of breaking taboos propels some women to explore their burgeoning attraction to other women. Eight of the women I interviewed started to date other women after they began working in the sex industry. Five of these eight were San Francisco dancers.

I found, however, that the intimacy Beatrice described dancers sharing (leading sometimes to romantic and sexual liaisons) was not unique to San Francisco or the O'Farrell Theater dancers. Melinda observed a similar phenomenon among Silverton dancers:

> I think they finally see other women. You can look at yourself and see yourself as a woman but not be attracted to yourself. But to sit there and look at women all day long who are trying to be attractive, if you have any bisexual tendencies, you're going to find one that you're attracted to. And you're going to want to do something with that because I don't think you can help it. They're beautiful. They're trying to be sexy. There's going to be an appeal.

Similarly, Jenna explained that dancing encourages women to be more open to sexual possibilities:

> Dancing encourages exploration and coming into your sexuality. I think, on a whole, we're all bisexual. It allows dancers to look a little more closely at that. I think a larger percentage are bisexual because they have had a chance to explore their sexuality more. They've had to deal with the sexuality more than a lot of other people do. It's a natural thing; it's a great thing.

Kelly concurred:

> Most dancers are bisexual here [San Francisco]. To be a sex worker you have to be comfortable with your sexuality. And it's a highly sexual environment, and you are surrounded by gorgeous women. I think sex workers definitely explore their sexuality.

The environment of the strip bar encourages sexual exploration. Similarly, the taboo-breaking process can work in both directions. A lesbian has already violated a cultural taboo by having sex with another woman for her own pleasure. She thus may be more open to considering exotic dancing.

Lesbian Dancers

I discovered that some lesbian and bisexual women may choose to work in the sex industry *because* they are not attracted to men. Some lesbian and bisexual women I interviewed shared that they felt dancing was easier for them than it would be for heterosexual women because they can sustain a clearer boundary between the work of feigning desire for men and the more "authentic" desire they feel for women.[14] Some believed, like Darby, that the boundaries between performance and pleasure, as well as between clients and partners, are simpler to maintain because men are not attractive to them. Darby explained that she feels that being a lesbian has helped her remain emotionally detached from her customers:

> It's a heck of a lot easier to keep yourself from getting emotionally attached. You can keep your mind on your money, because these little straight chicks, they get drunk, they meet some cutey, and then start dating him. He don't want them to dance no more. I've always found it easier to be a lesbian 'cause you can keep a total emotional detachment. You make a heck of a lot more money. You keep your mind on your money.

Like Darby, Vera and Sara, friends who traveled from New England to San Francisco to dance at the Lusty Lady, also feel that sex work is more emotionally demanding for the dancers who are heterosexual. Vera explains:

> I think it would be sad for a dancer who was straight because it would really disillusion her. If I could only be sexual towards men, I'd be in a big problem right now. I guess it would show me the real true gems of men who are out there, very few and far between.

Furthermore, Sarah thinks that lesbians cope with the abusive clients better than heterosexual women because they don't have to go home to a man:

> I think it's good that lesbians do it [dancing], because they can handle men being assholes better. You come home, you're not bringing any of

that stuff with you. Whereas if you get off work and you go to a bar and guys are treating you the same way as they did at the club, that's got to suck. I don't ever want to experience that.

Logically, then, it would be harder for a lesbian to dance for or prostitute herself with a woman and remain emotionally distant. Darby, who has worked as an escort as well as a stripper, shared that she has violated her own boundaries about having sex—with her female clients. Nevertheless, she struggles not to do this, especially when she is in a relationship. Darby explored this complicated situation:

If they're really good-looking, if they turn me on, I go there. I can't help it. That's why I don't think I could be straight and do this job 'cause if it turned me on, I'd be, "Hey, getting paid to do something I'd do for free here." But with women, one out of every three times, I've did it [had sex with them], but I don't see many women. I see a lot of couples. And couples, some of them want sex, and I won't give it to them. A lot of them just like me to be in the room while they have sex. I think it would be a hell of a lot harder if I weren't gay. That's the only time I've ever had sex for money is with women, and that's just really 'cause I would do it for free. I figure, "Hell, I can get paid for something I do for free." Except for when I was with Shannon. When I'm dating somebody, I don't believe in cheating. But that hurts my money. 'Cause I got a couple of women clients that do call me on a regular basis. Actually, I don't know why they pay. I'd come give them the sex without them having to pay me.

Beatrice also became involved with one of her female customers. In her case, the bond was both sexual and romantic, and they maintained a relationship outside the club. As the emotional connection grew, Beatrice felt uncomfortable accepting money from her. She explained:

There was a customer that came in, and I ended up having a relationship with her. I cut off any customer relationship with her. She would come in and give me money to talk to her. And we ended up having a relationship. And I told her that if she comes into the club, I'll sit with you and spend time with you, but I don't want money. I just don't feel right about it.

Beatrice did not "feel right" about taking money from her lover as the line between partner and client blurred. That line is inevitably blurrier for women involved in, or seeking, heterosexual partnerships. Some straight women, as Dana explained in an earlier chapter, avoid this emotional conundrum by staying single.

Man Problems

As the women quoted here abundantly demonstrate, exotic dancing exposes women to an often repugnant side of men and masculinity. As late-career dancers who suffered the toll of stripping—being insulted, poked, licked, rejected, and propositioned—some of my interview subjects said, "The heck with men. There's all these sexy women around who are nice and funny. I could be with a woman instead of a man." Hence, the third reason bisexual women may be so highly represented among sex workers is because sex work teaches them contempt for their clients and, then, for some, contempt for men in general. Beatrice said this explicitly:

> That's another reason that women get turned off to men—just working in the job. They just get turned off because they see a sexual side of men that they don't like. And it makes them more appreciative of women.

Similarly, Darby observed her co-workers growing tired of men and approaching one another. She argued that working in the sex industry will turn a woman queer:

> They get sick of men. They just would get fucked up. There's always one in the crowd, and that makes all the straight ones think about it. They get drunk, and they get tired of putting up with all them men. And they try it, and they like it: "I can have me a woman instead of one of these fucking men." Because putting up with men all the time, it just turns you off towards them. Working in those clubs, being around so many men, so much, it just turns you off towards them 'cause you meet so many assholes and pricks and you think, "God, are all men like this?" And you stereotype men. And you don't have

nothing to do with them because they get on your nerves. Then you get with a chick and she flips your shit upside down, and there you go.

Rachel distinguished between the male customers and the men with which she otherwise associates, the customers a category of individuals too loathsome to even identify as "men." She explained:

> When people say, "Doesn't that make you hate men?" or stuff like that, to me the customers are not men; they're this whole other species. All the men I know in my real life would never go to these places and just have nothing to do with that whole culture. And so, to me, I don't really count them as real people. They aren't people I would interact with for free in real life. They are people I only see as part of a business interaction.

The male customers rarely hold an erotic appeal to the dancers. The sexual version a client expresses in a strip club is necessarily narcissistic and selfish. The structure of the topless bar—of men and women as buyers and providers of sexual services—necessitates this. Accustomed, then, to sexually servicing men, to giving but not receiving specialized sexual attention, some dancers begin to feel that men are disinterested in pleasing women and only concerned with meeting their own needs. Most dancers shared that they began to feel degraded and disposable, invisible as individuals, just another in a long line of "Stepford" strippers the longer they worked in the sex industry. Again, this is part of the toll of stripping.

The institutionalized environment of the strip bar, and the unequal barter of flesh that makes up the sex industry more generally, forces a man, regardless of his intent or political orientation, into the role of selfish sexual dominator. Richard Perry and Lisa Sanchez's article "Transactions in the Flesh" supports this claim.[15] Their work documents the subordination, coercion, and objectification their informants experienced in the sex industry, finding that sex workers struggle, unsuccessfully, to remain subjects in the eyes of customers and other men in their lives.[16] The authors analyzed specific instances when clients and pimps deliberately treated the sex workers they encountered as property that they could both trade and consume. These men took advantage of the marginal location sex workers inhabit to improve their social standing with one another and to provide evidence of their sexual mastery within their social sphere. The women, then, were simply the commodity men bartered to enhance their masculine status. Indeed, Perry and Sanchez argue that what nude dancers really sell is not the opportunity to gaze at a naked form but the possibility for men to buy a position of sexual dominance in the eyes of sex workers and other men.[17]

But this is not the case with women, even the female customers, and especially not the other dancers. Because the strip bar is an environment organized for men, in a male-dominated society, and because the women in topless bars are supposed to play one role or not be there at all, in the language of the poststructuralists, a woman's gaze on another woman's body subverts the heterosexual hegemony of the strip bar. Or, put more simply, a woman looking at another woman in a strip bar is not automatically a sexual dominator. Another woman can see the dancer as a person with talents, needs, kids, a sick aunt, and three cats. Men, dancers learn, see a stripper. Thus, working in the sex industry teaches women to read the actions and presence of men and women differently —with men in a negative cast—and see in other women the possibilities for romantic intimacy. This paradigm-shifting perception—men = bad, women = maybe—is not confined to the insides of strip bars but enters into the general lexicon that a dancer uses in other aspects of her life.

Manifesting Queer Desire

Exotic dancers express lesbian and bisexual desire in myriad overlapping forms. Strip bars are liminal sites where, under the right circumstances, rules about "appropriate" sexual behavior might be temporarily suspended. They are places where dancers learn disdain for men and develop attractions for one another, where they take off their clothes in public, where they might welcome the sexual gaze of another woman. Exotic dancing may challenge a woman's sexual paradigm; then, having broken one taboo, it's easier for her to break others. Many elements are present that invite women to interact with one another sexually: access, attractive women, a sexual environment, the taboo-breaking process, irritation with men, and the need to separate the sexuality one engages in for work with the sexuality reserved for one's pleasure. For women who are already lesbian or bisexual, dancing is a way to make a lot of money and be around other queer women. For a woman interested in exploring her bisexuality, deciding to be romantically involved with another woman is one way to alleviate the toll of dancing. For both, being with a woman may function as a buffer against the insults of male clients and as a way to preserve a not-for-sale sexuality of one's own.

As I have previously discussed, feminist theorizing on the sex industry has largely emerged out of the "sex wars": a polarized debate between radical and sex-radical feminists about whether women's labor in the sex industry is altogether exploitative or holds the potential to empower women as well as oppress them. One implication of my research on queer desire among sex workers is that it confirms *both* radical and sex-radical theories about sex work. As the radical feminists so vividly describe, the sex industry abuses women and, more generally, perpetuates patriarchal attitudes about women's sexuality. Consequently, one way women might adapt to the worst parts of the labor—the physical and emotional abuse, the insults, the objectification, the rejection, the disgust they feel for the clients—is to develop romantic and sexual relationships with other women. Dancers who choose to expand their sexuality by exploring their attractions to other women thus illustrate the perspective of the sex-radical feminists: they are empowering themselves through a subversive act.

At the close of our interview, Darby gleefully described participating in an all-woman orgy in the dressing room of a strip bar in Silverton:

Oh man. One time in Lace and Lashes we had a big queer happening. All the dancers got suspended, or at least eight of us did. I was in the dressing room. I don't know who started it, but I was in the dressing room at Lace and Lashes. I was kind of young. All of a sudden the lights got flipped off. We all got smashed that night. This was back when everybody used to be real tight. And somebody flipped off the lights, and I got dragged onto the floor for this big gay women orgy. We're back here, we're supposed to be closing up, and nobody's paid their tip-out— 'cause at the end of the night you got to take your tip out and pay the bar for working there. Oh god, he opened up the door and flipped on the lights, and my face was the first he saw. I was like all up in this, got somebody back here, somebody right here, couple people here and here. We all got suspended. The dancers just—I don't know, I guess it's where you're around women so much. I really don't know what it is. I think it's where the women put up with men so much.

Manifestations of queer desire such as this, as well as others I have discussed, complicate feminist analyses of gender relations in the sex industry. They also warm my subversive heart. Hence, the originally counterintuitive concept of a lesbian or bisexual dancer becomes more logical
with rumination. For many women, then, exploring the romantic and
sexual possibilities of lesbian relationships is among the most significant
responses they make to the toll of stripping.[18]

6

Sticking Together

In the documentary *Live Nude Girls Unite!* director and peep-show dancer Julia Query shares a story about a random street meeting between her co-workers and her mother, who did not know she was working in a peep show. As she exchanged enthusiastic waves with her peep-show acquaintances, Query felt panic set in when she realized she only knew her co-workers by their stripper names—"Cayenne, CoCo, and Octopussy"—which would surely raise her mother's suspicion. Fortunately, accessing what Query described as "instant stripper ESP," each woman immediately understood the precarious situation, smoothly introduced herself, graciously finessed the social encounter, and Query's mom was none the wiser (at least not then). These kind of interactions encourage women to both appreciate and deepen their bonds with one another.

For many, working as a stripper for a length of time entails shouldering a loaded pack of social condemnation and self-loathing. The longer she works in the sex industry, the heavier the pack becomes. Some women cope with the extra weight by taking figurative steroids—drugs and alcohol. Some trudge along, adjusting to the mass until they eventually collapse under its impossibly heavy burden. Some pause, put the backpack on the ground, open it, do some serious reorganization and rid themselves of some of the items they collected that they really don't need anymore. Mom's disapproval—toss that one out. Impossible beauty standards—chuck it in the river. Sexual double standard—set it on fire. Competition with other women—watch it disappear in your palm. "Slut," "whore," "bitch"—gone, gone, gone. The closer our hypothetical dancer examines the items weighing down her pack, the lighter it becomes. In other words, the more a dancer develops a critical perspective on sexist stereotypes about exotic dancers—the more she notices, gets pissed off about, deconstructs, and critiques the injustices she experiences—the more tools

129

she has to survive and, for a finite period, even prosper in the sex industry. This is because the battlefield of the sex industry encourages women to develop female solidarity and critique social inequality.

Hanging Out in the Dressing Room

Like being gay in a homophobic culture or a person of color in a racist environment, a woman in a male-dominated society routinely endures institutional barriers in her life. And working as a stripper only ratchets up a woman's daily experiences of sexism. Think of the most common words we use to insult women—*slut, 'ho, tramp, whore, cunt, skank*—these terms all reference a women's sexual availability, implying that a woman's sexual organs are themselves dirty and disgusting. A society that denigrates a woman based on her perceived sexual activity reserves a special vitriol for the woman who literally puts a price tag on her sexual body. The fact that in some cases a woman "chooses"[1] to be a stripper or a prostitute does not erase the heavy whore stigma she bears.[2]

The strip club is a volatile environment. Exotic dancers are simultaneously affirmed, adored, and showered with money, and abused, rejected, and dismissed, depending on how attractive the men in a particular club find them. In this atmosphere, exposed both to the worst extremes of sexist degradation and to slavish worship, and sequestered for long periods with only one another for company, they have the opportunity to share their perspectives with like-minded others. And exotic dancers are marginalized in the strip bar not only physically but also figuratively, by the repellent social stereotypes associated with sex labor. As anthropologists have well researched, women isolated by idiosyncratic social norms about female purity and pollution—in the menstrual hut, the convent, the prison, the harem, and the topless bar—may use this social isolation to deepen their connections to and form bonds with one another. Anthropologist Michelle Rosaldo wrote in the introduction to her edited volume *Woman, Culture, and Society* that "the very symbolic and social conceptions that appear to set women apart and to circumscribe their activities may be used by women as a basis for female solidarity and worth."[3]

In his book *Domination and the Arts of Resistance*, anthropologist James C. Scott conducts a detailed analysis of how subordinate groups resist domination through the use of what he terms a "hidden transcript" of their thoughts about and experiences of oppression, as opposed to a public revolt. The hidden transcript is a vehicle that allows subordinate groups to conduct sophisticated critiques of their dominators among themselves, in private. Scott explains that

> the hidden transcript will be least inhibited when two conditions are fulfilled: first, when it is voiced in a sequestered social site where the control, surveillance, and repression of the dominant are least able to reach, and second, when this sequestered social milieu is composed entirely of close confidants who share similar experiences of domination.[4]

The dressing rooms of most strip bars engender just these conditions for exotic dancers. The dressing room is a sequestered social site that "dominators" rarely enter, shared by women who each experience the toll of stripping. And under these circumstances, dancers develop close, supportive relationships.

Given how central women's relationships with one another are to their experiences of the sex industry, there has been surprisingly little academic analysis written about this phenomenon. There are two primary reasons for this. First, most academic studies on sex workers tend to examine women's relationships to the clients, the management, or the industry itself, instead of the relationships dancers form with one another. This might be because cultural stereotypes of women in general, and sex workers specifically, as backbiting, shallow, and two-faced color what researchers see and choose to focus on. Such biases are inevitable within a patriarchal system—a consequence of our conscious and unconscious complicity in misogynist stereotyping.[5] Second, a significant portion of the sexuality literature is composed of dancers' autobiographical accounts of their experiences in the sex industry.[6] Although some dancers have discussed in these narratives how other women helped make sex work a positive experience for them, the majority of writers focus on their personal journeys into the work itself.[7] Dancers have only recently begun to publicly share their personal narratives; thus, their stories are still new to themselves and to the culture. It is logical that the writers of such a young genre would still be processing their own experiences. Dancing is inherently a profession that requires a certain degree of self-involvement. Dancers must paint and perfume their bodies and watch themselves reflected in mirrors nude and half nude much of their working hours. Consequently, most dancers' narratives center on their own feelings, transformations, pleasure, and pain. Nonetheless, although most dancers do not highlight their relationships with other dancers in their written accounts, my research suggests that the friendships women form with one another are crucial in managing the toll of the sex industry.[8]

"Girls Here, We'll Stick Together"

The importance of friendship was especially apparent among the Vixens dancers on the day shift. One morning, before the shift started, Carol went to a local grocery store to pick up food for everyone. She generously offered to bring me food too. This is something they do every day: they cook special dishes for one another and share costumes, makeup, hair spray, cigarettes, and marijuana. Marcy, Susan, Carol, and Tracy explained how important their friendships are with one another in the following exchange:

> *Tracy*: Girls here, we'll stick together.
> *Marcy*: Family.
> *Tracy*: Yeah, it's family.
> *Marcy*: We get mad at each other, but we make up.
> *Tracy*: We're like sisters.
> *Marcy*: But then the day shift is like a big slumber party.
> *Tracy*: If we argue with one another, it's still time out.
> *Marcy*: The next day we talk, and it's over.
> *Bernadette*: How do you work it through?
> *Tracy*: We've been around each other for so long.
> *Carol*: We've all been around each other for so long, we couldn't stay mad at each other for too long.
> *Tracy*: You're used to fighting with your sister, right? And automatically the next day you're fine, or sometimes it will last a week and then it's over with. We do pretty much love each other.
> *Marcy*: We keep sometimes a lot of contact outside of here too.
> *Bernadette*: And you take care of each other if anyone gets upset or hurt or mistreated?
> *Marcy*: Yeah.
> *Carol*: Yeah, you have to, because who else is going to?
> *Susan*: We got each other's backs.
> *Bernadette*: So you watch each other while you're out there?
> *Marcy*: Always.

Tracy: Always.

Susan: Always.

Bernadette: Do people ever get upset? Do dancers ever just sort of lose it?

Marcy: Yeah, I had to quit dancing for a while.

Tracy: I think we've all at one time or another quit dancing for a while because it gets so stressful in your head. And then you feel like you're
going nuts because you can't deal with everybody and everything.

Marcy: But then you miss everybody and you have to come back.

The Vixens dancers explicitly claim one another as "family." For them,
being family means helping one another through the bad times and cele-
brating the good times. The relationship entails soothing, succoring, and
supporting others, even when doing so is inconvenient, annoying, and exhausting.

Moreover, in addition to experiencing social isolation, to suffering the
often callous disregard of management and the abuse by clients, each exotic dancer also shares in common the stripper stigma that brands her as
a fallen woman in the eyes of mainstream culture. Thus, a woman's job
in the sex industry complicates her relationships outside it. Maureen, another Vixens dancer who was present during our focus group but too shy
to speak out, agreed with the others privately:

It's like a little family. We stick together. I don't have friends other than
people I work with. Once they find out you're a dancer, you feel alien-
ated. 'Cause when I walk in the room everybody gets real quiet. I just
figure they're not really my friends if they're going to do that. I shouldn't
even waste my time. I get mad once in a while. I think it's discrimination
'cause you really don't even know me. Like a book, you got to open it.

Dancers, like gays and lesbians, learn to make their own families when
they are rejected by others. And like soldiers in a combat situation,
dancers need each other for protection in a sometimes hostile environment. The dancers I spoke with were conscious that the support they provide one another far outweighed any petty battles or spiteful moments between them, though they do acknowledge, as I also observed, that there
are real tensions between some of the women. Families feud as well as de-
fend.

Dancers do not always and inevitably respect one another and form
cooperative support networks. For example, in chapter 3, I analyzed how

dancers "other" fellow workers by perceiving themselves as more virtu-
ous, smarter, or psychologically healthier to manage stripper stigma. Yet
even when dancers engaged in potentially conflictual "othering," it sel-
dom dismantled their immediate support systems. Usually, the dancers
characterized as "bad" and as "making it worse for the rest of us" were
not employed in the same workplace. Those I interviewed rarely identified a specific woman, or women, as responsible for problems they experienced. Thus, in their individual lives dancers formed close networks
with co-workers, while sometimes they collectively stigmatized the hypothetical or "straw" dancer.[9]

Furthermore, when a woman does experience antagonism from another dancer in a strip club, it might be motivated by something other
than competition for clients and money. To illustrate, Tara, a former
dancer in Honolulu, shared that one of the most salutary parts of dancing for her was discouraging young girls from stripping:

> I think one of the good things that I did as a dancer is that we did have
> a lot of underage girls that would try to get in with their fake IDs and
> try to work, and I would discourage them from that. Sometimes I
> would have to be a bitch, if you want to call it, to get them out of there.
> I felt, being that young, it was no place for them to be. The youngest
> girl we had try to come in was fourteen. Looking at her even with a
> fake ID there was no way you could think she was of age. They would-
> n't stay for long. I had one girl I was so mean to she cried. I had already
> been doing it a couple of years so I knew what it was all about and the
> type of guys you get in there. There are a lot of nice guys, but occasion-
> ally you get a few that think that because you take off your clothes for a
> living they can do what they want to you and say what they want to
> you. It's not something I thought someone of her age should have to ex-
> perience.

That one of the most positive experiences Tara took away from stripping
was pushing a young girl out of the sex industry by any means necessary,
rather than, say, reminiscing about the night she made five hundred dollars in an hour, demonstrates the complex range of emotional and psychological connections between the dancers. Tara, a self-described
"chubby girl" in high school who was emotionally neglected by her father, shared that she identified with the fourteen-year-old. She explained,
"When I see young girls like that I want to protect them." Tara revealed

that protecting younger dancers was also a way of honoring, and nurturing, the wounded fourteen-year-old still inside herself.

But the private space in the dressing rooms of strip clubs and the abusive actions from male managers and clients provide only the fertile soil for female solidarity. Solidarity grows when dancers discard the stereotypes of female cattiness and competition and learn to appreciate one another. Beatrice, working at the elite Mitchell Brothers club in San Francisco, quickly realized this:

> We're always supportive, even for the girls who don't do as well. We'll always clap and whistle and try to make them feel good. That was something surprising to me, because I thought the girls would be more snobby when I tried out. I thought they were judging me, picking me apart, and "Oh, look at that girl. She thinks she can be one of us." But actually they are real supportive.

Outside the dressing rooms, strip clubs can be precarious environments. The mix of cash, nudity, and alcohol with the potential for rejection, abuse, and sexism can become "very stressful in your head," as Tracy observed. One way that some dancers relieve that stress is to take emotional responsibility for one another in and out of the strip bars. they comfort one another if one of them has a bad night, makes very little money, interacts with an insulting client, or becomes distressed onstage. They have each other's back.

"I Like Everybody That Works There"

Most of the women I interviewed explained that forming connections with other women was one of the best aspects of stripping. Darby shared:

> Women's a good part of it. It's a soap opera really. In a club, it's like living in one big soap opera. It's kind of cool. But the women in the clubs, they're all good-looking. Half of them bisexual. You have parties. You're kind of really close friends. At Lace and Lashes, it was like one big happy family. Everybody liked each other and hung out and stuff. It's changed, but everybody that worked there when I first started working there agrees. We used to go to amusement parks and everything. The women are just cool.

Janeen, who had stopped dancing by the time I interviewed her and was more critical than most of the dancers about the toll dancing had taken on her, still had only positive things to say about the other dancers:

> I liked being around all those women all day long, wearing cool costumes, feeling like it's glamorous. It's free. I'm really free. I can come and go as I please. I don't have to be accountable. I don't have to work nine to five. I get to live in this sort of fantasy world. I used to watch Wonder Woman as a child, and she lived on Paradise Island. The strip part wasn't Paradise Island, but the women part felt like it. They reminded me of that. And they're totally cool. And they're wearing Wonder Woman–type outfits, so you get to wear the Wonder Woman outfit, and it was like the whole Paradise Island thing. I loved that. I miss that so much.

In addition to working at the Market Street Cinema and Mitchell Brothers Theater in San Francisco for a time, Janeen also danced at the Lusty Lady. As I explained earlier, because the dancers do not compete with one another for clients and tips, the Lusty Lady nurtures even closer relationships between dancers than other stripping venues. At the Lusty Lady two of the more insulting things customers can do are motion to a dancer to move away because he wants to watch another dancer or make a fish-type gesture with his hands to indicate that he wants her to spread her legs on the glass. At the Lusty Lady, the women demonstrate support for one another by refusing to dance for clients who behave rudely. Sarah explained that meeting and growing close to the other dancers was one of the best parts about working there:

> We work with the sexiest, smartest, wonderful-est women in the entire universe. I like everybody that works there. I can sit down and chat with anyone. And, I'm not the most sociable person. It's great. We have marvelous discussions in the dressing room about a seventeenth-century Flemish painter or philosophy or our favorite dildos, anything ranging from mundane stuff to really deep stuff. And just being onstage with them is wonderful. They are so supportive. If somebody tries to motion to another dancer, your friend onstage will come running over and beat them up, if you don't get to them first. And it's just really great to be in that atmosphere. Our club is special because we can have that. At other clubs, you're begging for tips. And that's another reason why I like being

at the Lusty Lady is because I don't have to fight for tips and I can be friends with the dancers.

But I found that even at topless clubs where dancers *are* dependent on tips, the women offer one another support and camaraderie. Melinda, a Silverton dancer, shared a story illustrative of the kindness dancers express toward one another:

> Last night there was this girl, she was one of the older dancers and she just recently started putting makeup on and curling her hair. And she's still not very attractive—she's got two teeth in the bottom of her mouth. Well, she made a lot of money last night. Somehow she managed to make up to $140, and she was feeling really good about herself. She kept talking and talking about it. And there's this one girl must make four hundred to five hundred dollars a night. She really works. And she just kept making the girl feel good about herself. She was like, "Can I borrow twenty-five dollars off of you bitch?" She was just harassing her and giving her a hard time about how much money she had made, and the girl just felt so good about herself. It was really neat. And that girl doesn't even like her, but she just knew. She just now started making money; she usually only makes about twenty dollars a day.

Morgan, also a former dancer at Lace and Lashes, joked that dancing with other women was one of the few fringe benefits that she had at work:

> A lot of customers like for the girls to dance for each other and will pay both girls to dance together and stuff like that. Well, you know, "Hey, it's a dirty job but somebody's got to do it. Oh no, please, twist my arm, don't pay me to sit here and let this girl dance for me. It sucks to be me." That's a fringe benefit. We don't have a dental plan, but we have that. We don't have worker's comp but we do have that. We can touch the entertainers.

Most of the women I spoke with, especially the women working at the Lusty Lady, preferred dancing with one another to dancing for the men. Some clubs, like the Mitchell Brothers, as I noted earlier, require their dancers to perform live sex shows and dance with one another. Such job requirements can also foster intimacy. As Morgan said, "We can touch the entertainers." And they do. A lot. I observed a great many signs of affection during my time in the clubs: touching, hugging, kissing, and snuggling. I watched as dancers freely complimented each other on their outfits, hair, music, and makeup and tipped one another onstage. It is likely that some dancers' physical demonstrativeness with one another is a performance for the customers—to create the impression that the strip bar is a place for pleasure and partying and to further stimulate the clients by touching that which is deemed forbidden. The dancers' affectionate behaviors encourage customers to relax, hang out, have another beer, and spend money. So when I was at Desire in Honolulu observing and chatting with a rotating succession of dancers and five different women encouraged me to watch for Jasmine, "a fabulous performer," each exclaiming with some variation of "whose pole work is spectacular," it is difficult to determine whether these compliments were motivated by genuine appreciation or economic self-interest.

But in the "back stage" arena of the dressing room, where Vixens dancers characterized one another with insight and compassion—Maureen was the shy one, Susan would take anyone on, Tracy was the most articulate—their interactions illustrated connections they shared with one another unrelated to clients' perceptions.[10] Historian Deborah Gray White noted a similar phenomenon among female slaves in her book *Ar'n't I a Woman? Female Slaves in the Plantation South.* White explained, "Because black women of a given plantation spent so much time together they inevitably developed some appreciation of one another's skills and talents."[11] In the antebellum South, stable heterosexual relationships between slaves were difficult to sustain as owners broke up families, separating spouses according to whim or profit. In such an environment, where the future of male-female relationships was so unpredictable, White elaborated, "the female network and its emotional sustenance was always there."[12]

The constraints and toll of stripping in the contemporary United States little resemble the complete suffocation of the self in a slave society (although some radical feminists might argue this point). But the lives of strippers and female slaves of that period do have in common unstable heterosexual relationships—by choice, aversion, or coercion—a marginalized status in society, and social isolation. These factors encourage community building and solidarity. In his analysis of the cohesiveness of the hidden transcript among the working class, James C. Scott described groups who share a common, clear, antagonistic view of their employers, or oppressors, as "communities of fate."[13] To illustrate this, Scott distinguished occupations such as mining, working at sea, and forestry from the general working class because, like stripping, these jobs involved "an exceptionally high level of physical danger and required a commensurate degree of camaraderie and cooperation to minimize that danger."[14]

The Stripping Community

Dancer after dancer shared that meeting other dancers and making friends with them was an unexpected reward of stripping. "Cool," "wonderful," "funny," "smart," and "supportive" were the adjectives dancers most often used to describe one another. This finding is an explicitly feminist dimension of dancing that warrants further exploration. It shifts the focus of analysis from stereotyped conceptions about dancers' competitiveness and self-involvement to their real and necessary cooperation. Treating one another with dignity, affection, and respect is a feminist response to the toll of stripping and provides the foundation for a deeper critique of social inequality.

Stripping unexpectedly, and unintentionally, propels a woman into a "community of fate," thus encouraging her to develop camaraderie with and to cooperate with other dancers. The stigma, the dangers, and the isolation of stripping foster first a hidden transcript and, consequently, connections among exotic dancers. The women I interviewed formed close friendships and partnerships with one another, supported one another through difficult times, and appreciated and centered other dancers in their lives. Sometimes these friendships were short-lived, because dancers tend to change places of employment frequently. The experience and stigma of stripping, however, offers dancers and ex-dancers immediate access to the hidden transcript and, thus, to a community, even at a new club or with new co-workers.

Morgan, a former Silverton dancer now pursuing a medical degree, confided that she still feels a far stronger identification with other dancers —whom she frequently called "my people" in our interview—than she does with her fellow medical students. Morgan explained, "I have never met a dancer who was reasonably intelligent who did not have a social conscience." Unfortunately, she could not make the same claim about medical students. It is more common, and certainly far easier, for members of marginalized groups to recognize their own experiences of oppression than it is for members of the majority to perceive their own privilege.[15] Strippers' daily activities—sharing information about customers while they apply makeup, soothing a co-worker crying over a nasty insult, bringing lunch to a woman whose boyfriend dumped her, being naked and vulnerable and mistreated *together*—create the conditions for critical reflection.

Developing Social Consciousness

Put simply, there's nothing that will wake up one's critical consciousness more quickly than being mistreated for no good reason, especially if one has the opportunity to analyze these instances with like-minded individuals. Just about every woman I interviewed expressed an organic understanding of social inequality, including analyses of class, gender, and racial discrimination. Many offered sophisticated critiques of social systems—most obviously, Janeen, Kelly, Joscelyn, and Rachel, who organized to improve working conditions for sex workers in San Francisco and whose activism I discuss in the following chapter. But a dancer does not need to live in San Francisco, go to Exotic Dancer Alliance meetings, or create performance art to recognize sexual hierarchies and hypocrisies. In 1998, the mayor of Silverton proposed new legislation to severely curtail the amount of contact permitted between customers and dancers, as well as how much skin a dancer could reveal. This legislation was extremely threatening to the dancers because it directly affected their incomes and sensationalized them in the local public eye as misbegotten victims or whores. Vixens dancers Marcy and Tracy discussed the potential impact of the mayor's legislation on their livelihoods and the community:

> *Marcy*: If she closes the titty bars down, welfare is going to go up. You're going to have everybody taking food stamps, welfare, social services. She's going to put them on the street, prostitution.
> *Tracy*: They're already cutting welfare. There are too many single mothers. There's young girls that are trying to put themselves through college. We have so many bills to pay, and we're not asking the government or anyone to help us. We're paying our taxes, we're doing what's right, and here she wants to come in and destroy jobs for dancers, waitresses, bartenders, bouncers.

Marcy: And what she's going to do is put them on the street to do prostitution, which will bring up disease, murder, rape. Drug use is going to go
sky high 'cause they're going to be out on the street corners pulling
tricks.

Tracy: What are they going to do? There are so many people out there that
can't get jobs—they don't have the education. They have been trying to
get off welfare but have been knocked down so far that they can't get off
welfare to get a damn job, to even go to school. They say they have all
these programs out there for people, but who in the hell do you see getting into these programs?

Marcy: And then the programs are only for so long. You're allotted only so
much time out and then they cut you off.

Tracy and Marcy analyze stripping both as a way to support themselves
and as a better option to financial hardship than going on welfare or engaging in prostitution. Most women do not aspire to be strippers. Sex
work is a temporary and imperfect solution to a larger social problem: a
lack of economic alternatives for women in a male-dominated, capitalist
society. Although Marcy and Tracy did not frame their analysis in the sociological language of "institutional constraints," they nonetheless recognize that closing local strip bars would not feed a dancer's children,
pay for her college tuition, or help her ailing parents. Shutting down strip
bars does nothing to address the lack of economic opportunities for
women.

Moreover, dancer after dancer drew parallels between working at a
strip bar and other forms of labor exploitation. Although the toll of stripping is high, working in any low-paying, repetitive labor exacts psychological, emotional, and material costs.[16] Tara, born and raised in Hawaii,
quit dancing when she became pregnant. She still misses it, though, especially the autonomy she had as a dancer and, of course, the money. At the
time of our interview, Tara worked in a local mall in the food court. She
compared working in a "respectable" job to dancing:

My reason for wanting to go back now [to stripping] is for the money. I
did it for three years, making my own hours and coming and going as I
please. I would go in every night with a set limit in my head, "Okay, I'm
not leaving with less than two hundred dollars tonight." Whether that
took me two hours or eight hours, I wouldn't leave until I got it. Now,

after I left dancing, I really work hard for the chump change I am getting. It is ridiculous. That makes me want to go back even more because you have to work twice as hard when it's honest.

You have all these bosses that shit all over you. When you're in the strip industry no one is bullshitting you. You are there to take off your clothes and make money for yourself. In a regular job, they can't say it like that, but you're their workhorse. You're going to bust your ass for them so they can pay for their Mercedes-Benz and their condo and whatever else they have. And they dump all over you and treat you like shit. For that, I might as well be dancing. At least it's honest, because I know people are there to see me naked. At least I'm not getting lied to to my face to keep me there on the clock making them money.

Similarly, as Lily Burana has pointed out, whenever a dancer needs to convince herself that her job situation isn't so bad, she can say, "Well, it beats working at McDonald's."[17] Dancer after dancer reminded me that there are parts of any job that make it difficult. Morgan, for instance, said she would not want to be waitressing at Waffle House for the rest of her life. Joscelyn explained that "there are certain things that other workers have to do in their own jobs, and sometimes it may be demeaning. And you do it anyway because that is what's expected of you and that's what brings in your paycheck."

Reflecting on what it is about working as an exotic dancer that encourages a woman to be more attentive to social problems, Morgan offered the following analysis during our second interview:

I think, because you see a lot, you have to be damn near comatose after a while to not notice some things like wasted potential and unfortunate patterns that get repeated. A lack of education, opportunities, health care, a lack of lots of things. A lack of respect. It's difficult not to see. This is not universal. This does not happen to everybody. I think some people probably tumble to it more quickly than others.

Unlike people of color in a racist society, dancers are not born stigmatized. Women who work in the sex industry adopt and are labeled with a stigmatized identity. This offers dancers a kind of double vision: they experienced being treated one way before they began stripping and another afterward. Like gays and lesbians who come out as adults, exotic dancers can experience the world as privileged members as well as stigmatized deviants. These contradictions, accompanied by the social isolation and solidarity I discussed, also foster a critical gaze on social life.

Working in the sex industry provides women with the conditions necessary to produce what W. E. B. Du Bois, the eminent African American scholar of the early and mid-twentieth century, theorized to be a form of "double-consciousness," with one's warring identities mediated by a "veil." Du Bois first wrote about the veil in his book *The Souls of Black Folk*:

> The Negro is a sort of second son born with a veil, and gifted with a second sight in this American world—a world which yields him no true self-consciousness, but only lets him see himself through the revelation of the other world. It is a peculiar sensation, this double-consciousness, this sense of always looking at one's self through the eyes of others, of measuring one's soul by the tape of a world that looks on in amused contempt and pity. One ever feels his two-ness—an American, a Negro; two souls, two thoughts, two unreconciled strivings; two warring ideals in one dark body, whose dogged strength alone keeps it from being torn asunder.[18]

Strippers, like the members of other marginalized groups, can see themselves as normal, productive, unstigmatized members of society—nice girls, daughters, moms, students—as well as through the eyes of mainstream assumptions and prejudices about sex workers. The "veil" that Du Bois describes keeps these two perceptions of self separate, helping the individual occupying an oppressed status from absorbing the attitudes and beliefs of the oppressors. Since the 1903 publication of *The Souls of Black Folks,* a vast array of feminist, race, class, and sexuality scholars has expanded Du Bois's concept of double-consciousness beyond an analysis of racism to include multiple oppressions that might more contemporarily be understood as multiple consciousnesses.[19] The dancer, then, may not have only one veil between herself and her stigmatized identity, stripper, through which she may observe injustice and inequality but several. She is an exotic dancer and a woman, perhaps a lesbian, working class, a woman of color, and so on.

Understanding Inequality

Like the members of other marginal groups, dancers' experiences of domination and coercion are periodically intense and extreme. Simply experiencing discrimination, however, does not transform one's consciousness or inspire the activism that might change the larger structural issues at work in society. Enduring oppression can foster a critique of social inequality, but it can also breed resignation and internalized oppression. If this were not so, legions of battered women would have revolutionized domestic-abuse and rape laws years ago. Unlike the isolated social lives of domestic-abuse victims, however, exotic dancers share a private, communal area—the dressing room—in which they can critique injustices with like-minded and supportive others. For example, a stripper denied housing, like Maureen, can call it "discrimination" or can believe she deserved to be mistreated because only bad women work as exotic dancers. The woman who is spat on, called a slut, licked, or ignored takes the healthier road when she can perceive this abuse as a consequence of social inequality—a manifestation of oppression—that does not reflect her or how she deserves to be treated. And the more her peers reinforce this perception, the easier it is to sustain it. Thus, the dancers who form the most stable support networks best survive the toll of the sex industry.

Participating in a support network and adopting a critical gaze on the sex industry will not mitigate all the effects of becoming a social outcast or the overall toll of stripping, but it can help a woman maintain her sanity—for a time. Unfortunately, though individually beneficial, these acts function as temporary stop-gaps to social problems. Social change requires collective activism, the topic of the next chapter. The women I interviewed with the most well-developed critical perspectives on sex work, those most conscious of institutional inequality and exploitative working conditions, publicly challenged unfair labor practices by forming the first unionized place of employment for sex workers in the United States, at the Lusty Lady in San Francisco.

7

"Everything Is Not Okay"

I don't have a problem with the work itself; I never did. I don't have an issue with women doing prostitution or women doing anything they want to do with their bodies. I think that is their choice. But I do take issue with women being exploited, and I do think that women are entitled to fair treatment and they are entitled to great working standards. I don't think that women should have to apologize for making a lot of money. This is the one area where women make money far beyond what men make. And I don't think women should have to apologize or accept substandard working conditions because they make a lot of money. I think they should make as much money as they possibly can and be happy in their jobs and be treated fairly by their managers. I don't think that is too much to ask.

—Joscelyn

The women quoted in *Stripped* suffered from and responded to the toll of dancing in the myriad ways I have explored: they established and negotiated boundaries, developed support networks, and experienced changes in their sexuality. In San Francisco, some dancers, like Joscelyn quoted in the epigraph, also coped with the toll of the sex industry by becoming social activists; they challenged owners and managers to improve working conditions and organized the first unionized strip club in the United States, SEIU Local 790. Each activist I interviewed shared that she found this political work immensely rewarding. For these women, organizing to improve working conditions for sex workers catalyzed a change in their self-perception from sex workers to sex activists, a much more "respectable" profession to themselves and others. This chapter explores women in the sex industry who turned to sex activism. My focus will mostly be on San Francisco because the women there, for reasons that I will elaborate on, are more politicized and therefore more likely to become activists. I regard this evolution into political organization and social activism as largely an empowering act for these women and, consequently, see this move as a more positive outcome, like the freedom to explore one's sexuality, of the toll that sex work takes on the lives of women.

So what makes a woman so disgruntled with the sex industry that she begins organizing for labor reform? Why did the first sex-worker union in the United States emerge in San Francisco rather than in Boston, Chicago, or New York City? In May 1999, I flew to San Francisco to answer these questions. I was particularly interested in examining whether dancers working in the Bay Area, a politically and sexually progressive environment, enjoyed their labor in the sex industry more than dancers in Silverton, in the middle of the Bible Belt. I imagined that living and working in a less sexually repressed area of the United States would influence how women perceived dancing. My interviews suggest that it does, but not in the way that I originally imagined. As you may have already observed from comments made by San Francisco dancers, women working in the Bay Area are much less satisfied with their working conditions than dancers in Silverton and Honolulu. Rachel, a San Francisco sex activist, described these conditions succinctly: "San Francisco is a pioneer when it comes to heinous violations of the labor code and horrendous working conditions in the sex industry, especially in strip clubs."

Visiting San Francisco

Seedy, dark, and physically indistinguishable from other peep shows, the Lusty Lady has nonetheless inspired a rash of academic articles and personal narratives.[1] During the mid-1990s and throughout the unionization effort, feminist scholars flocked to the Lusty Lady to do research, some even dancing in peep shows. Although there is little in the physical environment of the Lusty Lady to explain the attraction of so many to the club, the transformation of dancers into writers, and the impetus behind the union, during taped interviews with San Francisco dancers I felt a tangible atmosphere of empowered women. This positive, at times explicitly feminist, energy radiates through the academic and autobiographical writing on the Lusty Lady and through the film documenting their unionization, *Live Nude Girls Unite!*

The arrangement of dancers and customers at the Lusty Lady differs from the physical setup at strip bars like the Velvet Lounge. At a peep show, the dancers are separated from the clients by glass windows and the performers are paid by the hour, not through tips and table, lap, or couch dances. This results in a noncompetitive atmosphere without the dancers needing to vie for men's attention. Because the dancers are separated from the clients by a partition, with most customers there to see crotch shots and masturbate, not chat and drink, the dancers generally perform a set routine of eight to twelve positions of maximum exposure.

I visited the Lusty Lady around 11 A.M. on a Sunday—Mother's Day, in fact. Although this was not the most raunchy time of the day, week, or year, there was still a thin scattering of customers at the peep show. Entirely unfamiliar with peep-show protocol and disoriented by the sudden darkness, I asked a lounging, disinterested man at the front desk to instruct me in how the booths work. He explained that customers enter into a single booth and that vacancy lights over the booths indicate which are empty. Unsatisfied with the level of detail he provided but aware that he was not going to lead a workshop on peep-show processes, I gingerly ventured inside a cramped, dark, sticky booth and fumbled for a seat.

The booth was so dimly lit it took me several moments before I could locate the proper slot to insert a dollar bill. When the money processed through the machine, a partition separating me from the dancers rose electronically. I peered into a mirrored room, dubbed a "fishbowl" by many performers, containing four dancers garbed in a variety of lace, denim, heels, feathers, and wigs. The clothing the dancers wore was solely for the purpose of eroticizing and enhancing their sexual parts. Management required each woman to expose her breasts and genitals at all times. From my location I could see the dancers but not the occupants of the other booths. I knew at least one other booth was occupied because a dancer was performing to one of the windows in an adjoining area.

When my screen rose, the dancers looked at each other and said, "I don't believe it; it's a woman." One woman, Ann, sauntered over to me. I told her a bit about my project. She quickly understood that I hadn't come to stare at her crotch and settled down next to me to chat. The screen closed immediately. One dollar lasted me one minute. I put in a five-dollar bill and waited for the screen to rise again. Our conversation was difficult because of the soundproofing in the booth. Customers can hear the dancers when they speak, but the sound system blocks most customer comments. Muting the clients is one way to filter obscene and abusive remarks. Ann had to strain to hear every word I said. In spite of the effort, she seemed happy to talk with me for the few minutes my five dollars afforded us. She pointed to a white stain on the window and made a disgusted comment about how they should really clean that up. Looking about the booth now that I could finally see, I noticed a box of tissues, a trash can, and several other semen splotches.

In retrospect, perhaps I should have gotten the pussy show like the men, if only so that I could compare my observations to others'. I could have seen the eight to twelve standard positions the dancers described and noted my own reactions to the display. Ultimately, though, I felt too uncomfortable to peep in the peep show. I wanted to interact with a person, not a crotch. Trying to interact with a person and a crotch, behind glass, with an inadequate sound system seemed wildly formidable. My five dollars up, Ann waved enthusiastically as the partition closed. I slipped out into the bright, cold San Francisco morning, relieved to breathe in fresh air.

Unionizing at the Lusty Lady

San Francisco is a more sexually progressive city than Silverton and, for that matter, than much of the United States. Materially, this is manifested in fewer city regulations about public nudity and sexual acts. One consequence of this sexual freedom is that customers expect more graphic sex for their money. For example, if one dancer is unwilling to give a client a naked lap dance or hand job, he can likely convince another. There are more dance clubs, with more women, competing for a limited number of customers. Furthermore, in formal interviews and casual discussion, dancers in the Bay Area shared that working conditions in many clubs are both dangerous and illegal. Dancers suffer dilapidated dressing areas and bathrooms, high stage fees, no sick time, capricious pay cuts, and sexual harassment. The political activists I met theorized that the competition for jobs and customers in San Francisco is so fierce that management experiences little incentive to maintain decent working conditions for their employees. Joscelyn explained that she has witnessed a deterioration in working conditions for sex workers:

> It has been anywhere from an increase in stage fees and people paying more money to actually go to work to more sexual assault, sexual ha-

rassment, and increased sexual activity in terms of prostitution but also a reshaping of people's boundaries. A lot of women wanted to continue working in these clubs as dancers but are finding that they are competing with women who are either voluntarily doing full service or doing it as a result of economic means because they are having to pay so much in stage fees.

Dancers working in San Francisco uniformly expressed frustration with the high stage fees—averaging $100 to $150 a shift—that management forced them to pay for the "privilege" of coming to work. Moreover, clubs expect dancers to pay for their shifts when they are scheduled, regardless of whether they are actually working. Thus, the San Francisco dancer may owe her place of work up to $150 if she misses her shift for any reason. In contrast, a dancer in Silverton pays between $25 and $50 in stage fees and is not expected to pay her stage fees if she is absent from work. Honolulu dancers are actually paid for their labor by the club at a rate comparable to the base salary of a waiter. Rachel, one of the union organizers, discussed the strip-club policy of requiring dancers to pay the clubs:

> There is a quota system. You must sell at least ten dances at $20 each and give the house 50 percent of what you make. So you have to sell a minimum of ten dances, plus they get $50 for something else; but it adds up to $150. The owners make their money no matter what, even if nobody comes in the door. Their workers are paying them. If no one comes in, the workers suffer, because they have to pay whether it's a slow night or not.

Although the management at the Lusty Lady billed itself as a "feminist" peep show, the union organizers found the working conditions to be every bit as poor as in other San Francisco clubs.[2] Rachel perceived the "feminism" that the owners advertised as a marketing strategy to attract women:

> That was just a hollow marketing ploy that worked well because everyone thinks that; that is how they market themselves, but they're just as brutal. The only thing that made them any more fair to the workers were the changes made by the union. They rule with an iron fist there. There were way more rules there than there were at any other clubs. The

only thing they had going for them was that they paid the workers, which is pretty sad. If you say we're feminists because we comply with the labor code?!

The "ploy" was successful in the cases of Vera and Sarah, who drove all the way to San Francisco from Massachusetts to work at the Lusty Lady because of its feminist reputation. Vera shared:

> Sarah graduated college two years after I did. I was off in Israel for a while. She was finishing college and transferred. Then we drove here. Then we didn't stop, we didn't pass go, we went right to the Lusty Lady Theater. We knew we wanted to dance on my birthday, which was September. It was right after we moved. I went to just about every club in the city, and I didn't like a lot of what I saw at the other clubs, and I've heard a lot of horror stories about prostitution being in the clubs. It was the only club I'd heard of where they gave you a form to fill out asking you to theorize on women's place in society and how you saw others' sexuality, which was a very good sign to me. At least the managers wanted to hear about your intelligence.

It is important to note that although Vera and Sarah had only positive things to say about the working conditions at the Lusty Lady, the union had already been formed by the time they started dancing there. Sarah, suffering from Chronic Fatigue Syndrome, might have had a much rougher time working at the Lusty Lady before the unionization. Rachel describes the sick-leave policy at the Lusty Lady before the dancers established the union:

> They had a really, really inhumane sick policy or no policy. There was no justification for being sick. If you missed a shift for being sick, your pay would be cut in half, and if you tried to replace your shift, you had to find someone who was the same race, had the same hair color and breast size as you. And if you couldn't find people who met those criteria when you were sick, that was just too bad; you'd get your pay cut or you'd have to come to work sick, which is what a lot of people did. People used to be in tears because they were in so much pain at work. People would come to work with strep throat and pass it around. People puking, totally sick, because there was no excuse. Or extreme menstrual cramps.[3] They were just brutal.

Compare this to Silverton dancer April's description of her relationship with her managers and her cavalier attitude about even going into work:

> You don't hear a lot of feedback from your superiors. Well, you don't really have a superior. They're there because you're there. If no dancers showed up, they wouldn't have a job, and they know that. It's like this pyramid: dancers are at the top. And it's not like I'm conceited; it's just part of the structure. That's the way it works. It's the only job that you only go in when you're in a good mood. What job can you call in and say, "Listen, I can't come in. I'm in a bad mood. I'm going to have sex today. I've got a hang over. I'm on my period today." You call in and you're very blunt and you're very last minute, but it is the autonomy of it. You just decide when you're going to do it. If you feel like it, you do it, 'cause it don't matter 'cause they can't fire you. So you start thinking that, and you're just on a rampage. You're just like, "Open up the curtains. I'm coming in!"

I met my first San Francisco dancers at a monthly Exotic Dancers Alliance meeting held in a union space in a building on Market Street. The Alliance's mission statement as described on their website at www.eda-sf.org reads,

> Our mission is to address the lack of civil, human and labor rights on behalf of exotic dancers and other sex industry workers. Our primary objective is to support all sex industry workers by providing information, referrals and non-judgmental, empowerment-based services while collectively advocating for sufficient working conditions for everyone including Asian, Black, Latina, Native American communities and other people of color; lesbian, gay, bisexual, transgender, queer and questioning individuals; persons with disabilities; low-income women, and those who may have barriers accessing services.

At the May 1999 meeting of the Exotic Dancers Alliance, those present discussed the situations of two dancers who were wrongfully terminated from their place of employment. About eight women were present; of these, at least five were directly involved with, and therefore fluent in, union organization and dancers' rights under the law. They provided one another with information and support. For example, Joscelyn is a full-time activist who has filed lawsuits against every club she danced for.

During this meeting, she agreed to accompany two less experienced dancers to court the next day. The dancers I met at EDA were successfully working the system. Rachel, also present at this EDA meeting, agreed to speak with me afterward about the union. At that time, the Lusty Lady had been unionized for a year.

The culminating event that catalyzed the dancers at the Lusty Lady to organize, Rachel explained, was not the inhumane sick policy or capricious pay cuts. Rather, dancers discovered that customers were videotaping performers in booths with one-way mirrors without their knowledge or consent. Even worse, employees' concerns about being secretly videotaped were not taken seriously by management. The dancers' privacy was violated; they were economically exploited and, finally, ignored by management. Rachel described this cycle:

> There were a lot of problems that are endemic to the industry anywhere you work, but the one issue that was unique to our workplace, and the issue that united us, was the fact that we work in a peep show. And we're in a big box surrounded by windows. Some windows used to be made of one-way glass, and customers would routinely tape us and take pictures and then sell the videotapes and pictures as marketable porn, without our consent, without compensation, and without our knowledge. We would just notice when we'd see a flash or the red light on the video camera that they would forget to cover. Lots of times they would get away with their film intact. We complained to management for months and actually found a video with Lusty Lady dancers on it that has since been pulled off the market, and the distributor is being sued. But who knows what else is out there or what's been put on the Internet without our consent? And the managers didn't do away with the one-way windows for marketing reasons. Their attitude was: if you don't like it, get another job.
>
> So we started meeting and decided to organize the union because we learned that we had no legal protection if we spoke out and we weren't protected. We hooked up with the Exotic Dancers Alliance, and they have this loose arrangement with the Service Employees International Union. And the EDA finally convinced an initially reluctant group of higher-ups in the organization. At first, they weren't convinced that we were committed, and they had never represented anyone in this industry. No one has. This is the only unionized strip joint in the country right

now that has successfully followed through with a campaign and negotiated a contract.

And during the course of these meetings, we discovered that a lot of things that people were bitching about under their breath, in the dressing room, were widespread injustices. They were injustices that you would find in any strip joint—from favoritism to erratic and unwritten disciplinary policies. Some people would be harshly punished for things that others would totally get away with.

This unionization process required that Rachel and Kelly, among my informants, dedicate an enormous amount of personal time and energy: the grueling contract negotiations between management and employees took months of effort (documented beautifully by Julia Query and Vicky Funari's film *Live Nude Girls Unite!*). Unfortunately, although the activists individually demonstrated great commitment and energy to improving the working conditions of sex workers, the consequences of the lawsuits were not always favorable to the employees of other strip clubs.

Management Fights Back

Predictably, owners and managers of strip clubs and peep shows in San Francisco did not respond positively to the unionization at the Lusty Lady, nor to the lawsuits dancers filed against their workplaces. Prior to the formation of SEIU Local 790, several women—including Lily Burana, author of *Strip City*, and Joscelyn, among the women I interviewed—filed a class-action lawsuit against the Mitchell Brothers Theater to be compensated for lost wages and stage fees. The Mitchell Brothers Theater reacted to the lawsuits by raising stage fees for all their currently employed performers. When questioned about the sudden increase, managers blamed the former dancers who were suing the clubs. Joscelyn rightly identified this management tactic as a divisive practice. Indeed, she expressed that being scapegoated by management and watching owners pit dancers against each other were among the most disappointing aspects of her sex activism. Although her intent was to improve working conditions for all dancers, management used her lawsuit and the others as wedges to divide dancers. She explained:

The main things that I didn't like were the practices of management, and that went anywhere from the labor violations to the sexual harassment. I didn't like seeing the women pitted against other women. It was really disheartening to see that, especially, when we were organizing. And to watch that division as a result of management's greed. They would like nothing more than to see women divided. It's something we still deal with. Women are told certain things by managers, and whether they believe it or not, they have to adhere to it if they want to keep their jobs.

The management really used us as scapegoats with the other women. They would actually say things like, "It's those girls' faults that I'm raising your stage fee." So we were really used to justify the continued mistreatment. The women were pitted against us, and we were the ones trying to get retribution and improve the working conditions. When you come forward, you always risk that type of misconception from other people. It's hard to deal with that, especially if the manager is telling you one thing and we are saying exactly the opposite. It was hard to watch women actually believe what these people were saying.

Fearing additional lawsuits and further unionization efforts, the O'-Farrell Theater used a strategy of divide and conquer: they raised stage fees and deflected the responsibility for this to the dancers themselves. And in many instances they were effective in undermining the credibility of sex-worker activists. The following is what Beatrice understood to be the reasons former dancers filed lawsuits at the Mitchell Brothers Theater:

A bunch of girls got together and had a class-action suit against the club because they said they should have been employees all along, and so they were suing for back wages. The story goes that these girls had been fired because they had become overweight and were missing their shifts and bad for business. And so, in retaliation, they sued the owner and won. And one of the things they wanted to change, besides getting a lot of money, they wanted us all to be made into employees, and they were successful in that.

It definitely worked against the girls there because we probably wouldn't be paying that much money to work there if Jim didn't have to pay such a big lawsuit; he has to pay millions to these girls and attorney fees. It's really taking its toll on the girls who still work there. He's not going to let his business go under. He's not going to take it. He's not going to take that loss; he's just going to raise the price at the door and the price that the girls have to pay. So it's coming out of our pockets.

Having just met and spoken with a number of women involved in the EDA, I shared with Beatrice that I suspected the last thing the dancers filing lawsuits, and unionizing, wanted was for their efforts to penalize other dancers. She responded, "I think they really didn't care. They just wanted the money. They were opportunists. I believe they were just in it for the money." Unfortunately, regardless of whether the women suing the Mitchell Brothers were motivated by greed, altruism, or the pursuit of social justice, it is clear that Beatrice did not, at that time, understand what she had in common with them.

Beatrice's interpretation surprised me. Throughout our interview, she repeatedly demonstrated a complex understanding of her treatment as a woman in the sex industry. She was critical of the clients, the stereotypes about sex workers, and the increasing pressure women felt to perform more graphically sexual acts in strip bars. Yet the management of the O'-Farrell Theater convinced her that "other dancers"—disgruntled, fat ones—were responsible for upping her stage fees, not the club owners and managers. Ultimately, our exchange illustrated the level of control management can exert over the discourse surrounding sex workers' efforts to improve working conditions for themselves—for example, "It's her fault; she was just angry because she couldn't take care of herself and got fat." And, in fact, dancers *could* be fired for being overweight at the O'Farrell Theater, as well as for any other reason they dictated. Lily Burana, one of the original plaintiffs in the class-action lawsuit against Mitchell Brothers, in her book *Strip City* described the way capricious managerial actions engendered feelings of fear and paranoia among her co-workers:

You can make a lot of money at Mitchell Brothers if you apply yourself —a thousand dollars a shift is not uncommon, though my average is considerably less. But that money comes at a substantial cost. The club harbors a savage atmosphere of paranoia because you can be let go at any time, for any reason—being overweight, underweight, too old, frequent tardiness, and the absurdly cruel "over-exposure." You have to keep on top of everything, especially your looks. We all feel the pressure. One night, I stand at the mirror in the bathroom between two women laboring over their makeup and one says to the other, "God, I can't wait to get married, have children, get fat, and just let myself go."[4]

Joscelyn recognized that some dancers will believe the misinformation of management and ignore and deny poor working conditions as a protective device to enable them to come into work day after day and continue to make money. Thus, denial is another way dancers manage the toll of stripping. She explained: "Some women just live in denial to protect themselves from that whole environment. It's easier to think it is not happening to you because that enables you to work the next day and make money."

Interestingly, though, at the same time that management will squelch dancers' efforts to unite, they will support individual dancers when they are angry or upset with customers. In other words, a dancer's perspective that clients in general are insensitive and hateful is not disputed by male managers, owners, DJs, bouncers, and bartenders. To the contrary, managers will openly acknowledge that their clients are largely a bunch of "horny assholes," as Allen, the Vixens DJ, vividly described them. Such assertions do not compromise the real power management wields over employees, and they serve the function of creating a public face of support and protection. Recall the manager at the Pink Cave who explained to me that I could not come to the club unaccompanied by a man because he could not guarantee my safety around a bunch of drunk and rowdy customers. While I knew that that was not the entire reason, or even the largest part of why he did not want me to come in alone, it was still weirdly soothing to hear: *A man in power cared about my safety as a woman.* Dancers absorb this paternalistic message daily in their workplaces. An essential aspect of masculine socialization is that men protect "their" women—daughters, wives, friends, sisters, and mothers—from the potential sexual violence of other men. Thus, the dancers in a particular club fall under the custody of management both literally—management must ensure dancers' physical safety so they can perform—and figuratively.

At the same time, protecting dancers from abusive clients extends only so far as the club's profits remain unaffected. Whereas management experiences little conflict of interest in defending one of its dancers against the inappropriate advances of a drunken customer, it will turn a blind eye to illegal sexual activity between dancers and clients when it benefits them, even if this creates more stressful working conditions for all its employees. To the degree to which profit depends on the desires of its customer base, management will ignore certain behaviors. One consequence of management's "blind eye" is that the women working in an unregulated, competitive environment have to engage in increasingly more explicit sexual activities with customers in order to make the same amount of money they made before for doing less sexually graphic acts. Further, unctuous staff encourage unhappy dancers to blame other dancers for this problem. Women learn, then, to accept management's version of events and shift their dissatisfaction onto other dancers for the bad working conditions, rather than recognize the exploitation they all share in common.[5] Joscelyn explained:

> It is coming from management but also from customers, and the two are linked. Because when you have a situation that is "anything goes" and the club owners aren't saying, "This is illegal, so please don't do this on the premises," they've given the green light to customers to come in and expect certain sexual practices for less money than was ever expected before. It's in their interest to keep the customers coming back and to keep them happy. If the customers are paying an entrance fee and the dancers are also paying fees to rent their rooms or to just have their shift that day, and there are six customers and fifty workers, then the women are going to do whatever they have to do to make money. It sets the precedent. The customers have almost become entitled in wanting what they want for very little money. Unfortunately, this has happened all around this city.

When sex workers unite to fight both the material conditions of inequality, such as paying for shifts when they are sick, and the psychological stress of negotiating customers' increasing expectations, it threatens to revolutionize the sex industry. This could potentially affect clubs' profit margins. Under American capitalism, threats to profit are taken seriously. In addition to forcing dancers to pay high stage fees, offering no benefits, and, in some cases, refusing to clean or maintain their facilities, clubs will also blacklist dancers who challenge their policies.

Dealing with the Toll: Changing from Stripper to Sex Activist

Dancers in San Francisco endured the worst working conditions among the women I interviewed and, anecdotally, among all women dancing in the United States. The "highs" that San Francisco dancers described from bonding with other women and forming a union were tempered by horrible working conditions and aggressive customer demands. Like the circumstances that led to the emergence of second-wave feminism in the 1960s, the dual elements of a politicized environment and extremely oppressive working conditions propelled sex workers in San Francisco to unite and unionize. Lily Burana, like Joscelyn, Rachel, and Kelly, recognized the exploitation exotic dancers experience, challenged these exploitative labor practices, and attempted to form connections with sex workers struggling with similar problems. This involved devoting a considerable amount of unpaid personal time and energy to organizing. As Joscelyn noted plainly, "We're all volunteers." After our interview, Rachel mailed me a thick manual of materials about how to unionize in the sex industry, along with a note that I was free to make copies and distribute the information to any dancers interested in learning how to organize effectively. Joscelyn, Rachel, Kelly, and Janeen had each become a sex-worker activist, and in May 2003 the dancers at the Lusty Lady transformed from employees to owners. The Lusty Lady continues to be a ground-breaking establishment in the sex industry. After years of contract negotiations, the club's owners decided to close the business. In response, the dancers bought the business and reorganized the Lusty Lady as a cooperative. Self-ownership, however, has brought with it a new set of challenges for the dancers, most of which entail managing a profitable business in a cutthroat market while meeting the financial, emotional, and psychological needs of the workers.

In San Francisco, I received the impression that, compared to other parts of the country, it is hip to be a sex worker. Sex workers were the causes célèbres at the turn of the millennium. At the time of my visit, I observed a plethora of writing, films, and performances related to sex workers and the sex industry, including a two-day sex-worker film festival at the Roxie Theater in the Mission that sex activists had organized. The week before I arrived in the city, Janeen had performed a one-woman show about her experiences in the industry. At the film festival itself, Kelly danced live before one segment of films related to exotic dancing, and

Vera was selling a zine that she, Sarah, and Mel had produced and written for and about sex workers.

Sex activism is a path to a more respected social identity and, potentially, an avenue out of the sex industry. Like changes in a dancer's sexuality, sex activism is also a means of coping with the toll of stripping. If a dancer can't tell her parents she is a stripper or maintain a primary partnership, if the customers are driving her crazy, the money is drying up, her sex drive is frozen, at least in the Bay Area the sex activist can celebrate, appreciate, and derive esteem performing political work for other sex workers—whether that work is organizing, counseling, creating performance art, writing a magazine, or forming a union. Those are accomplishments for which a dancer, though still marginalized in some circles, can feel unambivalently proud.

Of the dancers I interviewed that were involved in political organizing, four were no longer dancing. Joscelyn had stopped dancing by the time of our interview partly because she was blacklisted and partly because she found it increasingly difficult to work under the conditions that she was fighting to change. In Joscelyn's case, as she became aware of the ways she was mistreated, dancing became intolerable:

> It was really hard being an activist, knowing I'd filed these complaints, and then going back into the job the next day and seeing these conditions right in my face. So towards the end of my employment, it was really difficult for me to go into work. The last month of my employment, I must have called off half of my shows and didn't go in because it was so overwhelming. And even though I was making money, it was hard for me to justify it because I really felt like my integrity was sacrificed.

Among my informants, Joscelyn seemed the most satisfied with her life. At the time of our interview, she had completed her master's degree in social work and spent most of her time organizing with the Exotic Dancers Alliance.[6] She did all the grant writing for the EDA and was working with the Health Department and other community organizations to start a clinic for sex workers. Joscelyn transformed from sex worker to sex-worker activist.

Rachel, another union organizer, was still working at the Lusty Lady at the time of our interview. She expressed disgust and anger with the management, the owners, the industry, and the customers. The toll of dancing was noticeable in her responses. Rachel expressed that except for the company of the other women and her sex activism, there was little she liked about dancing. It seemed unlikely she would still be dancing were it not for the positive experiences she had organizing the union at the Lusty Lady. During our interview, Rachel was surprised when I asked her personal thoughts about dancing. She was prepared to discuss the unionization, not how she felt about working in the sex industry. Rachel centered her identity on being an activist, not on being a stripper. This illustrates yet another way women manage stripper stigma: by displaying a more personally or socially acceptable identity as an activist rather than a sex worker.

Like Joscelyn and Rachel, Kelly described her sex activism as very rewarding in contrast to the actual sex work:

> I have to say, the flip side of that was that I was also working at the Lusty Lady, which is a peep show. It was a low-paying end of sex work, but we unionized. I was really involved with that. So I had these two conflicting things. I didn't particularly like the job at Lusty Lady, but the unionization was really empowering, and I felt like I could take my politics from college and do something that was actually going to change something. I felt really proud of it. I got really involved in organizing and negotiating contracts. So that was really good. It helped me kind of deal with the dancing. I stayed at the Lusty pretty much for the union.

Unlike Rachel, however, Kelly was willing to explore with me her feeling that dancing had become an increasingly self-destructive profession for her over time. Prior to our interview, Kelly felt she'd had few opportunities to reflect on the toll of stripping. She explained that her public work as a sex activist constrained her from critiquing the negative aspects of exotic dancing. Kelly elaborated that she felt comfortable criticizing the owners, the managers, and working conditions at the clubs but feared that analyzing the negative repercussions of sex work in her personal life had the potential to empower those she directly opposed—such as the Christian Right, the Moral Majority, and antisex radical feminists—and that such criticism supported derogatory stereotypes about sex workers. Even worse, like Janeen, Kelly worried that speaking out about the toll of stripping made her vulnerable to censure from other sex activists. Kelly warned me that any woman who described the negative aspects of stripping risked being misread as suggesting that sex work is intrinsically bad:

It is so politicized that I can't even have a bad day without "See, you shouldn't have been doing it in the first place." I'm not one of these for power, super pro–sex workers. My sex-worker activism is about working conditions. It's not about being, "I'm proud to be a sex worker." That doesn't work for me. I'm really like, "It's a job." It's interesting and complex, and, of course, if affects my identity, but I'm not so wrapped up in the sex-worker identity or anything.

Sex activists willing to discuss the downside of being a sex worker articulate an unpopular and suspect perspective in the Bay Area. Even the much loved, well-known, and respected Annie Sprinkle—alternatively performance artist, sacred prostitute, and sex activist—carefully offered a caveat before addressing the issues of sex worker burnout in her article "We've Come a Long Way—And We're Exhausted":

Women in the sex industry have come a long way. Things have improved. There is now an international network of sex-worker organizations. In some areas, to be a young feminist working her way through college as a stripper has become not only acceptable but chic. Women are making and distributing their own pornography their way. . . . To make our businesses and our lives even better, it is time to be totally honest, to be more critical, to come out of any denial, to speak out about and confront the problems from an insider's, pro-sex-work perspective. This is difficult and dangerous to do, because we often sound terrifyingly like our enemies and can inadvertently fuel their flames, which could get us into a big pickle.[7]

In other words, it's a thin line between honest critique and undermining evaluation. Similar to the divisions between the writers of the sex wars, dancers may also be divided along ideological lines. If you are a sex activist in San Francisco, critiquing the labor like Kelly was beginning to do or discussing sexual abuse among sex workers as Janeen had complicates the "sex positive" paradigm. During our interview, Janeen expressed a great deal of frustration with how difficult it is to talk about sexual abuse in San Francisco. She described her fellow sex workers and sex-worker activists in San Francisco as unrealistically positive about the experiences of women in the sex industry. Janeen, who also produced a one-woman show about her experiences as a sex worker, explained this phenomenon to me:

I'm sorry, but I look at my own experience, and 99 percent of the women I've talked to, I see similarities. And you say one thing, and you hear, "Don't put people in a box." So even in my show, I left my sexual abuse part out of it—not on purpose; it just never wound up in the show. I did put child abuse in there. Somebody said they thought it was refreshing that I didn't put sexual abuse in it. And I was like, "What do you care? You're not even in the sex industry." So it's something I'm struggling with. San Francisco is all sex positive, and that's the backlash of people being so oppressed. But people go to the other extreme and think, "Everything's fine. Everything we do is wonderful here." No, everything is not wonderful. You got to have a balance between Andrea Dworkin or whatever the hell her name is . . . Everything is not okay. So that's where I am. And that's how I'm trying articulate that and get people to hear me.

Janeen, steeped in the politically correct culture of San Francisco sexual politics, would not actively align herself with Andrea Dworkin or the radical feminist position on sex work that the Council for Prostitution Alternatives advocate, even though her own experience and analysis of that experience resonate strongly with a radical feminist, material critique of the sex industry. Paradoxically, even while Janeen criticized the politically correct sex activists for silencing dialogue about sexual abuse, she reinforced their condemnation of radical feminists like Andrea Dworkin.[8]

Andrea Dworkin, who sadly died during the writing of this book, has been, and continues to be, singled out as the scary face of radical feminism by individuals across the political spectrum. I have listened to people as diverse as sex workers, clients, bouncers, friends, students, and even random guests at cocktail parties express pejorative stereotypes about Dworkin specifically and about radical feminists more generally— as angry, man-hating, ugly dykes—as vicious and caricatured as those hurled at sex workers. Throughout my interviews, Dworkin's name was mentioned more than once in terms that framed her as an emblem of all things wrong with a radical feminist, or anti-sex-work, position. This was the case even when women, like Janeen, were articulating ideas that at least partly supported a radical feminist perspective. I think this is because Dworkin embodied and represented a constellation of cultural anxieties about contemporary womanhood. She was a big, loud-mouthed woman, unafraid to speak her mind, an active prosecutor of patriarchy in every manifestation she perceived—especially in the sex industry—and completely opposed to feminine beauty standards. Much like an Old Testament prophet, Dworkin's writing and speeches warned us of things that are not comfortable to hear.[9]

Feminism and Stripping

Although I do not summarily agree that sex work *is* violence against women, nor with what I read as the sexual puritanism of radical feminism, I did find radical feminist analyses of sex work a more useful framework for situating the voices and experiences of my informants than I originally anticipated. My interviews indicate that women do begin stripping for the financial benefits they derive in a society that still reserves its highest paying and most prestigious jobs for men. The fact that stripping is such a lucrative occupation, relative to other low-skill jobs, traps many women in the industry, a consequence of the intersecting forces of capitalism and patriarchy. Thus, the longer a woman strips, the more her feelings about her labor reflect the validity of the radical feminist perspective. But few women that I interviewed were in it for the money alone. Most enjoyed the sexual abandon and ego gratification as well, the experience of erotic power emphasized by sex-radical feminists.

That gratification, however, is precarious and short-lived, as the varied dimensions of the toll wear away a woman's pleasure in breaking taboos and receiving flattering attention, compliments, and money. The longer the women I interviewed danced, the more dissatisfied each grew with the labor, no matter how much compensation she received. Several women I interviewed who described these processes, who found fewer and fewer of their needs satisfied by dancing, quit sex work at this point. More women would quit if they could easily transition into an alternative well-paying job. Thus, one of my major findings is that over time women move from feeling empowered to feeling oppressed in the sex industry.[10] Both individual factors—the daily highs and lows dancers endure in the clubs—and institutional forces—such as media representations of sex workers and deindustrialization—motivate women's changing feelings about their work.

There are many reasons for this cumulative disappointment, most of which support the structural analysis of the radical feminists. The sex industry complicates a dancer's personal relationships, threatens her self-esteem, reinforces psychological issues of abuse, warps her relationship to money, and teaches her manipulation as a way of life. Sex workers are also severely stigmatized. Several of my subjects reported discrimination in obtaining housing, employment, and medical care. Some, when finances were tight and other dancers were making more money, agreed to participate in abusive, invasive, or dangerous sexual behaviors that they previously felt violated their boundaries. This all illustrates the toll of the sex industry.

Rather than enhancing their sexual confidence, or even teaching them to develop stronger defense mechanisms against the internalization of abuse, the Möbius strip–like aspect of working in strip clubs ultimately made the women I interviewed feel worse about their bodies, their sexuality, their intelligence, and, finally, their overall identity in the social world. However, dancers can recognize all this and still choose to dance if it is the best economic option they have. It is essential to analyze women's sexual labor in a larger cultural context, especially in the deals we all make to survive destructive systems. Just because a woman works in the sex industry does not mean that she is necessarily a dupe of patriarchy, the critique often made by the sex radicals about radical feminist analyses of the sex industry. At the same time, it is possible to make an informed choice to strip and still be damaged by the experience, a fact the sex radicals sometimes obscure. In each of our lives we do things we know are damaging to us because it is the best, or only, option we perceive at the time. Radical and sex-radical feminists have struggled to find common ground because they are both correct, depending on whether a woman is an early- or late-career dancer. Our acts and behaviors have multiple, not singular, meanings and consequences. Thus, we need both radical and sex-radical feminists to understand how women experience the sex industry.

The women I interviewed illustrate that sex work often takes an unhealthy toll on exotic dancers, especially over time. They have also demonstrated great creativity in resisting this toll. Many have explored romantic and sexual relationships with other women, and most have depended on one another for emotional support and companionship. Within the strip bar, a microcosm of extreme patriarchy, women have formed communities with one another and, in some cases, learned to critique social inequality and work for social justice. Many of the women I interviewed in the Bay Area were involved in the unionization effort at the Lusty Lady and, hence, more accustomed to articulating their understanding of their experiences, including their awareness of exploitative working conditions and institutional inequality, than a random sample of dancers might be. Yet although the language they used to describe their lives was, in some cases, more sophisticated than that used by the dancers in Silverton and Honolulu, most of the women, in all three locations, expressed similar problems with the toll of dancing. I also found that the more a dancer—like Kelly, Janeen, and Joscelyn in San Francisco and April and Morgan in Silverton—became aware of the impact that stripping was having on her self-perception, her sexuality, and her overall health, the harder it became for her to continue dancing.

I have always felt that my own feminist work is to increase options for women, not remove them. Because of this, I do not agree with the radical feminist position that sex work should be abolished. Sex work may be the best option available for a woman at a certain time in her life, even though it may become damaging to her self-esteem over time and, more generally, reinforce patriarchal conditioning about women's sexuality. Feminist activism that focuses concurrently on increasing women's control in the sex industry and providing options for women who want to leave the industry is still the best feminist praxis for the women involved. Indeed, enacting state-sponsored policies that alleviate women's economic inequality—such as nationalized health care, community-sponsored day care, and free higher education—has the potential to change women's participation in the sex industry far more dramatically than any city ordinance, moral commandment, or consciousness-raising group. I hope to see it happen.

Notes

Notes to the Preface

1. Hochschild 1983.
2. Barry 1995; Chapkis 1997; Davis 2000; Nagle 1997; Wahab 2003.
3. Burana 2001, 136.
4. Frank 2002; Chapkis 1997; Weitzer 2000; Nagle 1997; Chancer 1993; Queen 1997.

Notes to the Introduction

1. Brandy is a composite character derived from the recorded interviews of many dancers who shared such experiences with me. The Velvet Lounge is a pseudonym for an actual site I researched. For other descriptions of topless bars, see Burana 2001; Eaves 2002; Mattson 1995; Prus and Irini 1980; Ronai and Ellis 1989; and D. Scott 1996.

2. All the clubs I researched in "Silverton" are pseudonyms, as is the name of the city itself. Because San Francisco is a famous site of sex activism, and the clubs I visited in the area so well known in the sex literature, I have not changed those names in this book; I have used pseudonyms for the clubs in Hawaii, however, but not for the cities of San Francisco or Honolulu. I also use the real names of certain well-known chain clubs such as Pure Gold and Déjà Vu, when doing so does not violate the confidentiality of the informant or the location.

3. "Silverton" is a midsized city in the Southeast.

4. Brenda owned Vixens with her husband and had operated the club through a number of incarnations—a local bull-riding establishment, a burlesque club, and finally a strip bar. She explained that people had a number of preconceived assumptions about her as well as the dancers. Brenda does the books and other business functions in the mornings at Vixens, between 10:30 A.M. and noon, just before the clubs open. One reason she spoke with me was because the mayor was instigating a citywide crackdown on strip clubs at the time, and I introduced myself as a researcher and someone interested in writing an editorial to the paper. Later I did write an editorial, and it was published in the local newspaper. I have since heard that a dancer from Vixens cut out the ed-

itorial, framed it, and hung it on the dressing-room wall, although I cannot verify this.

5. I observed strip clubs in Silverton two evenings a month for about twelve months, each session lasting from one to five hours.

6. In addition to being stood up, approximately 30 percent of my subjects canceled and rescheduled the interview. After a dancer canceled with me for the third or fourth time, she felt embarrassed, I was irritated, she avoided me, and, eventually, I stopped calling her.

7. The ways in which a woman's experience of childhood sexual abuse motivated her to work in the sex industry was not the most important question to me when I first conceived of this project. It is loaded, problematic, and stigmatizing. More significant to me was a woman's overall experience as a stripper. Nonetheless, I do tackle childhood sexual abuse in the next chapter.

8. Using a snowball sampling technique, I asked each dancer I interviewed to share with me the names of other dancers who might be interested in talking with me. I conducted tape-recorded interviews with thirty-six dancers, four clients, one owner, one bouncer, one DJ, and three partners of dancers. This approach is common in ethnographic research but perhaps especially so among groups of stigmatized subjects, as those who anticipate harsh judgments are often reluctant to talk to "middle-class" researchers.

9. I conducted my interviews, including an impromptu focus group, in the dressing room of Vixens, and another focus group in Risque in Honolulu, from April 1998 through June 2003. Interviews were open-ended and lasted from one to two-and-a-half hours. I interviewed subjects in a place of their choosing, usually their home, my home, or a quiet public space like a park. All the subjects' names in this book are pseudonyms, except for Morgan, who requested that I use her real name. Most of my female participants were active dancers during the interview period. The exceptions were a woman who danced twenty years previously, a woman currently working for an escort agency who had danced in the recent past, and a woman who had stopped dancing but used it in her performance art. I also sought out and interviewed three women at the Lusty Lady in San Francisco who had been instrumental in forming the very first exotic dancers' union. The interviews with male clients were easier to arrange. I met two of the men in strip clubs. One has been going to the same bar, Vixens, for twenty-five years. The other worked in several clubs as a DJ. The men were eager to share their insights.

10. Carol Leigh, a.k.a. the Scarlot Harlot, invented the term "sex work" in 1978 both to demonstrate that women in the sex industry are actively engaged in a form of labor and to change the focus from women being "used" to women who work in a profession.

11. Prior to our tape-recorded interview each dancer signed a consent form that described the interview process and assured her that she could refuse to an-

swer any question for any reason. Using a semistructured interview guide, most of my questions explored respondents' experiences as exotic dancers. I asked each woman why she started dancing and what she liked and did not like about the experience. I asked the dancers to identify, compare, and evaluate the clubs that employed them, their patrons, and management. I elicited specific examples of good and bad experiences at work and sought their impressions of other dancers. I inquired about their sexual orientations, racial backgrounds, reactions of family and friends to the job, and experiences of social stigma or rejection. I also asked each dancer to describe her routine on a typical day. My goal was to gain a nuanced and detailed picture of the life and world of the stripper.

A large percentage of the women I interviewed identified as lesbian or bisexual. Of the thirty-six dancers I interviewed in-depth, fifteen identified as bisexual. Of these, two were in long-term committed relationships with women, but most were not. Four dancers identified as exclusively lesbian and seventeen as heterosexual. I discuss the issue of sexual orientation and dancing at greater length in chapter 5. My research suggests that the greatest proportion of dancers are bisexual, with an unusually high percentage of lesbians, or women who identify as bisexual in lesbian relationships, compared to the general population. My findings on the sexual identities of dancers may indicate bias, however, as queer dancers may have been more likely to trust me because I came out to them during our interviews. I also interviewed eight dancers in San Francisco, a region with a high gay and lesbian population in general.

My informants included five African Americans, three mixed Hispanic-Asian, two Native Americans, and twenty-six white women, four of whom were Jewish. The dancers in my sample ranged between twenty and forty-two years of age, with most in their midtwenties. Youth, or the appearance of youth, is a job requirement. Exotic dancers, like professional athletes and ballerinas, have a short window of employment opportunity, as the work is physically demanding in addition to being psychologically stressful. Dancers endure knee, back, and foot injuries, in addition to suffering from the effects of second-hand smoke, loud music, alcohol, and late hours. Thus, even women who want to continue dancing are often forced to quit when they are past their prime or perceived to be.

It was difficult to ascertain the socioeconomic background of the dancers I spoke with. Most sociologists define class by education, occupation, and income, yet the dancers in my sample tended to make similar amounts of money regardless of their educational level. Education attainment in my sample ranged from some high school to undergraduate, graduate, and professional degrees, and income ranged from twenty thousand to sixty thousand dollars a year in Silverton, and even higher in San Francisco and Hawaii. Three dancers I interviewed were working their way through college and hoped to pursue graduate degrees. Twelve dancers had already attained a postsecondary degree, most of these bachelor's degrees. The dancers with more education generally tended to work in the more upscale clubs, in contrast to those with less education, who most often danced in working-class bars. Morgan, a college student studying pre-med at the time of our first interview, preferred to perform in a more working-class environment because she felt it was more honest and less pretentious. Or, as she put it, "It's all boobs and beer no matter how you dress it up."

12. This category corresponds to a model identified by Sweet and Tewksbury (2000a) in their paper "Entry, Maintenance, and Departure from a Career in the Sex Industry: Strippers' Experiences of Occupational Costs and Rewards."

13. This group, especially, supports Christine Overall's (1992) analysis that what is bad for women about prostitution arises not so much from the sexual acts themselves as from the lack of other economic opportunities in a capitalist patriarchal system.

14. In some cases, women expressed the feelings common to a late-career dancer *earlier* than three years. Only one informant, however, described the feelings common to early-career dancers after several years working in the sex industry. This particular informant represents the only variation in my theoretical model. Instead of her sense of the sex industry moving from positive to negative, it remained positive, but she is unique in several ways. She dances at the Mitchell Brothers Theater in San Francisco and makes up to fifteen hundred dollars in one shift. She has been a *Penthouse* centerfold and has been photographed for the publication *High Times*. She has also been on the Howard Stern show. Her experience of the sex industry is more varied than that of most women. She has therefore received affirmation from a number of sources. Organizing my findings by early- and late-career experiences, I offer a longitudinal perspective on dancing that is lacking in most other research, which is cross-sectional in design. I recognize, however, that this study does not conform to the precise definition of longitudinal data collection, as I gathered most of my data on each informant at one sitting.

15. Schlosser 2003; Ultimate Strip Club List 2005.

16. Schlosser 2003, 283.

17. Ultimate Strip Club List 2005. Academic studies that quantify strip bars are hard to generate because clubs open, close, and change owners and names regularly.

18. Schlosser 2003, 114.

19. Ibid., 113—114.

20. For this research, I have focused exclusively on strip bars in the United States, largely because an international comparative analysis of the women who work in strip bars was beyond my budget. For insights into the experiences of global sex workers, see Altink 1995; Chapkis 1997; Ehrenreich and Hochschild 2002; Farley 2003; Kempadoo 1998, 2004; Odzer 1994; and Thorbeck and Pattanaik 2002.

21. Clubs devise strategies either to adapt to or circumvent city regulations

that force dancers to stay a far distance from customers; otherwise the club would experience a serious drop in customers.

22. Ritzer 2000; and Hausbeck and Brents 2002.

23. See Collins 2000 for a description of the "Hoochie Mama."

24. For theoretical analysis on the performance of gender, see Goffman 1973; and Butler 1990.

25. For additional discussion on the organization of sex workers in San Francisco, see Chapkis 2000; Kempadoo 1998; and a first-person account in Burana 2001. This unionization effort is also the subject of the highly acclaimed documentary *Live Nude Girls Unite!* I interviewed some of the same individuals as directors and producers Julia Query and Vicky Funari. I will discuss dancers' efforts to organize in detail in chapter 7.

26. I am greatly indebted to Professor Ellen Rosenman for her contribution of the Möbius strip metaphor.

NOTES TO CHAPTER I

1. Brooks 1997; Funari 1997; Langley 1997; Lewin 1984; Mattson 1995; Sweet and Tewksbury 2000b.

2. Ronai and Ellis 1989.

3. PayScale.com 2005.

4. J. Johnson 2002. For another illustration of the struggles in surviving on a low-paying service job, see Ehrenreich 2001.

5. In fact, exotic dancing offers women more opportunities to find a job outside the sex industry than many low-paying retail, fast food, or factory jobs because sex workers have more time to job hunt, a higher income, and potentially greater savings to tide them over between jobs.

6. Pollet and Hurwitz 2004.

7. Thompson and Harred 1992.

8. For a discussion of sex workers' sexual victimization, see Barry 1995; Dworkin 1997; and Farley 2003. For a discussion of sex workers' control over their choices, see Chapkis 1997; Dudash 1997; Frank 2002; and Leigh 2004.

9. Chapkis 1997.

10. For example, Barry 1995; Dworkin 1974, 1987.

11. The April 1982 Barnard conference titled "Towards a Politics of Sexuality" marked the eruption of the sex wars. For a wide range of sex-radical perspectives presented at this conference, see Bright 1997; Califia 1994, 2002; Chapkis 1997; and Vance 1984.

12. Frank 2002, 2.

13. Davis 2000. CPA has closed since Davis printed this article; see Farley 2003.

14. Davis 2000, 150.

15. Frank 2002; Reed 1997.

16. For an excellent analysis of how the stigma of "slut" brands a young girl, causing devastating harm, see Tanenbaum 2000.

17. Lindy and Wilson 1994, 62.

18. Although I have no way to gauge the percentage of women in my study who were sexually abused, or the impact that abuse had on those who did not broach the topic, some informants themselves suggested that the number of abused dancers is high; one dancer, a psychology major, has collected data that indicates that 70 percent of the women in her club were sexually abused.

19. National Research Council 1993, 94. Another set of figures reported that 15–33 percent of women had experienced childhood sexual abuse (J. Johnson 2002, 172).

20. Farley et al. 2003; Leidholt 2003. Almost 50 percent of the dancers Wesley (2002) researched reported histories of sexual abuse.

21. Sociologists examine cultural patterns as well as individual motivations to understand why people do what they do. To illustrate, sociologist Jennifer K. Wesley explores the connection between a woman's history of abuse and becoming a sex worker in her article "Growing Up Sexualized: Issues of Power and Violence in the Lives of Female Exotic Dancers" (2002). Wesley observes that the overall sexualization of young girls in our society influenced the ways her informants perceived their own sexual selves. The women Wesley interviewed learned early in their lives that they could use their sexualized bodies as currency to barter for power, money, and male attention.

22. Analysis of my informants' experiences suggests the possibility that working in the sex industry has the potential to help a woman work through some of the issues associated with sexual abuse so long as she exits the sex industry as an early-career dancer or before the on-the-job experiences reinforce the abuse more than they help her work through it. This would be an excellent topic for further inquiry, as it complicates much clinical and radical feminist literature and research on sex workers.

Notes to Chapter 2

1. Silverton dancers such as Melinda tended to have a better relationship with management than San Francisco dancers, for reasons I discuss in more detail later.

2. Sloan and Wahab 2004.

3. Wendall 2000.

4. See also Sweet and Tewksbury (2000b), who found that of the exotic dancers they interviewed four out of five suffered from "ugly duckling" syndrome.

5. McGhan 2003.

6. Maslow 1970.

7. Harner 1980.

8. "Dreaming" is an altered state of consciousness described by Carlos Castaneda (1984).

9. See Chapkis 2000; Forsyth and Deshotels 1998; and Wesley 2003a for further discussion on sex workers' drug and alcohol use, especially the functions drugs and alcohol meet.

10. SAMHSA 1998.

11. Bennett and Lehman 2003.

12. Burana 2001; Eaves 2002; Lewin 1984.

13. Hochschild 1983, 7.

14. Bordo 1993b; Wolf 1991.

15. For a thoughtful, in-depth examination of dancers' fluid body boundaries, see Wesley 2003b.

16. Bordo 1993b; MacKinnon 1989; Wolf 1991.

17. Benard and Schlaffer 1997.

18. For more discussion on the Möbius strip qualities of exotic dancing, see Barton 2002.

19. Other researchers (e.g., Bell and Sloan 1998; Forsyth and Deshotels 1998; M. Johnson 1998; Sweet and Tewksbury 2000a) have noted a similar pattern.

20. Hochschild 1983.

NOTES TO CHAPTER 3

1. Daly 1978; Dworkin 1974; S. Johnson 1987.

2. Tanenbaum 2000, xiv.

3. "Holy whore" is one way Fabian (1997) describes herself.

4. de Beauvoir 1952.

5. Goffman 1963, 5.

6. See Bell and Sloan 1998 for a similar analysis of internalized stigma.

7. See Bruckert 2002 and Ronai and Cross 1998 for analyses of informants who create "straw" women against whom they can compare themselves favorably.

8. hooks 1994; Ronai and Cross 1998.

9. For additional discussion of dancer personas, see Burana 2001 and Eaves 2002.

NOTES TO CHAPTER 4

1. J. Johnson 2002, 64.

2. Collins 2000; de Beauvoir 1952; S. Johnson 1987; Smith 1998.

3. Bordo 1993b, 1997; Kilbourne 1999; Wolf 1991, 1997.

4. For examples, see Bordo 1993b; Kilbourne 1999; and Wolf 1991.

5. For an excellent autobiographical description of the liberating potential of stripping, see McGhan 2003.

6. Thompson 2003, 331.

7. Marx writes in "Alienation and the Proletariat," "The propertied class and the class of the proletariat present the same human self-alienation. But the former class finds in this self-alienation its confirmation and its good, its own power: it has in it a semblance of human existence. The class of the proletariat feels annihilated in its self-alienation; it sees in it its own powerlessness and the reality of an inhuman existence" (McLellan 1990, 134).

8. Schor 1998.

9. Brownmiller 1975; Russell and VandeVen 1976.

10. For a detailed autobiographical exploration of the toll stripping takes on partnerships, see Lewin 1984.

11. It is important to note that neither Kelly, Janeen, nor April had children to support, and April had the additional resource of a loving partner who financially helped her transition out of the sex industry.

12. For other illustrations of first-person narratives that describe the author's experience of the toll of the sex industry, see Burana 2001; Funari 1997; Lewin 1984; and Mattson 1995.

NOTES TO CHAPTER 5

1. I am using the word "queer" in this chapter in the academic context of queer theory, a branch of theoretical inquiry that breaks cultural gender binaries, especially with regard to sexuality. Thus, any sexual identity or behavior outside the heterosexual, patriarchal norms may be constituted as "queer," including gay, lesbian, and bisexual acts. With some effort, one might construct stripping as queer because of the way it violates certain gender norms for women.

2. Mulvey (1999) used psychoanalytic and feminist theory to demonstrate that audiences perceive most films through the gaze of patriarchal privilege, in other words, the "male gaze." This male gaze defines women as the bearers, not the makers, of meaning. By this, Mulvey theorized that the female presence in most films is passive and eroticized. When a woman appears, she freezes the moment in erotic spectacle. The heroine does not act with the agency of the hero. She is the catalyst for his transformation, not her own. The power of the male gaze comes from knowing without being known, seeing without being seen, invulnerability watching vulnerability—a social construction that defines knowing and seeing and invulnerability as the exclusive right of men.

3. See, for example, Hollibaugh 2000; Patton 1997; Queen 1997; and Zoticus 1997.

4. For example, Erika Langley (1997), in her photographic essay and text, documents her experiences working at the Lusty Lady in Seattle, including her burgeoning romantic interest in women.

5. Andrea Dworkin was married to a man but identified as a lesbian.

6. David Scott's *Behind the G-String* (1996), a sociological study of strippers, provides an illustration of the attitudes and biases of researchers examining sexual orientation. The book includes detailed interviews with dancers, who are quoted freely throughout the text. Scott's analysis focuses primarily on the images dancers project (such as "Demon" and "Goddess")and the audience's reception of and responses to dancers. Scott relies heavily on psychoanalytic theories of attachment to explain the unique place the dancer inhabits in the consciousness of male audience members. Although he notes that there is a cultural stereotype that many dancers are lesbian, his entire discussion of this phenomenon spans less than half a page and is illustrated by the comments of only one dancer. These comments support uncritical negative assumptions about both strippers and lesbians. Research that does examine the sexual identity of sex workers include McCaghy and Skipper 1969; and Pendleton 1997.

7. For illustrations of researchers who discuss the deviant identity of topless dancers, see Bell and Sloan 1998; Forsyth and Deshotels 1998; McCaghy and Skipper 1969, 1972; Ronai and Cross 1998; Sweet and Tewksbury 2000b; and Thompson and Harred 1992. For discussions about sex workers' self-esteem, see Forsyth and Deshotels 1998; Ronai and Cross 1998; Ronai and Ellis 1989; and Thompson and Harred 1992.

8. McCaghy and Skipper 1969, 1972; D. Scott 1996.

9. Lerum 1998, 9.

10. I say this not to belittle male researchers but because conversation after conversation with dancers has demonstrated to me that many of them have conflicted, often negative feelings about their customers. Dancers expressed that they feel almost no actual arousal. They are, in fact, most often bored, drunk, dissociated, or on an ego trip, which is not necessarily erotically charged.

11. From Jones 2001: "Estimates of a general queer population are necessarily difficult because of both fear of identification and also because of the lack of any public or private mechanism for enumerating people by their sexual orientation. The work of Kinsey (Kinsey et al. 1948, 1953) and subsequent authors (Fay et al. 1989; Laumann et al. 1994; Rogers and Turner 1991) have developed the measure that 10 percent of Western population groups are predominately or exclusively homosexual in their sexual behavior." Estimates of bisexuality are equally difficult to make, with figures ranging from 10 percent to 40 percent of U.S. citizens engaging in bisexual activity.

12. Of the dancers Dudash (1997) interviewed, 50 percent identified as lesbian or bisexual as well.

13. Langley 1997; Patton 1997; Pendleton 1997; Queen 1997; Zoticus 1997.

14. Pendleton (1997, 75) argues that queer women choose sex work as a labor, not an identity, to leave "their lesbian sexuality intact."

15. Perry and Sanchez 1998.

16. Perry and Sanchez's work (1998) resonates with my own findings about the more negative aspects of working in the sex industry. They researched a range of sex workers including street prostitutes, drug-addicted prostitutes, and strippers. Street prostitutes who are addicts feel the toll of sex work more quickly than exotic dancers.

17. Uebel (2004) argues a strikingly different interpretation of customer actions, likening strip bars to an arena of masculine debasement in which the clients express a form of masculine masochism in their interactions with exotic dancers.

18. It is my sense that many of the bisexual women who explore and enter into lesbian relationships while working in the sex industry will return to heterosexual relationships some time after exiting sex work. I suspect this because being gay in our homophobic culture is cumulatively exhausting. I expect that once out of the sex industry, many bisexual women would seek the social acceptance of a mainstream heterosexual relationship. If this is indeed the case, what my findings demonstrate is not that the sex industry turns women into lesbians but that it provides a set of factors that encourage lesbians to choose sex work and bisexual women to explore being involved in lesbian relationships. My hypothesis would make an interesting longitudinal study.

Notes to Chapter 6

1. I exclude sexually trafficked women (for examples, see Altink 1995) and those pressured by dire economic circumstances to enter the sex industry to support their families.

2. Pheterson 1989.

3. Rosaldo and Lamphere 1974, 39.

4. J. Scott 1990, 120.

5. Bruckert (2002) describes and analyzes several key aspects of working as an exotic dancer, including the intersection of class and sexuality in the sex industry, how women negotiate the stigma of being a stripper, and the impact of working conditions on performers. Though Bruckert's data reveal her subjects to be catty and competitive some of the time and supportive and protective at others, she does not highlight or analyze this contradiction.

6. Brooks 1997; Bruckert 2002; Burana 2001; Dudash 1997; Frank 2002; Funari 1997; M. Johnson 1998; Langley 1997; Mattson 1995; Queen 1997; Ronai and Ellis 1989.

7. Dudash 1997; Langley 1997.

8. My data regarding friendship among dancers in the clubs may contradict

some of the sex literature because the sites I focused on, the Lusty Lady in particular, have built-in mechanisms to reduce competition among dancers. Furthermore, Vixens dancers tend to be older and more established, mature, and respectful of one another's needs. For example, if a dancer already has forty regulars, she may be less likely to take offense when a newcomer violates a spoken or unspoken boundary.

9. Bruckert 2002; and Ronai and Cross 1998.

10. For an analysis of "front stage" and "back stage" behaviors, see Goffman 1973.

11. White 1985, 128.

12. Ibid., 132.

13. J. Scott 1990, 134.

14. Ibid.

15. Rothenberg 2005.

16. Ehrenreich 2001; Ehrenreich and Hochschild 2002; J. Johnson 2002; McLellan 1990.

17. Burana 2001, 55.

18. Quoted in Lester 1971, 15–16.

19. Collins 2000.

NOTES TO CHAPTER 7

1. Brooks 1997; Dudash 1997; Funari 1997; Langley 1997; Queen 1997.

2. The Lusty Lady marketed itself as feminist because it was run by women and claimed to allow more freedom of expression by the performers. In truth, the Lusty Lady called itself feminist to attract women in the socially conscious Bay Area. Since I performed my research, however, in 2003 the Lusty Lady became the first cooperatively owned strip club. So the Lusty Lady may now be able to support a claim that it is a feminist enterprise.

3. Having her period does not prevent most dancers from performing. A typical strategy is to cut the string off a tampon before inserting it. This is, obviously, a less precarious strategy for dancers who are only topless as opposed to fully nude.

4. Burana 2001, 217–218.

5. Friedrich Engels developed Karl Marx's analysis of class struggle by theorizing the attitude of identifying with one's oppressor as "false consciousness" and identifying with one's peers as "class consciousness," originally in a private communication with Marx. (For a detailed analysis of the concept of "false consciousness," see McCarney 2004). A number of feminist and poststructuralist scholars have critiqued the concept of "false consciousness" on the grounds that it erases individual agency and does not account for the nuances of resistance that members of oppressed groups make in relation to their oppressors. False

consciousness is a dangerous means of describing members of marginalized groups because such accusations may themselves be a kind of oppressive attack. It is my belief that false consciousness is a useful concept for understanding the dynamics of oppression but that it should be used carefully.

6. As of June 2005, the Exotic Dancers Alliance is no longer operating. Individuals in the industry who are interested in obtaining health care and social services are encouraged to contact the St. James Infirmary at www.stjamesinfirmary.org.

7. Sprinkle 1997, 66–69.

8. A brief illustration of Dworkin's thoughts on sex work: "When men use women in prostitution, they are expressing a pure hatred for the female body. . . . It is a contempt so deep, so deep, that a whole human life is reduced to a few sexual orifices" (1997, 145).

9. Thanks to Jules Unsel for her analogy comparing Andrea Dworkin to an Old Testament prophet.

10. Again, this finding applies to women who have at least some ability to determine their own actions.

References

Adler, Patricia A., and Peter Adler. 1998. "Observational Techniques." In Norman K. Denzin and Yvonna S. Lincoln, eds., *Collecting and Interpreting Qualitative Materials*. Thousand Oaks, CA: Sage, pp. 79–109.

Albert, Alexa. 2001. *Brothel: Mustang Ranch and Its Women*. New York: Ballantine.

Almodovar, Norma Jean. 1993. *From Cop to Call Girl: Why I Left the LAPD to Make an Honest Living as a Beverly Hills Prostitute*. New York: Simon and Schuster.

Altink, Sietske. 1995. *Stolen Lives: Trading Women into Sex and Slavery*. London: Scarlet.

Anzaldúa, Gloria E. 1987. *Borderlands/La Frontera: The New Mestiza*. San Francisco: Aunt Lute.

Barry, Kathleen. 1995. *The Prostitution of Sexuality: The Global Exploitation of Women*. New York: New York University Press.

Barton, Bernadette. 2001. "Queer Desire in the Sex Industry." *Sexuality and Culture*, 5:4:3–27.

———. 2002. "Dancing on the Möbius Strip: Challenging the Sex War Paradigm." *Gender and Society*, 16:5:585–602.

Bell, Holly, and Lacey Sloan. 1998. "Exploiter or Exploited: Topless Dancers Reflect on their Experiences." *Affilia: Journal of Women and Social Work*, 13:3:352–369.

Bell, Laurie, ed. 1987. *Good Girls/Bad Girls: Feminists and Sex Trade Workers, Face to Face*. Toronto: Seal.

Benard, Cheryl, and Edit Schlaffer. 1997. " 'The Man in the Street': Why He Harasses." In Laurel Richardson, Verta Taylor, and Nancy Whittier, eds., *Feminist Frontiers IV*. New York: McGraw-Hill, pp. 395–398.

Bennett, Joel B., and Wayne E. K. Lehman, eds. 2003. *Preventing Workplace Substance Abuse: Beyond Drug Testing to Wellness*. Washington, DC: American Psychological Association.

Berger, John. 1972. *Ways of Seeing*. London: British Broadcasting Corporation.

Bordo, Susan. 1991. " 'Material Girl': The Effacement of Postmodern Culture."

In Lawrence Goldstein, ed., *The Female Body.* Ann Arbor: University of Michigan Press, pp. 106–130.

———. 1993a. "Reading the Male Body." *Michigan Quarterly Review,* 32:4:696–737.

———. 1993b. *Unbearable Weight: Feminism, Western Culture, and the Body.* Berkeley: University of California Press.

———. 1997. *Twilight Zones: The Hidden Life of Cultural Images from Plato to O.J.* Berkeley: University of California Press.

Bright, Susie. 1997. *The Sexual State of the Union.* New York: Simon and Schuster.

Brooks, Siobhan. 1997. "Dancing Toward Freedom." In Jill Nagle, ed., *Whores and Other Feminists.* New York: Routledge, pp. 252–255.

Brownmiller, Susan. 1975. *Against Our Will: Men, Women, and Rape.* New York: Simon and Schuster.

Bruckert, Chris. 2002. *Taking It Off, Putting It On: Women in the Strip Trade.* Toronto: Women's Press.

Burana, Lily. 2001. *Strip City: A Stripper's Farewell Journey across America.* New York: Hyperion.

Butler, Judith. 1990. *Gender Trouble.* New York: Routledge.

Califia, Pat. 1994. *Public Sex: The Culture of Radical Sex.* San Francisco: Cleis.

Califia, Patrick. 2002. *Speaking Sex to Power: The Politics of Queer Sex.* San Francisco: Cleis.

Castaneda, Carlos. 1984. *The Fire from Within.* New York: Simon and Schuster.

Chancer, Lynn. 1993. "Prostitution, Feminist Theory, and Ambivalence: Notes from the Sociological Underground." *Social Text* (winter): 143–171.

———. 1998. *Reconcilable Differences: Confronting Beauty, Pornography, and the Future of Feminism.* Berkeley: University of California Press.

Chapkis, Wendy. 1997. *Live Sex Acts: Women Performing Erotic Labor.* New York: Routledge.

———. 2000. "Power and Control in the Commercial Sex Trade." In Ronald Weitzer, ed., *Sex for Sale.* New York: Routledge, pp. 181–201.

Collins, Patricia Hill. 1997. "Comment of Hekman's 'Truth and Method: Feminist Standpoint Theory Revisited': Where's the Power?" *Signs: Journal of Women in Culture and Society,* 22:2:375–381.

———. 2000. *Black Feminist Thought: Knowledge, Consciousness, and the Politics of Empowerment,* 2d ed. New York: Routledge.

Daly, Mary. 1978. *Gyn/Ecology: The Metaethics of Radical Feminism.* Boston: Beacon.

Davis, Nanette J. 2000. "From Victims to Survivors: Working with Recovering Street Prostitutes." In Ronald Weitzer, ed., *Sex for Sale.* New York: Routledge, pp. 139–155.

de Beauvoir, Simone. 1952. *The Second Sex.* New York: Vintage.

Delacoste, Frederique, and Priscilla Alexander, eds. 1987. *Sex Work: Writings by Women in the Sex Industry.* San Francisco: Cleis.

Denzin, Norman K., and Yvonna S. Lincoln, eds. 1998. *Collecting and Interpreting Qualitative Materials.* Thousand Oaks, CA: Sage.

Dominelli, Lena. 1986. "The Power of the Powerless: Prostitution and the Reinforcement of Submissive Femininity." *Sociological Review,* 34:65–92.

Dudash, Tawnya. 1997. "Peepshow Feminism." In Jill Nagle, ed., *Whores and Other Feminists.* New York: Routledge, pp. 98–118.

Duggan, Lisa, and Nan D. Hunter. 1995. *Sex Wars: Sex Dissent and Political Culture.* New York: Routledge.

Dworkin, Andrea. 1974. *Woman Hating.* New York: E. P. Dutton.

———. 1987. *Intercourse.* New York: Free Press.

———. 1997. *Life and Death: Unapologetic Writings on the Continuing War against Women.* New York: Free Press.

Eaves, Elisabeth. 2002. *Bare: On Women, Dancing, Sex, and Power.* New York: Knopf.

Ehrenreich, Barbara. 2001. *Nickel and Dimed: On (Not) Getting By in America.* New York: Metropolitan.

Ehrenreich, Barbara, and Arlie Hochschild, eds. 2002. *Global Woman: Nannies, Maids, and Sex Workers in the New Economy.* New York: Metropolitan/Owl.

Elkins, David N., L. James Hedstrom, Lori L. Hughes, J. Andrew Leaf, and Cheryl Saunders. 1988. "Toward a Humanistic-Phenomenological Spirituality: Definition, Description, and Measurement." *Journal of Humanistic Psychology,* 28:4:5–18.

Epele, Maria E. 2001. "Excess, Scarcity, and Desire among Drug-Using Sex Workers." *Body and Society,* 7:2–3:161–179.

Eurydice. 1999. *Satyricon USA: A Journey across the New Sexual Frontier.* New York: Scribner.

Fabian, Cosi. 1997. "The Holy Whore: A Woman's Gateway to Power." In Jill Nagle, ed., *Whores and Other Feminists.* New York: Routledge, pp. 44–54.

Farley, Melissa, ed. 2003. *Prostitution, Trafficking, and Traumatic Stress.* New York: Haworth.

Farley, Melissa, Ann Cotton, Jacqueline Lynne, et al. 2003. "Prostitution and Trafficking in Nine Countries: An Update on Violence and Posttraumatic Stress Disorder." In Melissa Farley, ed., *Prostitution, Trafficking, and Traumatic Stress.* New York: Haworth, pp. 33–74.

Fay, R. E., C. F. Turner, A. D. Klassen, and J. H. Gagnon. 1989. "Prevalence and Patterns of Same-Gender Sexual Contact among Men." *Science,* 243:338–348.

Fontana, Andrea, and James H. Frey. 1998. "Interviewing: The Art of Science."

In Norman K. Denzin and Yvonna S. Lincoln, eds., *Collecting and Interpreting Qualitative Materials.* Thousand Oaks, CA: Sage, pp. 47–78.

Forsyth, Craig J., and Tina Deshotels. 1998. "A Deviant Process: The Sojourn of the Stripper." *Sociological Spectrum,* 18:1:77–93.

Foucault, Michel. 1977. *Discipline and Punish: The Birth of the Prison.* New York: Vintage.

———. 1978. *The History of Sexuality, Volume One.* New York: Vintage.

Frank, Katherine. 2002. *G-Strings and Sympathy: Strip Club Regulars and Male Desire.* Durham, NC: Duke University Press.

French, Dolores. 1988. *Working.* New York: Windsor.

Friend, Tad. 2004. "Naked Profits." *New Yorker,* July 12 and 19.

Funari, Vicky. 1997. "Naked, Naughty, Nasty: Peep Show Reflections." In Jill Nagle, ed., *Whores and Other Feminists.* New York: Routledge, pp. 19–35.

Goffman, Erving. 1963. *Stigma: Notes on the Management of Spoiled Identity.* New York: Simon and Schuster.

———. 1973. *The Presentation of Self in Everyday Life.* New York: Overlook.

Greer, Germaine. 1970. *The Female Eunuch.* New York: Bantam.

Harding, Sandra. 1991. *Whose Science? Whose Knowledge? Thinking from Women's Lives.* Ithaca, NY: Cornell University Press.

Harner, Michael. 1980. *The Way of the Shaman.* San Francisco: HarperCollins.

Hausbeck, Kathryn, and Barbara G. Brents. 2002. "McDonaldization of the Sex Industries? The Business of Sex." In George Ritzer, ed., *McDonaldization: The Reader.* Thousand Oaks, CA: Pine Forge, pp. 91–106.

Hekman, Susan. 1997. "Truth and Method: Feminist Standpoint Theory Revisited." *Signs: Journal of Women and Culture,* 22:1:341–365.

Hochschild, Arlie Russell. 1979. "Emotion Work, Feeling Rules, and Social Structure." *American Journal of Sociology,* 85:551–575.

———. 1983. *The Managed Heart: Commercialization of Human Feeling.* Berkeley: University of California Press.

Hollibaugh, Amber L. 2000. *My Dangerous Desires: A Queer Girl Dreaming Her Way Home.* Durham, NC: Duke University Press.

Holmes, Stephen T., and Ronald M. Holmes, eds. 2002. *Sex Crimes: Patterns and Behaviors,* 2d ed. Thousand Oaks, CA: Sage.

hooks, bell. 1994. *Outlaw Culture.* New York: Routledge.

Jenness, Valerie. 1990. "From Sex as Sin to Sex as Work: COYOTE and the Reorganization of Prostitution as a Social Problem." *Social Problems,* 37:3:403–420.

Johnson, Jennifer. 2002. *Getting By on the Minimum: The Lives of Working-Class Women.* New York: Routledge.

Johnson, Merri Lisa. 1998. "Pole Work: Autoethnography of a Strip Club." *Sexuality and Culture,* 2:149–157.

————, ed. 2002. *Jane Sexes It Up: True Confessions of Feminist Desire.* New York: Four Walls Eight Windows.

Johnson, Sonia. 1987. *Going Out of Our Minds: The Metaphysics of Liberation.* Freedom, CA: Crossing Press.

Jones, Jeff. 2001. "Hidden Histories, Proud Communities: Multiple Narratives in the Queer Geographies of Lexington, Kentucky, 1930–1999." Ph.D. diss., University of Kentucky.

Kempadoo, Kamala. 1998. "The Exotic Dancers Alliance: An Interview with Dawn Passar and Johanna Breyer." In Kamala Kempadoo and Jo Doezema, eds., *Global Sex Workers.* New York: Routledge, pp. 182–191.

————. 2004. *Sexing the Caribbean: Gender, Race, and Sexual Labor.* New York: Routledge.

Kempadoo, Kamala, and Jo Doezema, eds. 1998. *Global Sex Workers.* New York: Routledge.

Kilbourne, Jean. 1999. *Deadly Persuasion: The Addictive Power of Advertising.* New York: Simon and Schuster.

Kinsey, A. C., W. B. Pomeroy, and C. E. Martin. 1948. *Sexual Behavior in the Human Male.* Philadelphia: W. B. Saunders.

Kinsey, A. C., W. B. Pomeroy, C. E. Martin, and P. H. Gebhard. 1953. *Sexual Behavior in the Human Female.* Philadelphia: W. B. Saunders.

Kipnis, Laura. 1996. *Bound and Gagged: Pornography and the Politics of Fantasy in America.* Durham, NC: Duke University Press.

Langley, Erika. 1997. *The Lusty Lady: Photographs and Texts.* Zurich: Scalo.

Laumann, E. O., J. H. Gagnon, R. T. Michael, and S. Michaels. 1994. *The Social Organization of Sexuality: Sexual Practices in the United States.* Chicago: University of Chicago Press.

Leidholt, Dorchen A. 2003. "Prostitution and Trafficking in Women: An Intimate Relationship." In Melissa Farley, ed., *Prostitution, Trafficking, and Traumatic Stress.* New York: Haworth, pp. 167–183.

Leigh, Carol, a.k.a. Scarlot Harlot. 1997. "Inventing Sex Work." In Jill Nagle, ed., *Whores and Other Feminists.* New York: Routledge, pp. 223–231.

————. 2004. *Unrepentant Whore: Collected Works of Scarlot Harlot.* San Francisco: Last Gasp.

Lerum, Kari. 1998. "Twelve-Step Feminism Makes Sex Workers Sick: How the State and the Recovery Movement Turn Radical Women into 'Useless Citizens.' " *Sexuality and Culture,* 2:7–36.

Lester, Julius. 1971. *The Seventh Son: The Thought and Writing of W. E. B. Du Bois.* New York: Random House.

Lewin, Lauri. 1984. *Naked Is the Best Disguise: My Life as a Stripper.* New York: William Morrow.

Lewis, Jacqueline. 2000. "Controlling Lap Dancing: Law, Morality, and Sex

Work." In Ronald Weitzer, ed., *Sex for Sale.* New York: Routledge, pp. 203–216.

Lindy, Jacob D., and John P. Wilson. 1994. "Empathic Strain and Countertransference Roles: Case Illustrations." In John P. Wilson and Jacob D. Lindy, eds., *Countertransference in the Treatment of PTSD.* New York: Guilford, pp. 62–85.

MacKinnon, Catharine. 1987. *Feminism Unmodified: Discourses on Life and Law.* Cambridge, MA: Harvard University Press.

———. 1989. *Toward a Feminist Theory of the State.* Cambridge, MA: Harvard University Press.

Macy, Marianne. 1996. *Working Sex: An Odyssey into Our Cultural Underworld.* New York: Carroll and Graf.

Maslow, Abraham. 1970. *Religion, Values, and Peak Experiences.* New York: Viking.

Mattson, Heidi. 1995. *Ivy League Stripper.* New York: Arcade.

McCaghy, Charles H., and James K. Skipper Jr. 1969. "Lesbian Behavior as an Adaptation to the Occupation of Stripping." *Social Problems,* 17:262–270.

———. 1972. "Stripping: Anatomy of a Deviant Lifestyle." In S. D. Feldman and G. W. Thielbar, eds., *Lifestyles: Diversity in American Society.* Boston: Little, Brown, pp. 362–373.

McCarney, Joseph. 2004. "Ideology and False Consciousness." Marx Myths and Legends Website. Available at http://marxmyths.org/joseph-mccarney/article.htm.

McElroy, Wendy. 1995. *XXX: A Woman's Right to Pornography.* New York: St. Martin's.

McGhan, Meredith. 2003. "Dancing toward Redemption." In Ophira Edut, ed., *Body Outlaws: Rewriting the Rules of Beauty and Body Image.* Emeryville, CA: Seal, pp. 165–175.

McLellan, David, ed. 1990. *Karl Marx: Selected Writings.* New York: Oxford University Press.

Miller, Eleanor M. 1986. *Street Woman.* Philadelphia: Temple University Press.

Millett, Kate. 1971. *The Prostitution Papers.* New York: Ballantine.

Montgomery, Heather. 1998. "Children, Prostitution, and Identity: A Case Study from a Tourist Resort in Thailand." In Kamala Kempadoo and Jo Doezema, eds., *Global Sex Workers.* New York: Routledge, pp. 139–150.

Morgan, Robin. 1968. *Going Too Far: The Personal Chronicles of a Feminist.* New York: Vintage.

———. 1970. *Sisterhood Is Powerful: An Anthology of Writings from the Women's Liberation Movement.* New York: Vintage.

Mulvey, Laura. 1999. "Visual Pleasure and Narrative Cinema." In Sue Thornham, ed., *Feminist Film Theory: A Reader.* New York: New York University Press.

Murphy, Alexandra G. 2003. "The Dialectical Gaze: Exploring the Subject-Object Tension in the Performances of Women Who Strip." *Journal of Contemporary Ethnography,* 32:3:305–335.

Nagle, Jill, ed. 1997. *Whores and Other Feminists.* New York: Routledge.

National Research Council. 1993. *Understanding Child Abuse Neglect.* Washington, DC: National Academy Press.

Odzer, Cleo. 1994. *Patpong Sisters: An American Woman's View of the Bangkok Sex World.* New York: Arcade.

Overall, Christine. 1992. "What's Wrong with Prostitution? Evaluating Sex Work." *Signs,* 17:4:705–724.

Paglia, Camille. 1992. *Sex, Art, and American Culture.* New York: Vintage.

Patton, Jessica. 1997. "500 Words on Acculturation." In Jill Nagle, ed., *Whores and Other Feminists.* New York: Routledge, pp. 136–137.

PayScale.com. 2005. "Real-Time Salary Survey Information for Executive Secretary or Administrative Assistant (United States)." Available at www.payscale .com/salary-survey/aid-8607/rid-79/fid-6886/RANAME-SALARY.

Pendleton, Eva. 1997. "Love for Sale: Queering Heterosexuality." In Jill Nagle, ed., *Whores and Other Feminists.* New York: Routledge, pp. 73–82.

Perry, Richard Warren, and Lisa Erin Sanchez. 1998. "Transactions in the Flesh: Toward an Ethnography of Embodied Sexual Reason." *Studies in Law, Politics, and Society,* 18:29–76.

Pheterson, Gail, ed. 1989. *A Vindication of the Rights of Whores.* Seattle: Seal.

Plachy, Sylvia, and James Ridgeway. 1996. *Red Light: Inside the Sex Industry.* New York: Thunder's Mouth.

Pollet, Alison, and Page Hurwitz. 2004. "Strip Till You Drop." *Nation,* 278:20–25.

Prus, Robert, and Styllianos Irini. 1980. *Hookers, Rounders, and Desk Clerks: The Social Organization of the Hotel Community.* Salem, WI: Sheffield.

Queen, Carol. 1997. *Real Live Nude Girl: Chronicles of Sex-Positive Culture.* San Francisco: Cleis.

Raphael, Jody. 2004. *Listening to Olivia: Violence, Poverty, and Prostitution.* Boston: Northeastern University Press.

Reed, Stacy. 1997. "All Stripped Off." In Jill Nagle, ed., *Whores and Other Feminists.* New York: Routledge, pp. 179–188.

Reid, Scott A., Jonathan S. Epstein, and D. E. Benson. 1994. "Role Identity in a Devalued Occupation: The Case of Female Exotic Dancers." *Sociological Focus,* 27:1:1–16.

Rich, Grant Jewell, and Kathleen Guidroz. 2000. "Smart Girls Who Like Sex: Telephone Sex Workers." In Ronald Weitzer, ed., *Sex for Sale.* New York: Routledge, pp. 35–48.

Ritzer, George. 2000. *The McDonaldization of Society,* 3d ed. Thousand Oaks, CA: Pine Forge.

Rogers, S. M., and C. F. Turner. 1991. "Male-Male Sexual Contact in the USA: Findings from Five Sample Surveys, 1970–1990." *Journal of Sex Research,* 28:491–519.

Ronai, Carol Rambo, and Rabecca Cross. 1998. "Dancing with Identity: Narrative Resistance Strategies of Male and Female Strippers." *Deviant Behavior: An Interdisciplinary Journal,* 19:99–119.

Ronai, Carol Rambo, and Carolyn Ellis. 1989. "Turn-Ons for Money: Interactional Strategies of the Table Dancer." *Journal of Contemporary Ethnography,* 18:3:271–298.

Rosaldo, Michelle Zimbalist, and Louise Lamphere, eds. 1974. *Woman, Culture, and Society.* Stanford, CA: Stanford University Press.

Rothenberg, Paula S. 2005. *White Privilege: Essential Readings on the Other Side of Racism,* 2d ed. New York: Worth.

Rubin, Gayle. 1984. "Thinking Sex: Notes for a Radical Theory of the Politics of Sexuality." In Carol S. Vance, ed., *Pleasure and Danger: Exploring Female Sexuality.* Boston: Routledge and Kegan Paul, pp. 267–319.

Russell, Diana, and Nicole VandeVen. 1976. *International Tribune on Crimes against Women.* Millbrae, CA: Les Femmes.

Russo, Ann. 2001. *Taking Back Our Lives: A Call to Action for the Feminist Movement.* London: Routledge.

SAMHSA. 1998. "Workplace Resource Center—Prevention Research." Available at http://workplace.samhsa.gov/WPResearch/BasicResearch/WPSA.html.

Schlosser, Eric. 2003. *Reefer Madness: Sex, Drugs, and Cheap Labor in the American Black Market.* Boston: Houghton Mifflin.

Schor, Juliet B. 1998. *The Overspent American: Why We Want What We Don't Need.* New York: HarperPerennial.

Scott, David A. 1996. *Behind the G-String: An Exploration of the Stripper's Image, Her Person, and Her Meaning.* Jefferson, NC: McFarland.

Scott, James A. 1990. *Domination and the Arts of Resistance.* New Haven, CT: Yale University Press.

Shrage, Laurie. 1989. "Should Feminists Oppose Prostitution?" *Ethics,* 99:347–361.

Sijuwade, Philip O. 1995. "Counterfeit Intimacy: A Dramaturgical Analysis of an Erotic Performance." *Social Behavior and Personality,* 23:4:369–376.

Sloan, Lacey, and Stephanie Wahab. 2004. "Four Categories of Women Who Work as Topless Dancers." *Sexuality and Culture,* 8:1:18–43.

Smith, Barbara. 1998. *The Truth That Never Hurts: Writings on Race, Gender, and Freedom.* New Brunswick, NJ: Rutgers University Press.

Sprinkle, Annie. 1997. "We've Come a Long Way—And We're Exhausted." In Jill Nagle, ed., *Whores and Other Feminists.* New York: Routledge, pp. 66–69.

Steinem, Gloria. 1978. "Erotica and Pornography: A Clear and Present Difference." *Ms. Magazine* (November): 54.

Sweet, Nova, and Richard Tewksbury. 2000a. "Entry, Maintenance, and Departure from a Career in the Sex Industry: Strippers' Experiences of Occupational Costs and Rewards." *Humanity and Society,* 24:2:136–161.

————. 2000b. " 'What's a Nice Girl Like You Doing in a Place Like This?': Pathways to a Career in Stripping." *Sociological Spectrum,* 20:3:325–344.

Tanenbaum, Leora. 2000. *Slut! Growing Up Female with a Bad Reputation.* New York: HarperCollins.

Thompson, William E., and Jackie L. Harred. 1992. "Topless Dancers: Managing Stigma in a Deviant Occupation." *Deviant Behavior: An Interdisciplinary Journal,* 13:291–311.

————. 2003. "Hanging Tongues: A Sociological Encounter with the Assembly Line." In Douglas Harper and Helene M. Lawson, eds., *The Cultural Study of Work.* Lanham, MD: Rowman and Littlefield, pp. 313–334.

Thorbeck, Susanne, and Bandana Pattanaik, eds. 2002. *Transnational Prostitution: Changing Global Patterns.* London: Zed.

Tisdale, Sallie. 1994. *Talk Dirty to Me: An Intimate Philosophy of Sex.* New York: Anchor.

Uebel, Michael. 2004. "Striptopia?" *Social Semiotics,* 14:1:3–19.

Ultimate Strip Club List. 2005. Available at http://www.tuscl.com/sc-Listings.ASP?mode=S&ID=co0000&Display=U.S.+Clubs.

Vance, Carol S., ed. 1984. *Pleasure and Danger: Exploring Female Sexuality.* Boston: Routledge and Kegan Paul.

Wahab, Stephanie. 2003. "Creating Knowledge Collaboratively with Female Sex Workers: Insights from a Qualitative, Feminist, and Participatory Study." *Qualitative Inquiry,* 9:4:625–642.

Weitzer, Ronald. 1991. "Prostitutes' Rights in the United States: The Failure of a Movement." *Sociological Quarterly,* 32:1:23–41.

————. 2000. "Why We Need More Research on Sex Work." In Ronald Weitzer, ed., *Sex for Sale.* New York: Routledge, pp. 1–13.

————, ed. 2000. *Sex for Sale.* New York: Routledge.

Wendall, Susan. 2000. "The Flight from the Rejected Body." In Anne Minas, ed., *Gender Basics: Feminist Perspectives on Women and Men.* Belmont, CA: Wadsworth, pp. 54–64.

Wesley, Jennifer K. 2002. "Growing Up Sexualized: Issues of Power and Violence in the Lives of Female Exotic Dancers." *Violence against Women,* 8:10:1182–1207.

————. 2003a. "Exotic Dancing and the Negotiation of Identity: The Multiple Uses of Body Technologies." *Journal of Contemporary Ethnography,* 32:6:643–669.

———. 2003b. " 'Where Am I Going to Stop?' Exotic Dancers, Fluid Boundaries, and Effects on Identity." *Deviant Behavior,* 24:483–503.

White, Deborah Gray. 1985. *Ar'n't I a Woman? Female Slaves in the Plantation South.* New York: Norton.

Wilson, John P., and Jacob D. Lindy, eds. 1994. *Countertransference in the Treatment of PTSD.* New York: Guilford.

Wolf, Naomi. 1991. *The Beauty Myth: How Images of Beauty Are Used against Women.* New York: Anchor.

———. 1997. *Promiscuities: The Secret Struggle for Womanhood.* New York: Fawcett Columbine.

Zoticus, Les Von. 1997. "Butch Gigolette." In Jill Nagle, ed., *Whores and Other Feminists.* New York: Routledge, pp. 170–176.

Index

About the Author

Bernadette Barton is Assistant Professor of Sociology and Women's Studies at Morehead State University, in Morehead, Kentucky.